AMERICAN POVERTY

BIG FOUR (*clockwise from bottom*): Abraham Lincoln, Theodore Roosevelt, Franklin D. Roosevelt, and Lyndon B. Johnson did the most to eliminate poverty in America. *Illustration courtesy of Miggs Burroughs*

AMERICAN POVERTY

PRESIDENTIAL FAILURES AND A CALL TO ACTION

WOODY KLEIN

FOREWORD BY WILLIAM J. VANDEN HEUVEL

Potomac Books
Washington, D.C.

Library of Congress Cataloging-in-Publication Data
Klein, Woody, 1929–
   American poverty : presidential failures and a call to action / Woody Klein; foreword by William J. vanden Heuvel. — 1st ed.
       p. cm.
Includes bibliographical references and index.
ISBN 978-1-61234-194-1 (hardcover : alk. paper)
ISBN 978-1-61234-195-8 (electronic)
   1. Poverty—Government policy—United States—History. 2. Economic assistance, Domestic—United States—History. 3. United States—Economic policy. I. Title.
HC110.P6K547 2013
362.5'5610973—dc23

                                                                        2012040611

Printed in the United States of America on acid-free paper that meets the American National Standards Institute Z39-48 Standard.

Potomac Books
22841 Quicksilver Drive
Dulles, Virginia 20166

First Edition

10 9 8 7 6 5 4 3 2 1

To my wife,
Audrey Lehman Klein,

*my guiding light, my intrepid editor for all seasons,
and my devoted partner for the past fifty-one years*

CONTENTS

FOREWORD

THE AMERICAN POVERTY CRISIS REVISITED

William J. vanden Heuvel

William J. vanden Heuvel served as the special assistant to Attorney General Robert F. Kennedy and was his close aide during Kennedy's run for the presidency in 1968, advising him on poverty issues. He previously served as the ambassador and deputy representative of the United States to the United Nations in New York and was the founder and chair emeritus of the Franklin & Eleanor Roosevelt Institute and chairman of the Four Freedoms Park Conservancy. He is one of three editors, with historians Arthur M. Schlesinger Jr. and Douglas Brinkley, of the St. Martin's Press Series on American Diplomatic and Political History.

Michael Harrington taught us how to put poverty on the agenda for action for our country. In 1962 he published *The Other America*, a powerful, detailed account of the country we did not want to look at: namely, the impoverished millions of Americans who desperately needed assistance. But one special person read the book and was profoundly moved by it: John F. Kennedy, president of the United States, and that was the beginning of the war against poverty that President Kennedy and Lyndon Baines Johnson carried forward for a decade. Poverty is the most intractable social problem in human history. The first lesson of Woody Klein's important book is that unless the president of the United States is personally committed to rallying the resources and political will of a country behind him, there is little prospect of significant progress.

In 1937, in his second inaugural address, Franklin Delano Roosevelt surveyed the nation, which his leadership had led out of the greatest depression in its history, and said, "I see one-third of a nation ill-housed, ill-clad, ill-nourished." But unlike any of his predecessors, he finished his speech by saying to his countrymen, "The test of our progress is not whether we add more to the abundance of those who have much; it is whether we provide enough for those who have too little." Born into a patrician family of wealth, Roosevelt had a greater concern for the poor than had any other president, and he demonstrated a determination to assist them in improving the quality of their lives.

It is almost unimaginable, and it certainly should be unacceptable, that today, seventy-five years after FDR's great inaugural address, fifty million of our fellow citizens live below the official poverty line of $23,050 for a family of four. One out of every five of American children is ensnared in the web of poverty that will deprive them of hope and opportunity in the later years of their lives. The numbers living in poverty would be fifty million larger were it not for government assistance programs, programs that are under constant political attack and some of which are scheduled to expire.

The political history of our country is generally written in the context of presidential administrations. In this masterful book, *American Poverty: Presidential Failures and a Call to Action*, Woody Klein has rendered a national service by exploring the attitudes of every president toward poverty. His book gives us perspective on present events. The great recession that has gripped our country for the last several years is frequently compared to the Great Depression, which Roosevelt confronted and ultimately turned into a time of enormous opportunity for political and economic reform. But unlike the political environment in 1933, there is little talk today about the poor. Instead, it is the middle class that is considered under attack while the poor are left hidden behind the walls of poverty, and few if any political leaders are prepared to risk their elections by talking about national responsibilities.

FDR's New Deal transformed America. It established that the government had the affirmative and constructive obligation to help its citizens. It rebuilt America and in the process created millions of jobs that saved countless families from despair and destruction. It enacted a network of social programs, including Social Security and Unemployment Insurance, that includes probably the most successful and cost-effective social programs that our government ever adopted. In 1933, the group most severely impacted by the Great Depression was senior citizens. There were no jobs or government programs of assistance, and families that could hardly afford to do so were left to take in parents and grandparents without resources. The Social Security Act changed all of that. It enabled people to plan retirements. It gave senior citizens basic minimum income so they were no longer subject to the uncontrollable vagaries of our economic system. And none of them were "handout" programs, forcing people to live on the dole. Self-respect was an essential element of New Deal programs. FDR was insistent that Social Security be administered as an insurance program in which the intended beneficiaries were contributors. Social Security became a right that politicians could not take away in the name of budget pressures. For seventy-five years, that concept has protected our senior citizens—until now when, in the name of privatization, newly empowered political forces threaten to destroy a legacy that every president from FDR to Barack Obama has zealously protected.

The minimum wage was established as a powerful weapon against poverty. If it were indexed to inflation, as it should be, millions could be lifted out of poverty almost immediately. The Wagner Act of 1935 gave workers the right to organize. Unions went on to play a most significant role in enlarging the middle class while establishing working conditions and wage standards that ensured a living wage for Americans and their families.

World War II brought an end to the Great Depression, and the war-time economy created full employment. We saw for the first time what the impact of a full employment policy could mean for our country. America became the most powerful, productive force in world history. Our economy produced the weaponry that won the titanic struggle of the war. For the first time, leading political figures talked about a full employment policy with the government playing a role of assuring every able-bodied man and woman who sought employment that they could find a job. A successful full-employment policy would be the most powerful weapon against poverty. Senator Daniel Patrick Moynihan, a pragmatic and powerful voice in the struggle against poverty throughout his political career, used to say that what the poor needed more than anything else was money—not the bureaucratic intervention of endless reports reflecting their well-being but the payment of money that would enable them to have a home, to buy clothing, and to have sufficient food. The nature of the free enterprise system does not make full employment a goal of the capitalist leaders, who understandably measure their results by the bottom line of profits, but any shortfall in employment threatens the free enterprise system. Therefore, the private sector and the public sector should work together with the avowed objective of advocating and bringing about full employment. While fully realizing that total success is never possible, working for full employment as an objective of our economy and of our government will do much to make such evil as poverty a lesser force in our society.

The progressive administrations of Presidents Kennedy and Johnson showed that constructive action and determination could affect the powerful forces that had made widespread poverty an unacceptable stain on American standards of liberty. During that period, poverty was reduced by more than 40 percent. Such programs as Head Start reminded us that we had to begin early in the life cycle of the poor to really break down the barriers. Launched in 1965, the Head Start Program is a creative, cost-effective concept that provides development assistance to children in the American family while they are still young enough not to have had their spirits broken by the failure of educational opportunity and the continuing outrage of racism. Education became a major focus of federal concern.

When poverty and racism combined to deny children the most fundamental rights of being Americans, I worked as assistant to Robert Kennedy in such places as Prince Edward County, Virginia, to turn despair into opportunity. We learned that providing motivated teachers to motivated children could in fact succeed in reaching educational objectives. The Supreme Court decision in *Brown v. Board of Education* (1954) had lifted us out of the dark ages of hatred and discrimination and given us the opportunity to fight poverty at the most basic level of education for all of our children. In Prince Edward County, with the leadership of John Kennedy and Robert Kennedy and the partnership of the private sector, we were able to show how the unforgivable burden of hateful segregation and discrimination could be overcome. We do not delude ourselves. Racism remains a powerful force not only in our history but also in our contemporary life. If poverty is our enemy, racism is its most powerful ally.

President Ronald Reagan is widely quoted as having said that we fought a war on poverty—and poverty won. But the fact is, when forces that were prepared to commit the resources to allow victory led the war on poverty, substantial success was achieved. Decades of experience have taught us what needs to be done to reduce poverty; Lyndon Johnson knew what had to be done. He had known poverty, having seen it himself in the hill country of Texas, and no one was more determined than he to improve the lives of the poor. And he performed legislative miracles in signing into law programs like Medicare and Medicaid, which truly lifted millions to a new and better plateau of existence.

Profoundly dark forces in our society make the struggle against poverty incredibly difficult. Consider, for example, the impact of alcoholism among the poor. Consider the role of narcotics in the impoverished communities of America. Think of the role of poverty in our criminal justice system. For several years, I was chairman of the New York City Board of Correction and witnessed the centrality of poverty to our criminal justice system. America today has more than two million people in prison, a higher percentage of incarceration than any other country in the world. The poor and the very poor are the clientele of our prisons and our courts. Prisons are social institutions where people engaged in activities that are a threat to their fellow citizens are properly incarcerated to prevent violence. We spend an enormous amount of money on our prisons. It is calculated that it costs more to keep a person in prison for a year than it does to pay tuition at Harvard. Prisons can be a time of opportunity for its internees. These institutions can be understood as temporarily housing individuals who have a variety of problems, ranging from mental illness to narcotic addiction, and as where the time and resources of incarceration can be used to lessen the possibility of continued crime upon their release. They can teach prisoners how to read, instruct them in the basic rudiments of good public and personal health, and identify their problems of alcoholism and narcotics addiction and establish programs where they can be made better before returning the prisoners to their communities. Every public dollar spent in criminal justice should have the purpose of making our communities safer and the possibilities of a better life more available, for the overall majority of prisoners return to their communities, most of them communities of poverty. Common sense dictates the enormous resources that we commit to the criminal justice system should ensure that these individuals will return to their communities better able to survive and with employment opportunities and family sustenance.

Michael Gerson, a conservative columnist for the *Washington Post*, has written that when a situation of inequality develops in which those at the bottom cannot rise, it is a caste system. We are in danger of that system happening in America. The inequality of wealth and opportunity is advancing to such a degree that basic American values are in danger.

The labor union movement, which helped create the middle class, is under thoughtless and ruthless attack. We are forgetting the role that unions have played in creating jobs in manufacturing, in mines and steel mills, and in the food industry, jobs that established a middle-class economic base through the partnership of labor unions, private owners, and government. The right to organize is a fundamental right that has enormous economic consequences. We seem to have forgotten how to bargain collectively. The rights of workers must be recognized as a fundamental part of the social contract along with the rights of capital.

One area where enormous success has been made in the nearly eighty years is with the farming industry. In 1933, 25 percent of the nation's workforce could be classified as farmers. They were among the most oppressed victims of the Depression. In 2012, less than 2 percent of our workforce is classified as farmers, and agribusiness has been taken over most of our farming. Generous subsidies begun in the New Deal have taken the avoidable risks out of farming and ensured a living wage for those employed in this sector. This progress never could have been accomplished without a significant program of subsidies that continues, almost without public discussion, to this day.

Unemployment and the exhaustion of unemployment benefits have created a new spiral, causing millions of workers to face the future with fear and anxiety. As FDR used the Great Depression to rebuild America, so we should now do it again. We should rebuild our infrastructure, restore our schools, repair our homes and highways, replenish our parks, and in the process restore a public attitude that accepts the general welfare promised by our Constitution as one that belongs to all of our citizens.

Poverty has a way of being invisible because we simply do not want to see it. But the squalor of poverty has a way of touching all of our lives. If we are unwilling to confront it, our children will pay the price for our neglect. Great strength comes with confronting powerful adversaries. When the war against poverty was being waged in the 1960s, a feeling in the nation was that great things were happening, that our democratic values were being enhanced, and that we were becoming a stronger people. The war in Vietnam and the endless wars since have helped divert the resources and political will that might have slain the poverty dragon.

Woody Klein's book gives us the opportunity as a nation to see where we have been and what we have tried to do to liberate those imprisoned by poverty. It is an enormous task to reorganize a country like the United States and to recommit the resources and political will that the needy require to begin to share the hope of America.

We will live in a stronger country and be more assured of our freedom and our future, however, if we make that commitment.

PREFACE
POVERTY, A PERSONAL RETROSPECTIVE

After one reads the facts, either there are anger and shame, or there are not. And, as usual, the fate of the poor hangs upon the decision of the better-off. If this anger and shame are not forthcoming, *someone can write a book about the other America a generation from now and it will be the same, or worse* [italics added].
　　　　　—Michael Harrington, *The Other America: Poverty in the United States* (1962), the book credited with launching President Lyndon B. Johnson's War on Poverty in 1965

One half century has passed since writer–social activist Michael Harrington's seminal volume on poverty in America was published.[1] I wrote this book as a response to Harrington's prophetic challenge to examine the status of poverty in the United States "a generation" from the time he wrote his book fifty years ago because the "anger and shame" that he referred to was not fully "forthcoming" in the highly volatile 1960s— or since. Circumstances have interrupted what once was a dream of a slum-free America. The huge financial drain of the war in Vietnam, ironically, thwarted the quest of Presidents John F. Kennedy and Lyndon B. Johnson for a Great Society. And, in recent years, successive presidents—diverting valuable American blood and treasure to the wars in Afghanistan, Iraq, and in other parts of the world—have all failed to continue the nation's effort to eradicate poverty.

At the outset of 2013, a record number of Americans—one in three people—were squeezed by rising living costs and living in poverty or close to it, according to recent government figures.[2] The latest Census Bureau data depict a middle class that is shrinking as unemployment remains high, homelessness increases, and the government's safety net frays.

The inconvenient truth is that the alarming increase in poverty is now perilous to our economy, to our national security, and to our standing in the world at large.

Despite the gravity of the situation, our austerity-minded Congress has little enthusiasm for another declaration of a War on Poverty, though much has been reported about income disparity and saving the nation's middle class. The Church cannot be accused of remaining silent. The U.S. bishops and Catholic Charities USA, for example, have repeatedly spoken up for the least among us as the economy has soured.

Two well-known national poverty experts, radio talk show host Tavis Smiley and academic-activist Cornel West, generated a great deal of publicity in 2012 by urging Americans across the country to pay attention to poverty. They also wrote a book, *The Rich and the Rest of Us: A Poverty Manifesto*, to make Americans aware of this overlooked and misconstrued issue. Perhaps more than any other media celebrities, they made the case with the profound message that America is far more economically divided than most people want to acknowledge, and this chasm, if not dealt with now, could ultimately destroy the fabric of American life.

The issue of American poverty has been reported with greater frequency in the U.S. media in recent years, but it has thus far failed to stir the public with the same emotional grassroots passion as it did in the 1960s with the publication of Michael Harrington's treatise. Of course, there is the notable exception of the Occupy Wall Street movement, a grassroots organization of millions of people who began gathering in spontaneous public demonstrations in 2011 across the nation to reject the economic status quo. Despite all the publicity the Occupy movement has garnered, however, it has done little to motivate Americans to prompt the government to take action. Indeed, one can argue that we as a nation have not made much progress since the War on Poverty in the 1960s. My good friend and mentor, the late Dr. Kenneth Bancroft Clark, the black psychologist who created a nationally known antipoverty program in Harlem in the 1960s known as Harlem Youth Opportunities Unlimited (HARYOU), conceded in 1968 toward the end of the War on Poverty that "a serious war against poverty, like any other war, eventually has to be judged in terms of its results. It is the ultimate victory that counts. By this standard, the war on poverty must now be seen as approaching defeat."[3]

At the time of *The Other America*'s publication, Dwight Macdonald, the highly respected writer and editor of *Partisan Review* who also wrote for the *New Yorker*, said of Harrington's book in 1963: "In the admirably short space of under two hundred pages, he outlines the problem, describes in imaginative detail what it means to be poor in this country today, summarizes the findings of recent studies by economists and sociologists, and analyzes the reasons for the persistence of mass poverty in the midst of general prosperity."[4]

Poverty in America is even worse today than it was in the 1960s. Indeed, in my view—based on an in-depth study of the past five decades of presidential administrations since the 1960s—I think it can be stated with historical proof that the famed War on Poverty has been lost. Consequently, I believe that something must be done—immediately—to awaken the conscience of all Americans and to renew the sense of urgency that launched that initial history-making assault on poverty in the 1960s. Government, private enterprises, and foundations must join together in a fresh new charge against poverty. Poverty, in a phrase, is no longer in vogue. As one pundit put it in 2011 at the height of the Republican presidential primaries: "Poverty remains the taboo word on the campaign stump, among lawmakers, the media, and the general public. It remains even a taboo word among many of the poor."[5]

Meanwhile, providing a new sense of urgency on the long-ignored issue of poverty, in an Op-Ed article in the *New York Times*, journalist David Bornstein once again paid tribute to Michael Harrington when he wrote on January 12, 2012:

> Is it time to rethink our basic assumptions about the way we fight poverty? When Michael Harrington's landmark book on poverty, "The Other America," was published in 1962, Harrington startled the nation's leaders, including President John F. Kennedy, by shining a spotlight on the deep poverty that remained hidden in America. Harrington's book became an underpinning for the War on Poverty. Half a century later, the United States Census Bureau has produced what may become another landmark reference. Based on an updated method for assessing poverty, the bureau has found that far more Americans are scraping by than was previously known: 100 million Americans—one in three—are "deep poor," "poor," or "near poor."[6]

Bornstein continued: "Adding to the impact of this analysis is the growing realization that American society has become more calcified.

The decline of social mobility in the United States is now acknowledged as a serious problem by Democrats and Republicans alike."[7]

What does it mean to be poor? Definitions of "poor" and "poverty" have changed over the decades. Daniel P. (Pat) Moynihan, a Harvard sociology professor and one-time counselor to the late president Richard M. Nixon, once wrote in the 1960s: "The poor are those able-bodied adults and their dependent children whose lack of income and wealth places them at the bottom most layer of the distribution and whose sources of income lie in either welfare payments or in unskilled and poorly paid occupations."[8]

A more up-to-date definition of poverty in *Webster's New World Dictionary of American English* reads, simply:

> The condition or quality of being poor, indigence; a specific quality, etc.; inadequacy (poverty of the soil, her poverty of imagination; smallness in amount; scarcity; paucity). SYN: poverty, the broadest of these terms implies a lack of the resources for reasonably comfortable living; destitution and want imply such great poverty that the means for mere subsistence, such as food and shelter, are lacking; indigence, a somewhat euphemistic term, implies a lack of luxuries which one formerly enjoyed. Penury suggests such severe poverty as to cause misery, or loss of self-respect.[9]

The singular purpose of this book is to put poverty back on the front page of every newspaper and magazine in America, and on every radio, Internet, and TV newscast. It is intended to be a clarion call to action, primarily on the part of the federal government but also involving private enterprise and the not-for-profit sectors. This effort might seem counterintuitive at a time when our political leaders in a politically broken Washington are so much at loggerheads about budgets, deficits, taxes, and the underlying structure of our historically cherished safety net programs. One can reasonably argue that it is hardly the time to reignite a campaign against poverty while the country is in economic crisis, but the fact is that the middle class is now the "new poor."[10] The new face of poverty in America has a decidedly middle-class appearance. The Great Recession is still taking a heavy toll.

I would argue it is long past the time for action. If not now—when?

Unlike the 1960s, we now have the leading-edge technology, the insight, and the experience to create an innovative approach to eradicating poverty. Developing new ideas is what we are best at doing. It could certainly open a new pathway for badly needed jobs, educational opportunities, and long-range stability. We might as well face this issue up front and not allow debt to pile up decade after decade as it has for many of our other major social programs.

Despite the profound philosophical divide between the two major political parties about the appropriate role of government, I am firmly convinced that we must address the poverty crisis now. It is bitterly ironic that poverty has become a multimillion-dollar business in itself. The numerous studies and analyses of poverty—not to mention the many books, including this one—have become an industry of their own. It is an intellectual refuge for social scientists; consultants in demographics; psychiatry and psychology, housing, education, health, and welfare experts; futurists; and medical and more professionals. The many millions of dollars spent thus far on studying poverty and hiring people to design antipoverty programs could well have gone for improving many people's lives. As *New York Times* columnist David Brooks has written (presumably tongue in cheek): "The United States spends far more on education than any other nation, with paltry results. It spends far more on health care, again, with paltry results. *It spends so much on poverty programs that if we just took that money and handed poor people checks, we would virtually eliminate poverty overnight.* In the progressive era, the task was to build programs; today the task is to reform existing ones."[11][Italics added.]

I still believe, as Michael Harrington wrote in 1962, that "it is clear that the government is the only institution in the society capable of dealing with the problem [of poverty]."[12] The very foundation of our country—our national security—depends, in large part, on our economic stability and our political will to bring about long-awaited structural changes.

Foreshadowing the present, Harrington also said of his findings:

> Throughout, I work on an assumption that cannot be proved by Government figures or even documented by impressions of the other Americans. It is an ethical proposition, and it can be simply stated: In a nation with a technology that could provide every citizen with a decent life, it is an outrage and a scandal that there should be such social misery. Only if one begins with this assumption, is it possible to pierce through the invisibility of 40,000,000 to 50,000,000 human beings and to see the other Americans. We must perceive passionately, if this blindness is to be lifted from us.[13]

The solution? Many informed observers believe the answer is to resurrect President Lyndon Johnson's original goal: Welfare's aim should not be to provide more government handouts. Instead, we must focus on promoting prosperous self-sufficiency, increasing the number of Americans who can support themselves above poverty without welfare and, as a majority of politicians have said, take responsibility for themselves. Indeed, while poverty has intermittently come back into the news since 2010, not enough public officials are speaking about it. Washington must come to life. It must acknowledge that this nation cannot exist divided between the 1 percent who capture half of all the rewards of capitalism's growth and the many others whose lives grow ever more tenuous, with more and more people in the middle class descending into poverty.

On a personal note, I have had a lifelong interest in poverty, dating back to my formative years. I am still passionate about the subject even five decades after I first decided, as a young, ambitious reporter, to expose New York City's slums. One does not give up one's principle beliefs, even with the passage of time and the aging process. It is too easy to become cynical.

By way of background, I attended the Ethical Culture Fieldston School in New York City in the 1940s, a private institution that stressed every individual's responsibility to society and a progressive approach to education. Its students came mostly from the middle and upper classes financially. Those years were influential, helping me become an idealist who wanted to bring about social reform when I reached adulthood. During my teens I worked as a volunteer at the University Settlement House on Manhattan's Lower East Side and learned an important part of the immigrant story.

Afterward, I majored in sociology at Dartmouth College and learned to be an investigative reporter at Columbia University's Graduate School of Journalism. Subsequently, as a reporter, I covered LBJ's War on Poverty and worked with Johnson's Office of Economic Opportunity, led by R. Sargent Shriver Jr., head of the War on Poverty. As a journalist, I reported on the extent of poverty in New York City and moved into a slum at 311 East 100th Street in East Harlem. My ten-part series of articles titled "I Lived in a Slum" published in the *New York World-Telegram & Sun* in 1959 earned a nomination for a Pulitzer Prize.[14]

Living in a stench-filled, rat-infested, airless slum building for two months in the summer with dozens of other people sleeping side by side in tiny rooms was the most horrifying and, at the same time, most memorable experience of my professional life. I can still smell the slums. The air was stifling, and the apartments and hallways had a nauseating odor that filled my lungs with dirt. I had a desperate desire to escape. I lived with drug addicts who used needles in the basement when they thought nobody was looking. I spoke at length with several of these drug-addicted young men and listened to their stories. Stories of hopelessness. Stories of purposelessness. Stories of no yesterday and no tomorrow. I was sickened and scared by what I saw, smelled, and felt. I was slipping into the very morass I had come to write about. Depressing is hardly the word for what I felt. I went from disillusionment to hopelessness to fear and, finally, to anger—anger so heated that I could only pound my typewriter ferociously to get the story out. I wanted to upset all of the contented middle-class New Yorkers and those materialistic, self-involved suburbanites who lived so comfortably behind white picket fences, safe and sound in their own pockets of plenty.

Based on this nightmarish experience, I poured out my observations and emotions in a book on slums and poverty, *Let in the Sun* (Macmillan, 1964). My story covered the anatomy of that very slum on East 100th Street from its construction as a New Law Tenement in 1901 to its reputation as "the worst block" in New York City in the 1960s, as sociologist Nathan Glazer described the building in an article about the progress East Harlem had made since the 1960s.[15] Congressman (later New York mayor) John V. Lindsay, who introduced housing legislation to help New York City when he was in Congress, wrote the foreword to *Let in the Sun*. And I was honored to have Michael Harrington review *Let in the Sun* in the *New York Herald Tribune*.[16] After the book was published in 1964, NBC's producer of *David Brinkley's Journal* asked me to write a TV script about the building for Brinkley.[17] That project was a huge lift for me as a young reporter. After joining WCBS-TV as an on-air investigative reporter, I arranged for an exclusive interview with New York senator Robert F. Kennedy at the 311 East 100th Street building, since he had shown a keen interest in poverty at the time. He expressed dismay at what he saw there and pledged to clean it up.

I hasten to add that while writing about New York City's slums, I read over and over again the incisive books written by the Danish immigrant Jacob A. Riis, a crusading journalist-reformer who had immigrated to the United States in 1870. After years of living in extreme poverty and hardship in New York City, he finally found employment as a police reporter for the *New York Tribune* in 1877.

The following year, he went to work as a reporter and photojournal-
ist for the *New York Evening Sun*, a newspaper that eventually merged
with two other newspapers to become the *New York World-Telegram &
Sun* (where I later worked). Riis became one of the first reporters to
practice what has long been called muckraking journalism, or digging up
all the dirt and scandal he could to expose the evil practices of the slum
landlords who preyed on innocent poor people in dark, dank tenement
houses of New York. His first book, *How the Other Half Lives: Studies among the Tenements of New York*, was published in 1890 and was a
historic work, revealing "the sea of a mighty population held in galling
fetters [that] heaves uneasily in the tenements."[18] The volume caught the
ever-sharp eyes of Theodore Roosevelt, then the New York City Police
commissioner. He befriended and teamed up with Riis and ordered the
police to close down the local slum buildings described in Riis's book.

Like Riis, I was thoroughly imbued with the idea that the slums
could be eradicated. I still believe it. In 1964, I discovered that his second wife, Mary Phillips Riis, was still alive. I interviewed her at length
in her apartment on Manhattan's Upper East Side. During this interview, Mrs. Riis talked a great deal about her husband's friendship with
Theodore Roosevelt, at one point telling me that "Jake and Teddy were
close friends."[19] She shared with me a comment that Roosevelt had
made to her privately: "If I were asked to name a fellow man who came
nearest to being the ideal American, I should name Jacob Riis."[20] Riis,
whose autobiography, *The Making of an American*, was published in
1901, died on May 26, 1914.

Riis's reporting inspired me on a daily basis. He had been a menace
to the officials and slum landlords responsible, as he saw it, for the despi-
cable condition of the tenements where the poor lived. I felt as though
I were chasing the ghost of a great man, imitating his writing style, and
doggedly pursuing phantom owners of slum buildings who hid behind
blind corporate names. I even tracked many of them down in their luxu-
rious homes in the suburbs and confronted them with evidence of numerous violations in their buildings. In one instance, a landlord filed suit
against my newspaper and me, but he settled it before it came to trial.
He paid his overdue fines for his failure to provide the basic amenities of
life: hot water, heat, and electricity.

I was passionately indignant that businessmen without ethics or
compassion could take advantage of the poor. I felt that way in my very
bones, and I imagined the powerful impact Riis's crusades against slums
must have had on his newspaper's readers and on city officials.

Following the closing of the *World-Telegram & Sun* in 1966, I served as New York mayor John Lindsay's first press secretary, then as his assistant for housing and urban development, touring the slums of New York at his side. In addition, I spent some time with Lindsay when he and Governor Otto Kerner of Illinois were cochairs of President Johnson's bipartisan National Advisory Commission on Civil Disorders, which produced the all-inclusive 1968 Kerner Report. Its basic conclusion: "Our nation is moving toward two societies, one black, and one white—separate and unequal."[21] Race and poverty were so closely entwined that they were linked together in the public mind—and they still are today.

In 1968, when I was still serving the Lindsay administration as an assistant administrator for the city's Housing and Development Administration superagency, I wrote an article published by *New York Magazine* on May 6, 1968, titled "Why One of the Worst Slums in New York Hasn't Been Torn Down." I offered my newly gained insight as a city housing official—myself then *inside* city government—of the overwhelming bureaucracy and red tape involved in tearing down any single building in the city, let alone one slum building. It was finally demolished in a progressive public-private partnership program, sponsored by the Maremount Foundation and the U.S. Gypsum Company in the 1970s called Metro North, and replaced with low-rent apartments and playgrounds.

With all this experience serving as motivation, I began my journey to research and write this book about poverty in America and how each of our nation's presidents dealt—or failed to deal—with it. My findings, which vary from president to president, follow. Notwithstanding some presidents' strong social consciences and seeming determination to eliminate poverty, collectively, they have all failed to lesser or greater degrees. Thus, my desire grew over these many years to focus on poverty through the lens of presidential history to find out why.

My conclusions are based on my own subjective analysis. They do not necessarily reflect anyone else's from either major political party or, for that matter, any other individual in public or private life. I alone am responsible for the contents of this book.

I have traced policies and actions—or lack of them—in an examination of the records of all forty-four U.S. presidencies to date. When appropriate, credit is given to a president who made a sincere and tangible effort to help the poor. In many instances, however, presidents either failed to put poverty high on their agendas or became preoccupied with other matters, giving social welfare issues a low priority or ignoring them completely.

It is the story of accumulative neglect, interspersed with some herculean efforts—most notably those of Abraham Lincoln, Theodore Roosevelt, Franklin D. Roosevelt, and Lyndon B. Johnson. The study reflects the actions of each president, from George Washington to Barack Obama. Ironically, the latter pledged to wipe out poverty in the United States in a moving speech he gave in Springfield, Illinois, on February 10, 2007, when he announced his candidacy for the presidency. Only months later the U.S. economy came crashing down, obviously making it exceedingly more difficult for him to keep this pledge.

The realities of governing, with all of the ups and downs and surprises that confront American presidents, have not enabled any one president to make the kind of breakthrough most Americans seek. That failing may be a function of a two-term limit, or, more likely, it may result from the lack of vision and practical resources of any single president to rise to the challenge. Congressional deadlock, especially over budgetary issues, has also hampered the ability of recent presidents to carry out their agendas.

Nonetheless, overall, we have made some progress since the republic was founded in 1776. Looking ahead, it is possible that if the United States were to have a series of presidents with one consistent primary goal in mind—the elimination of poverty—the generations-old stain on America could be eradicated.

I should add that I firmly believe, even after more than fifty years of writing about poverty, that it is truly possible to rid America of its slums. I reject the traditional cynical wisdom that has prevailed through the ages. Instead, as author Peter Singer noted in explaining the reason he wrote his book *The Life You Can Save: Acting Now to Save World Poverty*: "I have been thinking and writing for more than thirty years about how we should respond to hunger and poverty."[22] As he noted,

> Moving images, in real time, of people on the edge of survival are beamed into our living rooms. Not only do we know a lot about the desperately poor, but we also have much more to offer them in terms of better health care, improved seeds and agricultural techniques, and new technologies for generating electricity. More amazing, through instant communications and open access to a wealth of information that surpasses the greater libraries of the pre-Internet age, we can enable them to join the world community—if only we can help them to get far enough out of poverty to seize the opportunity.[23]

While America has declared wars against poverty, drugs, and terrorism, I believe we must win the war against poverty at home first if we are ever to ensure our national security, turn back terrorism, and fulfill our potential as the most successful experiment in democracy in history.

Certainly, the Occupy Wall Street demonstrations and similar protests in cities across the country in 2011–2012 have shown that the young people are angry and frustrated. In Kansas in late 2011, President Obama tapped into this growing unhappiness in a campaign speech when he warned that the growing disparity between rich and poor meant that the United States was undermining its middle class and "gives lie to the promise at the very heart of America: that this is the place where you make it if you try."[24] He advocated that the government should play a strong role in taxing and regulating. Broadly interpreted, this effort would mean spreading the wealth. Obama said, "At stake, . . . is whether this will be a country where working people can earn enough to raise a family, build a modest savings, own a home, and secure their retirement."[25]

As a journalist and an activist, I have been disillusioned at times, but somehow I managed to hang on to the inner core of my beliefs. President Obama expressed it best in his book *The Audacity of Hope: Thoughts on Reclaiming the American Dream*, when he wrote: "We hang on to our values, even if they seem at times tarnished and worn; even if, as a nation and in our own lives, we have betrayed them more often than we care to remember. What else is there to guide us? Those values are our inheritance, what makes us who we are as a people."[26]

Michael Harrington's admonition fifty years ago is as applicable today as it was when he wrote it: "I would beg the reader to forget the numbers game. Whatever the precise calibrations, it is obvious that these statistics represent an enormous, an unconscionable amount of human suffering in this land. They should be read with a sense of outrage. For until these facts shame us, until they stir us to action, the other America will continue to exist, a monstrous example of needless suffering in the most advanced society in the world."[27]

In the same spirit Harrington's book ignited in the first War on Poverty a half century ago, I submit that it is the time for all Americans again to forge a strong coalition to win this generations-old fight once and for all. I sincerely hope that this book helps to serve as a spark to fire up American ingenuity, imagination, and creativity to rid our nation of poverty.

ACKNOWLEDGMENTS

First and foremost, I am deeply indebted to the invaluable assistance I received for the past two and a half years from Nancy Kuhn-Clark, a highly intelligent, professional, always upbeat, can-do reference librarian on the staff at the Westport Public Library. Without her painstaking research, this book could not have been written.

I am also most thankful to Hilary Claggett, senior editor at Potomac Books, for honoring with me the assignment to write this book about American poverty. She has been most helpful in guiding me through the editorial process and making constructive suggestions in the structure and contents of the book. In that process, I want to express my profound appreciation to Amanda Irle, associate production editor, for her superb work in shaping and adding her valuable insights to the manuscript and in steering it through the production procedure to its publication; and finally, my gratitude to Vicki Chamlee, copyeditor, for reviewing and editing the final pages.

I would also like to acknowledge the critical work of Peggy Daily, a detail-minded freelance copyeditor, who helped polish the entire manuscript from its inception. Her observations were insightful and helped the manuscript flow smoothly.

I am grateful as well to Westport Library director Maxine Bleiweis, who made her staff available to me. I also want to thank the library's Susan Madeo, interlibrary loan coordinator; and my special thanks go to Carolyn Zygmont, another Westport reference librarian, for studiously compiling the bibliography.

In addition, my thanks go to designer Miggs Burroughs, a good friend and colleague, whose talents as a nationally recognized illustrator have been on display in this and previous books I have written.

Finally, I want to express my heartfelt appreciation to my extraordinarily patient wife, Audrey, who has always been my toughest but most valuable critic.

INTRODUCTION

THE POLITICS OF POVERTY:
WHY IS IT STILL PLAGUING AMERICA?

Tear down the old. Build up the new. Down with the rotten, anti-
quated rat holes. Down with hovels. Down with disease. Down with
crime. Down with firecraft. Let in the sun. Let in the sky. A new day
is dawning. A new life. A new America!
—Mayor Fiorello H. La Guardia, New York, 1944

"The past is prologue"[1] is a centuries-old truism that applies perfectly to
the anatomy of poverty in the United States, beginning with the birth of
our nation in 1776. Only a thorough analysis of what has happened in
the fight against poverty in America during the past 237 years will explain
why the alarming spread of poverty now threatens our national security.

Pockets of poverty are rapidly spreading across America, as the nation's states and cities go broke and bankrupt. Economic stability is the
foundation of the United States' hold on world leadership. We are only
as strong as our weakest link—and that is why poverty should be on
the front burner of our domestic agenda again. Despite a series of tax
cuts since the 1980s, not only has inequality of wealth increased but the
pathway for individuals to rise out of their own economic class has also
narrowed.

As a result, poverty has climbed steadily to record levels during the
Great Recession, starting in December 2007. Further, the issuance of
food stamps expanded to proportions that once seemed unthinkable,
and Republicans derisively called President Barack Obama "the food
stamp president" during their primary campaign in 2012. The pundits
labeled the difference between the middle class and the poor the "great
American divide." Indeed, Obama made it one of the major themes of

1

his reelection campaign, kicking it off in his State of the Union address on January 24, 2012, by emphasizing that one of his most important goals for his next four years would be to ensure "fairness" for everyone in economic opportunity.

Many political observers believe that the president of the United States must take the lead in restoring job security, economic growth, and military readiness during this period of extended threats by worldwide terrorism. The number of Americans who are living in poverty is on track for a record increase, with the ranks of working-age poor approaching levels not seen since the 1960s, when the nation waged its first War on Poverty.

The message is stark: *one out of three Americans—or 100 million poor*—is a sobering indicator of the acutely ill health of America's current economic system. In May 2012, U.S. Census Bureau economist Kathleen S. Short explained how the census arrived at the calculation: "The Census Bureau found that there are 51.4 million in the group of people with income/resources between 100 and 150 percent of the Supplementary Poverty Measure [SPM] poverty thresholds. If you add to this 49.1 million people with income/resources below 100 percent of their SPM poverty threshold, there were a total of 100 million people with income/resources below 150 percent of the SPM poverty threshold. This represents one-third of the total U.S. population of 306.1 million people."[2] Short pointed out the many differences between the official poverty measure and the SPM by taking into account total income, food stamps, housing subsidies, energy assistance, geographic location, earned income tax credit, and cost of living index. Sheldon Danziger, one of the foremost experts on poverty, put it simply: "If I were using the Census Bureau data, I would say that there are about forty-six million people who are officially poor, another fifty-seven million who have incomes between the poverty line and twice the poverty line [a grand total of 103 million]."[3]

The greatest tension in American society is attributed to the increasing gap between the wealthy and the poor.[4] The reliable Pew Research Center conducted a survey and found that the message "regarding the increase in income inequality—branded by the Occupy Wall Street movement and pressed by Democrats—may be sweeping into the national consciousness."[5] The survey cited a 50 percent increase in income inequality since 1992 when immigration was perceived as the greatest source of tension between the rich and poor. Richard Morin, a senior editor at Pew Social and Democratic Trends, which conducted the survey, said, "Income inequality is no longer just for the economists. It has moved off the business pages onto the front page."[6]

Regardless of how income is distributed, many Americans fervently believe that despite the Great Recession, the United States is still the richest, most powerful nation in the world in 2013. But the trend has been—and continues to be—sobering. The past five years have seen the near bankruptcy of many of our previously rock solid financial institutions, stubborn high unemployment, increasing food prices, volatile gasoline prices, a collapse of the housing market, stock market uncertainty, and the fall of America's previously undisputed position as the world's leader in the automobile industry. Some Americans appear to have had their confidence in the capitalist system shaken, and they have all but lost trust in our national government, our immigration policies, and our two-party political system. The last has been accurately described as "dysfunctional," especially pertaining to the Congress since 2008.

This crisis is far worse than anyone could have predicted in the 1960s. The rising number of homeless people in America—a topic widely publicized in the media in recent years—clearly illustrates the fiercely urgent need for action in America today. The fact is that more and more middle-class Americans—many of whom lost their homes through foreclosures in the Great Recession—find themselves homeless. Nearly every day, we are confronted with heartbreaking video clips of people's despair at becoming homeless, with newspaper, magazine, and Internet stories vividly describing the excruciating suffering so many Americans are experiencing. It has become a fixture in our daily news diet and remains an anathema to many affluent Americans whose lives have been relatively undisturbed so far.

Even worse, little substantive dialogue in the presidential campaign of 2012—especially during the Republican primaries—focused on the urgent issue of poverty. The disconnect between the issues that the Republican candidates debated and reality was stark. It was almost as if the GOP contenders had an unspoken agreement not to touch the topic because, as was the case in the past, it does not grab most voters' attention. When it was raised in the last phase of the campaign with only two men (the president and Republican candidate Mitt Romney) left standing, the Obama administration was forced to defend its record on the inequity of income equality and the alarming increase in poverty, homelessness, and housing defaults, among other consequences of the Great Recession. How bad is the family homelessness problem in America? It's bad enough that 1.5 million American children are now homeless, or

38 percent of the entire homeless population, compared to 1 percent in 1988, according to a report by Dr. Ellen Bassuk, founder and president of the National Center on Family Homelessness.[7]

As stated in a trilogy of books, *Homelessness in America*, edited by Robert Hartmann McNamara,

> The American social landscape is littered with examples of homelessness, from men gathering outside a shelter near the end of the day in the hopes of a bed for the evening to middle-aged men with handmade signs that read, "Will Work for Food." Others may have observed women wearing layers of clothing pushing shopping carts full of items that most would consider trash. Still others might have encountered entrepreneurial individuals who sell newspapers or clean windshields at traffic lights in the hopes of a small donation. To the public, these scenarios serve as visible and tangible reminders of the plight of the homeless. However, this perception serves to desensitize Americans to the plight of the homeless. Because so many people have been exposed to the most visible dimension of the population, they have become used to their presence and, at the same time, annoyed by it.[8]

The facts are more complex. During these several years of the Great Recession, tens of thousands of people who had their homes seized through foreclosures now make up what might be called "the invisible poor." They are not necessarily on the streets or in shelters, but they have been forced to find a temporary place to stay. As various television programs have shown, such as *60 Minutes'* in-depth interviews with homeless families in Florida, these people have moved in with relatives, friends, or even, in the worst cases, in their cars or vans.[9]

Collectively, the breakup of families and losing their homes as a result of unemployment, the failure to create enough jobs for the jobless, the housing bubble, the Wall Street and corporate bailouts, the bitter bickering in Congress about how to solve the alarmingly increasing national debt, and the federal government's runaway deficits have all converged as a "perfect storm" of economic and social crises, the likes of which Americans have not seen since the Great Depression (1929–1940). It is time, therefore, for a long-overdue action plan, especially now that more and more people are slipping into poverty. Poverty was conspicuously absent as a major issue in the recent presidential campaign because the catastrophic effects of millions of broken lives does not attract votes. Slums are not sexy. They do not grab people's attention in the same way that job losses and foreclosures do. The uncomfortable reality is that the government in 2011 defined the poverty line as a meager annual income of $23,050 for a family of four and $11,170 for an individual—amounts on which it is virtually impossible to survive.[10]

Poverty has been—and still should be—arguably a huge concern in our national political dialogue in 2013 and beyond. The following stark figures tell the disturbing story of our critical national crisis: in 2013, one out of three Americans lives in poverty—or on the edge of poverty—twice as many as author Michael Harrington reported in his seminal book, *The Other America*, more than fifty years ago.[11] True, the population has increased 58 percent since 1962, but the quickening increase in the number of Americans mired in poverty is alarming. Consider, for example, these statistics:

- The number of Americans who lived in poverty in 2011—49.1 million whose income and resources fell below 100 percent of their SPM poverty threshold—is the largest number in the fifty-two years during which the U.S. Census Bureau has published poverty estimates.[12]
- Washington University in St. Louis published a study in 2011 that revealed nearly half of American seniors will face poverty in the future.[13]
- According to the National Coalition for the Homeless, between 2.3 million and 3.5 million people are homeless in America. Of these, an estimated 39 percent are children.[14]
- Twenty-five percent of very young children are living in poverty, according to the Census Bureau's analysis.[15]
- The number of people living in neighborhoods of extreme poverty grew by a third over the past decade, according to a Brookings Institution report, and erased most of the gains from the 1990s when concentrated poverty declined.[16]

Following are some additional figures supporting the observation that the country has made little, if any, progress in eradicating poverty in recent years: 2009 saw the largest single increase in our poverty rate since the U.S. Census Bureau began keeping figures in 1959. According to its official figures, in 2009, 43.6 million people were poor, up from 39.8 million in 2008 and 37.3 million in 2007. The nation's official poverty rate in 2009 was 14.3 percent, up from 13.2 percent in 2008—the second statistically significant annual increase in the poverty rate since 2004. In 2010, 45 million Americans lived in poverty, and in 2011, the poverty rate increased again owing to the job-killing impact of the Great Recession. In 2012, in 2013, and thereafter,[17] the trend is likely to continue to worsen unless the economy improves considerably. Too many middle-class Americans are slipping into poverty every year.

The disgraceful result? The United States has the third worst rate of poverty—measured by poor people's per capita income—among the developed nations as tracked by the Organization for Economic Co-operation and Development. Only Turkey and Mexico are worse. This finding alone should be enough to shame all Americans and awaken us to the huge cost of poverty on the American economy and, most important, on the American psyche. Moreover, since our national security depends, in large part, on the economic health of all Americans, at the outset of 2013 America needs to move from its tired, old approach and solicit both fresh ideas from young people with knowledge, skills, and commitment, and new strategies to rid our nation of poverty—once and for all.

It is ironic, I think, to close this introduction with an observation I made nearly fifty years ago in my first book about slums, *Let in the Sun*. Tragically, it is as applicable today as it was when I first put the following words to paper in 1964: "It is time the United States government launched the biggest and most effective attack on slums the world has ever known. The dark shadow of the house at 311 East 100th Street has loomed over this nation for generations. We must now remove it forever and let in the sun."[18]

Why is poverty still plaguing America? In the United States, where surface has always passed for substance, we have heard political rhetoric in every generation promising to rid the country of poverty, but inevitably each has failed to take serious, effective action. In this book is a chronological analysis of how each of our presidents coped with poverty.[19] The following chapters are intended to answer the question why we are still struggling with this generations-old, self-imposed curse on American civilization.

1

FOUNDING THE REPUBLIC (1789–1829):

WASHINGTON, JOHN ADAMS, JEFFERSON, MADISON, MONROE, JOHN QUINCY ADAMS

I never mean . . . to possess another slave by purchase; it being among my first wishes to see some plan adopted by which slavery in this Country may be abolished.

—George Washington, in a letter to his friend,
John Frances Mercer, September 9, 1786

GEORGE WASHINGTON (1789–1797) arguably had the most intimidating challenge of any president of the United States. When he took office on April 30, 1789, the fifty-seven-year-old former war hero and general faced an almost impossible task: he had to create from scratch an entirely new democratic government based on the Constitution that had been shaped earlier in Philadelphia at the Constitutional Convention.

Never before had a man taken on the awesome responsibility of forming a government based on the Enlightenment ideals of republican rule and individual rights. The fact was nobody—including those who had thrust the reluctant Washington into the leadership position he did not seek or want—knew what the outcome could be.

Giving Washington this responsibility was, perhaps, the boldest experiment in democracy in world history, especially since Washington had received no more than an elementary school education. His natural intelligence, his ability to listen, and his intuitive capability to make sound judgments made him stand out. He was one of ten children born into an aristocratic Virginia family. Nonetheless, by the time he was an adult, it was quite clear that he was a natural leader.

He developed into an awe-inspiring, athletic-looking military commander and a Federalist of Virginia. Washington stood ramrod tall—all six feet three inches of him—weighed 175 pounds, and had broad shoulders. On inauguration day on the Federal Hall's balcony on Wall Street in New York, while wearing a plain brown suit so as to avoid projecting an image of royalty or superiority of class, he was sworn in as the first president of the United States. A huge crowd cheered wildly. When Washington responded with a bow, the cheers grew even noisier and more enthusiastic. Then, Washington proceeded to the Senate chamber, where he made his first inaugural address before the members of both houses of Congress.

In that speech, Washington's modesty was on full display. He referred to his reluctance to assume the office and to his "lack of practice" in government administration. And he clearly referred to his desire that every citizen should benefit from the bounties that this new nation offered, stating: "There is no truth more thoroughly established, than that there exists in the economy and course of nature, an indissoluble union between virtue and happiness, between duty and advantage, between the genuine maxims of an honest and magnanimous policy, and the solid rewards of public prosperity and felicity."[1]

By linking the state of the nation's economy to "solid rewards of public prosperity and felicity," he introduced the concept of every man's right under the Constitution to earn a living and bear the fruit of his toil. Broadly speaking, one could interpret his fundamental philosophy as striving for economic success for everyone, thus preventing as many people as possible from falling into poverty.

The government—in particular, the presidency—was in a remarkably unformed stage. Other than organizing a government, Washington's biggest challenge as a protector of the people was to make certain that he looked after the best interests of all the people in the nation, including Native Americans, slaves, less fortunate white families among his constituents, and the homeless, many of whom begged for food on a daily basis.

One of the early federal policies that caused massive homelessness was the displacement of American Indians, especially tribes in the Southeast, who were essentially uprooted and moved west. In the 150 years before Washington's inauguration—beginning in 1607 when the first English settlers arrived in the New World—an American society had emerged distinct from their British predecessors; however, the newcomers were far from homogeneous. They were, in fact, an amalgamation of various national stocks from a number of European countries. Still, the English language bound them closely together, and their sense of general unity led to the formation of the colonies. By 1750, the thirteen colonies had nearly 1.5 million people. Most of the colonies developed quickly. Crime and pauperism were two social problems in most colonies, except in thrifty New England.

The one common challenge that all of the colonists faced was the need for economic security. The poverty-stricken people in the colonies who needed assistance were subject to a strict system of the original English Elizabethan Poor Laws, whose principles emphasized public responsibility for relief for the poor.

Washington enforced the Poor Laws, which had become far stricter than they had been when the early white settlers arrived in New England in the 1600s. Efforts to control costs through residency requirements and a passport system—arguably the first attempt to move people from welfare to work, a concept that would become politically acceptable centuries later—made it difficult for the Washington administration to reach out to the poor as much as it would have liked. "The number of poor greatly increased . . . and many persons, especially women and children, were destitute of employment and in danger of becoming a public charge," according to historians June Axinn and Mark J. Stern in their book *Social Welfare: A History of the American Response to Need.*[2]

"The Poor Laws," wrote Axinn and Stern, "were designed to protect those who held legal claim to settlement in particular localities. They offered protection against strangers who threatened the stability—namely, the morality and physical safety—of society singularly concerned with order and wary of new ways and different cultures."[3] They could be interpreted as the origin of what would become a "law and order" political slogan in future administrations in Washington, D.C., in the mid- to late twentieth century.

The Poor Laws also gave rise to what eventually became an accepted twentieth-century theory in social science: giving money to the poor indefinitely would only make them become involved in the cycle of poverty that would be passed down from one generation to the next. As Benjamin Franklin, a remarkable man of vision and insight, put it: "I have sometimes doubted whether the laws peculiar to England, which *compel the rich to maintain the poor* [italics Franklin's], have not given the latter a dependence that very much lessens the care of providing against the wants of old age."[4] As dire as those early laws may have been, it is important to note that the measures for military veterans were far more generous than those for the general public. They originated in 1626 when the Plymouth Colony declared that soldiers injured while defending the colonies were entitled to support,[5] depending on circumstances.

This directive could now be seen as the forerunner for what eventually became the GI Bill, originally known as the Servicemen's Readjustment Act of 1944.

Washington was up to the challenges he faced primarily because he was trusted and respected. As historians Allan Nevins and Henry Steel Commager expressed in their book, *A Short History of the United States*: "[Washington] commanded not merely obedience but a sort of awe, and he typified the idea of a union as nobody else could. Responsible men of every party and section trusted his fairness, breadth of view and sagacity."[6]

When Washington became president, he knew that every action he took would be examined carefully later. Extremely aware of his standing as the first president of the newly born Union, Washington wrote to James Madison on May 5, 1789: "As the first of everything, *in our situation* will serve to establish a precedent, it is devoutly wished on my part, that these precedents may be fixed on true principles."[7] [Italics in original.]

Therein lies the tale of how Washington conducted business as president—with an awareness that virtually everything he said and did was setting a precedent. Naturally, having served as the victorious general in the Revolutionary War, his management style was that of a military man: he delegated a great deal of responsibility to subordinates and gave himself the task of coordinating issues and making final decisions. One point was clear: Washington was the chief executive who gave orders as if he were still a general and head of the military but with less stridency. Executive authority, he believed, was strictly his own. Washington's reliance on department heads for advice, similar to his consulting his War Council during the Revolutionary War, set both a precedent for including the cabinet secretaries as part of the president's office and the tone for the entire nation. The country's population was then 3.9 million people.

One Washington biographer, Richard Harwell, described Washington this way:

> What he demanded for himself, he allowed with equal exactness to his fellow men. Anything that any person deserved at his hands, that person must receive on balanced scales, whether in monetary payment, reward, courtesy, candor or truth-telling. Justice could never walk with compromise. Nor did adherence to justice require that young Washington be a partisan of individuals. If injustice to any individual came under Washington's eye in his own command, he would correct it as a matter of course, but there he drew the line. He would do his

part to relieve human misery and he might be the champion of public causes. Rarely did he become the advocate of any man, lest support of one be injustice to another.[8]

Washington's election—with John Adams coming in second and therefore becoming vice president—served as the foundation of American politics and the reason to this day that he is still called the father of his country. He set the standards and the rules that put the nation on a path that has endured for more than two centuries, longer than any other democratic republic in history. He established precedents that have lasted for generations.

In at least two vital areas that would challenge America in the centuries to come—namely, those involving the relationship between the new American colonies and the Indians and the Negroes—Washington had the vision to articulate compassion, kindness, and a deep understanding of human relations. First, as the aristocratic French historian Alexis de Tocqueville wrote of Washington's early years in office: "In one of his messages to Congress Washington said: 'We are more enlightened and more powerful than the Indian nations; it behooves our honor to treat them with kindness and even generosity.'"[9]

Second, regarding Washington's attitude toward Negroes—most of whom were trapped in a minimum living standard in which they barely got by—he did not initially take issue with slavery publicly during the Revolutionary War. However, he confided privately to his friend and biographer David Humphreys, in late 1788 and early 1789, his sympathy for his slaves.

Washington contemplated freeing his slaves even before he was elected president. According to Henry Wiencek, a scholar and author of *An Imperfect God: George Washington, His Slaves, and the Creation of America*, Washington talked with Humphreys at Mount Vernon, Virginia, as he agonized over whether to attempt the presidency. Washington wrote:

> The unfortunate condition of the persons [slaves] whose labour [*sic*] in part I employed, has been the only unavoidable subject of regret. To make the Adults among them as easy & comfortable in their circumstances as their actual state of ignorance & improvidence would admit, & lay the foundation to prepare the rising generation [of slaves] for a destiny different from that in which they were born; afforded some satisfaction to my mind & could not hope to be displeasing to the justice of the Creator.[10]

Washington, in his will, directed that his slaves be freed after he died; however, he almost let them go free in 1789, the year he became president. Washington had "experienced a moral epiphany," according to historian Wiencek. "The hallmark of his plans for emancipation [of his slaves] was that they were drawn up in secret most of all from his family. This showed," Wiencek wrote, "that Washington had already decided upon emancipation as early as 1789, ten years before his death."[11]

While Washington kept his distance, physically, from people with whom he conversed, he was a sensitive person who showed his care for others—especially in his contact with slaves—in many small but important ways. For example, as historian Douglas Southall Freeman noted in his book *George Washington: A Biography*, in the spring of 1787, "the General had talked of buying a slave bricklayer, but when the Negro was made unhappy by the prospect of living at a distance from his wife, Washington changed the prospect to hire with the statement, 'I am unwilling to hurt the feelings of anyone.'"[12]

Washington has been criticized, along with other Founding Fathers, for owning slaves and keeping them in poverty compared to the living standards of the white population at the time. At one point, Washington expressed the sincere desire to see a plan adopted for the abolition of slavery, but he backed away from pressing the matter in Congress and kept his slaves in bondage during his lifetime. While not objecting to slavery, Washington could be classified, one could safely argue, as a benign slaveholder, whose progressive, humane intellect was a gift. In this way, he was far ahead of his time. Consequently, he could not do much about poverty, even if he wanted to, especially among the Negro slaves and the Indian tribes. He did however instill a strong moral and political foundation upon which future presidents could eventually bring about constructive social change.

Despite all that has been written about him, it should be noted that, above all, he was a reluctant leader. His selflessness was perhaps his most appealing characteristic. He never requested the positions and the high honors he received. When asked to head the Continental Army in 1775, Washington expressed concern that he might not have the natural abilities to take on the challenge. Again, when he was asked to chair the Constitutional Convention, he did so reluctantly, coming out of comfortable retirement in his Mount Vernon home to create nothing less than a brand-new government. At the close of the convention, everyone in attendance clearly thought that Washington was by far the best-qualified, most popular, and certainly the most publicly acceptable man to lead the United States as president. It was no secret that he did not want the responsibility of leadership of this history-making experiment in self-rule, but he obliged once again because of his overriding sense of honor and duty to his country.

As a first step toward transforming the ideas in the Constitution into a real government, Washington and Congress—the elected officials representing each of the states—passed the Judiciary Act of 1789, which established the judicial courts in the third branch of the federal government. This basic structure would later play a key role when future presidents actually mobilized the government in later years to address the increasingly burdensome social issue of poverty in the states. While the fundamental departments such as the secretary of state and secretary of the treasury were created, it was premature in America's growth for anyone to think of organizing separate departments for such key matters as health, housing, welfare, environment, energy, and even homeland security. Much of these groups were formed as a result of national and international crises.

Although Washington's tenure proved to be more inspirational than concrete in terms of addressing poverty, he laid the fundamental building blocks for social change. From the outset, Washington worked with Congress to pass legislation that would be helpful in keeping peace treaties with funds specifically labeled for that purpose. For example, he made certain that laws were passed that did not permit anyone "to carry on any trade or intercourse with the Indian tribes, without a license for that purpose under the hand and seal of the superintendent of the Indian department [appointed by the president]."[13] Washington also made certain that the government could employ Indians, if needed, in the course of its work in land settlement.[14]

Washington introduced hundreds of additional measures that Congress passed in an attempt to ease the tension between the government and the Indians. It can safely be concluded, as historian William F. B. Vodrey did in his article in *American History* magazine: "No one worked harder or did more than George Washington to see that the United States would become—and remain—one nation, indivisible."[15]

In the end, the key to America's future was based on Washington's belief that the Union was built on a foundation that would support "much purer civil liberty and greater public happiness than have hitherto been the portion of mankind," in the words of social historian Michael B. Katz.[16] Prophetically, he added the hope that America would "prove an asylum for the persecuted of all nations"—a dream that would be fully realized in future generations.

The government helped to set up outdoor relief (local communities forming assistance to destitute people) in Washington's time; they served as forerunners for the poorhouses (also known as almshouses) that evolved in the early nineteenth century for people too poor to support themselves. However, in those earliest days of transformation in government, no clear demarcations separated average citizens from those in need of help because the public and private sectors lacked structural solutions.

Postscript: An analysis of Washington's sterling character would not be complete without referring to what arguably was his most outstanding personal trait, civility. He promoted civility in politics and throughout American life. Just as he had in the military, when he issued orders against using profanity, Washington emphasized in his role as president the importance of good manners, honesty, and loyalty. This philosophy was evident in his dealings with virtually everyone with whom he came in contact, including minorities and the poor. Unfortunately, this particular legacy has not been passed down through the generations of Washington politics.

It is not an exaggeration to say that Washington achieved virtually all that he set out to do. He created a government and held it together during eight years of stress and strain. Washington's legacy, of course, was not altogether pure. As a slave owner himself, his place in history is slightly blemished, despite his personal feelings of admiration for his slaves and establishing terms for their freedom. On August 18, 1799—a decade after he first took office—Washington expressed his inner thoughts about slavery, looking back in a letter to a friend, Robert Lewis, in which he said that he was opposed to traffic in the human species. Conflicting reports say Washington's will stipulated that upon his wife's death that his slaves should be freed and that his heirs had to feed and clothe those who were incapable of supporting themselves.[17]

At the close of his second term, the economy was strong and the spirit of the people never better. Inspired by Washington—whom they perceived as being above politics—the Americans of his time believed with certainty that the country would continue to be exceptional. No doubt, this belief led to the relatively modern phrase "American exceptionalism," which Alexis de Tocquville first used in his seminal book *Democracy in America*, published in 1835.[18]

JOHN ADAMS (1797–1801), sixty-one, of Massachusetts and a Federalist like his predecessor, served George Washington mostly as a diplomat abroad for eight years while awaiting his turn to be president. He was an intellectual who is best remembered as a politician-diplomat. He served only one term, which began on a gloomy day in March 1797. He has been described as "insecure, ambitious, pretentious, opinionated, and prone to fits of anger."[19]

America's second president was a learned, well-read, thoughtful man, who is better remembered as a political philosopher than as a politician. Born in the Massachusetts Bay Colony in 1735, he was a Harvard-educated lawyer and an ardent patriot. As a delegate to the First and Second Continental Congresses, he led the movement for independence.

In his inaugural address on March 4, 1797, Adams praised the fundamental principles that came out of the Constitutional Convention in Philadelphia. He cited measures that were taken to create "a plan to form a more perfect union, establish justice, insure domestic tranquility, provide for the common defense, promote the general welfare, and secure the blessings of liberty. The public disquisitions, discussions, and deliberations issued in the present happy Constitution of Government." He summed up his service abroad under Washington this way:

> Employed in the service of my country abroad during the whole course of these transactions, I first saw the Constitution of the United States in a foreign country. Irritated by no literary altercation, animated by no public debate, heated by no party animosity, I read it with great satisfaction, as the result of good heads prompted by good hearts, as an experiment better adapted to the genius, character, situation, and relations of this nation and country than any which had ever been proposed or suggested. In its general principles and great outlines it was conformable to such a system of government as I had ever most esteemed, and in some States, my own native State in particular, had contributed to establish.[20]

It is instructive to note that Adams, as president, showed signs of his personal philosophical commitment to freedom and independence for all Americans in a document he wrote in 1765 while still in England. It reflected his keen interest in poverty and the law. Titled "A Dissertation on the Canon and Federal Law," it read, in part:

> Let the pulpit resound with the doctrines and sentiments of religious liberty. Let us hear the danger of thralldom to our consciences from ignorance, *extreme poverty* [italics added], and dependence, in short, from civil and political slavery. Let us see delineated before us the

true map of man. Let us hear the dignity of his nature, and the noble rank he holds among the works of God—that consenting to slavery is a sacrilegious breach of trust, as offensive in the sight of God as it is derogatory from our own honor or interest or happiness—and that God Almighty has promulgated from heaven, liberty, peace, and good-will to man![21]

Although he recognized man's dilemma of extreme poverty in his earlier years, he failed to follow through; rather, he occupied himself almost entirely with international matters, having served in diplomatic posts in France and Holland during the Revolutionary War and having negotiated the peace from 1785 to 1788. He made a big hit as minister to the Court of St. James, returning to serve under Washington.

Adams paid little attention to domestic affairs, virtually ignoring the economic and social conditions of Americans at home. The record shows Adams taking scant interest in the issues of slavery and Indian settlements. He looked abroad instead. His administration focused on America's relationship with France and, through skillful negotiations, was able to avoid a war with that country over diplomatic flaps.

In his first annual message to Congress on November 22, 1797, Adams made a single but most important reference to poverty in the context of promoting international trade:

The commerce of the United States is essential, if not to their existence, at least to their comfort, their growth, prosperity, and happiness. The genius, character, and habits of the people are highly commercial. Their cities have been formed and exist upon commerce. Our agriculture, fisheries, arts, and manufactures . . . In short, commerce has made this country what it is, and it can not be destroyed or neglected without involving the people in *poverty* [italics added] and distress. Great numbers are directly and solely supported by navigation. The faith of society is pledged for the preservation of the rights of commercial and sea faring no less than of the other citizens. Under this view of our affairs, I should hold guilty of a neglect of duty if I forbore to recommend that we should make every exertion to protect our commerce and to place our country in a suitable posture of defense as the only sure means of preserving both.[22]

Postscript: It is difficult to evaluate Adams's presidency in terms of whether he was even aware of or cared about slaves living in squalor or, for that matter, Indian tribes living in poverty-stricken communities in the nation. He did steer the country through what became known as the Panic of 1797, which proved to be an economic challenge that resulted from the bursting of a land speculation bubble and temporarily left the economy stagnant and the poor with less resources. The event did transform the American economy from an export-based to a domestic-based economy. "Adams's legacy," one research analyst stated, "is one of reason, virtuous leadership, compassion, and a cautious but vigorous foreign policy. At the same time, Adams's stubborn independence left him politically isolated. He alienated his own cabinet, and his elite republicanism stood in stark contrast to the more egalitarian Jeffersonian democracy that was poised to assume power in the new century."[23]

Indeed, **THOMAS JEFFERSON** founded an American political party, the Democratic-Republican Party (or Republican Party), in the early 1790s with James Madison. (Political scientists use the former name, while historians prefer the latter one; contemporaries generally called the party the "Republicans.") Fifty-seven-year-old Jefferson, a native of Virginia, assumed the presidency (1801–1809) on March 4, 1801, at the dawn of a new century. The first president to be inaugurated in Washington, D.C., he is said to have believed in his heart that he could bring about a "second revolution"—that is, a revolution of ideas. A philosophical tenet attributed to him was: "That government is best which governs least."[24] He was the first president to have articulated this now-familiar philosophy of government. Moreover, Jefferson's election marked the beginning of a new period of American history that ushered in a generation of Southern, agrarian-dominated Democratic-Republican rule.

In his first inaugural address in 1801, Jefferson summed up how he saw the role of government as it pertains to the poor. He did not describe welfare programs, as government support for the poor came to be known generations later; rather, he proposed "a wise and frugal government, which shall restrain men from injuring one another, shall leave them otherwise free to regulate their own pursuits of industry and improvement, and shall not take from the mouth of labor the bread it has earned. This is the sum of good government, and this is necessary to close the circle of our felicities."[25]

The aristocratic French historian de Tocqueville said of Jefferson: "In 1801 the Republicans finally got control of the government. Thomas Jefferson was elected President. He brought them the support of a famous name, great talents, and immense popularity."[26]

Jefferson, contrary to his popular image today of being an outgo-
ing man of extraordinary talents, was, in fact, a remote and casual
president who greeted people in his slippers. He was perceived at the
time as a bit eccentric and quite secretive.[27] Jefferson saw himself as
a man of the people and someone who practiced conciliation above
all. As with Bill Clinton, two centuries later, he liked to bring people
together, and he had enormous charisma and the ability to connect
with the average man or woman. Dealing with the press came easily to
him because he was the first president to realize fully how important
newspaper reporters were in the scheme of politics. The press gave him
full credit for all of his achievements, not the least of which was the
passage of social welfare laws, especially those guaranteeing financial
aid, which proved helpful during a series of economic depressions in
the early 1800s.

Thomas Jefferson was an enlightened leader. According to famed
sociologist Gunnar Myrdal, author of *An American Dilemma*, Jefferson's
following statement indicates he clearly saw the moral danger of the
institution of slavery:

> The whole commerce between master and slave is a perpetual exercise
> of the most boisterous passions, the most unrelenting despotism on the
> one part, and degrading submissions on the other. Poor children see
> this, and learn to imitate it. The man must be a prodigy who can retain
> his manners and morals underrated by permitting one half of the citi-
> zens to trample the rights of the other, transforming those into despots,
> and those into enemies, destroys the morals of one part, and the amor
> patriae of the other. . . . [Can] the liberties of a nation be thought secure
> when we have removed their only firm basis, a conviction in the minds
> of the people that these liberties are a gift of God? That they are not to
> be violated but with His wrath? Indeed, I tremble for my country when
> I reflect that God is just; that His justice cannot sleep forever.[28]

Historian Annette Gordon-Reed catalogued Jefferson's personal
opinion of slavery in her book *The Hemingses of Monticello: An American
Family*. She wrote: "Though he understood viscerally that slavery was
wrong, he resigned himself to the institution and rationalized that the
project of emancipation was best left to future generations."[29]

While Jefferson was undoubtedly one of America's most compassionate presidents, he could do little about poverty as president. Neither
the politics of his time nor the people were ready to hear about the poor.
Moreover, while it was not generally known at the time, Jefferson, in
fact, "disliked cities, great manufacturing interests, and large banking

and trading organizations—[he believed] they promoted inequality; though in later years he admitted that industrialism was necessary to give the country an independent economy."[30] In a phrase, "Jefferson's great aim was to give individual men a wider liberty."[31]

One positive development that occurred during Jefferson's tenure as president was that Congress passed an act that prohibited the importation of slaves into any U.S. port from any foreign land between 1808 and 1860. Nonetheless, during that period traders illegally imported more than 250,000 slaves.

It is interesting to note that long after he left the White House, Jefferson confirmed in 1821 in his own mind what the mood was when he was president. Myrdal attributed this quote to Jefferson: "It was found that the public mind would not bear the proposition of gradual emancipation, nor will it bear it even at this day. Yet the day is not far distant when it must bear it, or worse will follow. Nothing is more certainly written in this book of fate than that these people [Negroes] are to be free."[32]

Nonetheless, Jefferson left another—and far less public—legacy that some historians have written revealed a subtler and much more ambivalent side of the man. Gordon-Reed, who chronicled Jefferson's relationships with his slaves, has stated: "Jefferson observed black people (sometimes one wished he had not) and fancied himself an expert on the subject. Of all the white southern members of the founding generation, he devoted the most time to thinking about blacks as a group—what they did, what they were like, and how they responded to certain situations."[33]

Among those black people close to him at Monticello was a slave named Sally Hemings. Gordon-Reed asserts he had a long-standing affair with Hemings, confirming a generations-old rumor now generally accepted as fact. As concrete evidence of this affair, Gordon-Reed painstakingly researched the relationship and found "that the names of the children of Sally Hemings and Thomas Jefferson appear in a book [*Notes on the State of Virginia*] detailing the lives of slaves conveniently and poignantly encapsulates the tortured history of slavery and race in America."[34] In recent years, a DNA study was conducted that offered further evidence of Jefferson's fathering children by Hemings.[35]

Jefferson's successor, **JAMES MADISON (1809–1817)**, a fifty-seven-year-old Democratic-Republican from Virginia, was an understated president.

One account describes him this way: "Despite his bawdy sense of humor, light hair turned a bit gray, blue eyes sparkling, he was short, funny, soft spoken, and usually dressed in black. He was known to bow very low when he met his guests; his eyes were penetrating and expressive, his smile charming, his manners affable, his conversation lively and interesting."[36]

During his first term, Madison found himself on the verge of war with Great Britain. On June 1, 1812, because of the British imprisonment of American seamen and the seizure of cargoes, Madison felt impelled to give the order to go to war. The War of 1812, climaxed by Gen. Andrew Jackson's triumph at New Orleans, convinced Americans that it had been successful; therefore, an upsurge of nationalism followed. The New England Federalists who had opposed the war—and had even talked secession—were so thoroughly repudiated that Federalism disappeared as a national party.

Madison's tenure was marred—and the country suffered high unemployment again—as a result of the 1815–1821 depression, again leaving the poor to fend for themselves. This downturn resulted from the government having piled up heavy debts during the 1812 war that hurt the banks' capital supply. Land speculation broke out, the banks called in their loans, and many people defaulted, causing a number of banks to fail. Once again, for several years, unemployment rose and the economy went nowhere.

Postscript: In retirement at his estate in Orange County, Virginia, Madison spoke out against the disruptive influences of states' rights proponents that by the 1830s threatened to shatter the federal Union. In a note made public after his death in 1836, he stated, "The advice nearest to my heart and deepest in my convictions is, that the Union of the States be cherished and perpetuated."[37] And, indeed, it was.

The fifth president, fifty-eight-year-old Democratic-Republican **JAMES MONROE (1817–1825)**, was the last of the Virginia dynasty. Called the quintessential hero of the Revolution, Monroe was a tall man who wore britches, was well liked, and was judged to be honest in character and trustworthy. He was elected twice, having run unopposed for his second term, in an era of good feeling. Because he was a hands-off administrator and a slave owner himself, he did little to improve the living conditions of slaves. He did make it clear, however, that he would veto any legislation that restricted self-determination by any state on the question of slavery. And the slave trade was abolished during his tenure.

During his presidency, Missouri entered the Union as a slave state, and Maine entered as a free state. While the government established prohibitions on expanding slavery, Abolitionists, or those who would abolish slavery altogether, saw them as only a temporary solution. Monroe came up with his own plan. In what he thought was a progressive step, he proposed returning freed slaves to Africa and backed the American Colonization Society, which led to the founding of Liberia and its capital Monrovia, named for the president. This movement did little to solve the crisis at home, however, as the issue of slavery still simmered. Further, the country made little progress in terms of eradicating poverty. Monroe, the last of the architects of the new republic, was not really a politician. He was, rather, a statesman.[38]

JOHN QUINCY ADAMS was a fifty-seven-year-old Democratic-Republican of Massachusetts when he became the sixth president (1825–1829). As the son of the nation's second president, he strongly believed that the role of the president and the federal government was to improve the social and physical conditions of society.

In his first annual message to Congress, Adams articulated many lofty goals, including an ambitious program for creating a national spending plan that included roads, canals, a national university, a national astronomical observatory, and other initiatives. In addition, he wanted to explore and develop the western territories.

John Quincy Adams wholeheartedly supported the federal government's involvement in sponsoring projects and institutions designed to improve the conditions of society. He had no constitutional doubts about the authority of the president and Congress to construct a system of internal improvements, ranging from roads and canals to harbors and rivers. In this effort, he supported the "American System," an economic plan that Henry Clay first proposed while Clay was Speaker of the House. In addition, toward the end of Adams's tenure in office, he was faced with a mass wave of immigrants who tended to exacerbate the problem of poverty.

One of the most significant parts in John Quincy Adams's inaugural address on March 4, 1825, dealt with human rights—a necessary ingredient of a free society without poverty. Adams declared:

> It is a source of gratification and of encouragement to me to observe that the great result of this [American] experiment upon the theory of human rights has at the close of that generation by which it was formed been crowned with success equal to the most sanguine expectations of its founders. Union, justice, tranquility, the common defense, the general welfare, and the blessings of liberty—all have been promoted by the Government under which we have lived. Standing at this point of time, looking back to that generation which has gone by and forward to that which is advancing, we may at once indulge in grateful exultation and in cheering hope. From the experience of the past we derive instructive lessons for the future.[39]

Adams presented a rather full slate of innovative ideas to a somewhat hostile Congress. He had obviously come to the White House, many of his peers thought, hoping to overshadow his father's undistinguished record in office. He believed he could overcome the charge he had gained the presidency through corrupt bargaining in the deadlock for the presidency in the electoral college. The vote had been sent to the House, where he was elected by only a one-vote margin.

Congress then began resisting everything he presented, including his few efforts to pass laws that would help the poor. The result was gridlock—perhaps in its earliest incarnation—and no one even mentioned those citizens who were in dire need economically. Poverty was not on this president's agenda. One account of Adams's one-term presidency explains why he was a failure when it came to any legislation that would be designed to help the plight of the poor in America:

> Reared for public service, John Quincy Adams . . . proved [to be] the wrong man for the presidency. Aloof, stubborn, and ferociously independent, he failed to develop the support he needed in Washington, even among his own party. Faced throughout his term with organized opposition from the Democrats—who were committed to limiting Adams to a single term and replacing him with Andrew Jackson— Adams refused to forge the political alliances necessary to push his ideas into policy. His father, President John Adams, had also ignored the political side of the office and served only one term. History repeated itself with his son: John Quincy Adams lost his reelection bid to Andrew Jackson in 1828.[40]

Postscript: It is fair to conclude that, despite his well-meaning efforts, John Quincy Adams—like many presidents to come—was stymied by a Congress that was insensitive to the fundamental social needs of the people. That indifference may well have been because of lack of leadership from the White House itself.

2

THE ERA OF JACKSON (1829–1853):
JACKSON, VAN BUREN, WILLIAM HENRY HARRISON, TYLER, POLK, TAYLOR, FILLMORE

> It is to be regretted that the rich and powerful too often bend the acts of government to their selfish purposes.
> —Andrew Jackson, vetoing a bill that would have rechartered the Bank of the United States, July 10, 1832

Supporters of Tennessean **ANDREW JACKSON** (1829–1837) turned out in huge numbers to elect the sixty-one-year-old former general and hero of the War of 1812 as the seventh U.S. president in 1829. Jackson, who described himself as a Jeffersonian Democrat, was a strong leader who captured the imagination of the common man. His men called him "Old Hickory" because he never bent in battle. Jackson was a strict disciplinarian who stood six-feet-one but weighed barely 150 pounds,[1] according to historian James C. Curtis. Despite his wiry frame, Jackson came across as a tough, no-nonsense soldier who was not to be crossed.

The noted historian Arthur M. Schlesinger Jr., in his book *The Age of Jackson*, shared this view of the president: "Jackson did indeed bear the reputation of being intemperate, arbitrary and ambitious for power. As a general he had tended to do necessary things with great expedition, and to inquire afterward into their legality. His political opponents, building ardently upon incidents of his military past, managed almost to read into the record of history a legend of his rude violence and uncontrolled irascibility."[2] According to author Jon Meacham's account, "Jackson could absorb the essence of a situation at a glance. . . . To manage conflicting forces of emotion and pragmatism is the rarest of political gifts."[3]

Jackson was no stranger to slavery or the accompanying abject poverty it brought with it. He had grown up with the institution of slavery and accepted it. According to the social mores of his time, he bought and sold slaves and used them to work his plantation and to attend to his various needs.

In his first inaugural address on March 4, 1829, Jackson promised a tall order. He pledged to manage taxpayers' money wisely, to eliminate waste and corruption in the government, and to do away with the patronage system that he had inherited from previous presidents. His main goal was to keep the financial house of government in order, a theme that has resonated ever since in the White House and Congress and up to the present time.[4] It is worth noting that in his inaugural address, Jackson made a gesture to allay the Native Americans' fear of his new administration by saying: "It will be my sincere and constant desire to observe toward the Indian tribes within our limits a just and liberal policy, and to give that humane and considerate attention to their rights and their wants which is consistent with the habits of our government and the feelings of our people."[5]

Jackson's seemingly generous attempt to quell Indians' fears did not last long, however. His strict adherence to the Constitution—and by extension to its protection of the institution of slavery—also marked his tenure in office, and he failed to carry out his pledge to treat the Indians with "humane and considerate attention." Quite the contrary. His first legislative action—the Indian Removal Act of 1830, which passed Congress—served to keep the Indians poverty stricken and gave the strong-willed Jackson the power to forcibly evict all Indian tribes located east of the Mississippi River. The Indian tribes took their case to court. Chief Justice John Marshall ruled in favor of the Cherokee—one of five tribes—stating its people did not have to move. Jackson ignored the decision, though, and rounded up the Indians at gunpoint and forced them to move while seizing their property. His actions were labeled as "one of the saddest chapters in American history."[6]

In historian Marquis James's *Andrew Jackson: Portrait of a President*, Jackson's turnabout from his inaugural address was confirmed. "True to the spirit of the West," he wrote, "Jackson would push the red people further back, exchanging new promises for promises broken. Reversing the policy of [his predecessor] John Quincy Adams, he sided with Georgia in its violent measures to expel the peaceable Creeks and Cherokees from lands guaranteed to them by Federal treaty."[7]

Interestingly, as it turned out, Jackson's act, which removed the Indians from the political sphere of life in his time, was the only major piece of legislation passed at Jackson's request during his entire eight years in office. Jackson was obviously no friend of the Indians, yet he showed an ambivalence to their standing. He was critical of the policy he inherited from previous presidents who historically treated tribes as "foreign nations." He referred to this policy as an "absurdity" and maintained that because "Indians are subjects of the United States," they should be brought under congressional control, historian Curtis wrote.[8] The prevailing view of his actions at the time was that while he talked compassionately and sympathetically about the Indians' fate, Jackson's plan was to rid the country of the tribal structure and replace it with the strong arm of the federal government. Then the government could control them completely.

As for his role in the simmering slave controversy, Jackson had little sympathy for the slaves' plight. "Jackson may have opposed states' rights when it came to unification," Curtis wrote, "but on slavery, as on the Indian question, he was not interested in reform. Jackson, who believed in the virtues of democracy and individual liberties so clearly and so forcefully for whites, was blinded by the prejudice of his age."[9] He would continue to support slavery as the choice of each individual state.

Jackson found himself faced with organized groups of people from a number of states known as the Abolitionists. They began to flood the White House and the halls of Congress with petitions to outlaw slavery because it was morally wrong. In response, those who favored slavery argued that criticism of the issue threatened public safety. Furthermore, they felt such opposition should be made illegal.

Jackson, in turn, viewed both sides as a threat to sectional harmony and to the Union in general, and he condemned all of their public demonstrations. Nonetheless, Congress's response was severe. It adopted a series of "gag rules" to prevent debate on the institution of slavery from coming to the floor of either the House or the Senate. Further, Jackson eventually was forced to show his hand when he backed a series of practices by the Southern U.S. Post Offices, which refused to deliver pamphlets and other pro-Abolitionist mail to the public. Jackson himself publicly supported these flagrant actions and recommended that all of the Abolitionists' "incendiary publications" be suppressed. He also was critical of their attempts to incite the slaves to rebel.

Speaking of emotional battles, Jackson took on the Second Bank of the United States in an epic imbroglio that marked, perhaps, one of the most gratifying victories of his tenure. Jackson was dubious of the bank's monopolistic power. While the bank had served the nation well, Jackson—opposing the centralization of such economic power—vetoed a bill for its recharter in 1832. In 1833, he unilaterally removed the government's funds from the bank and deposited them in state banks in order to decentralize the Second Bank.

"Beyond question the bank had meddled with politics; beyond question it was also a private monopoly which had unduly enriched a small group of insiders," wrote historians Allan Nevins and Henry Steel Commager. "Public sentiment was behind Jackson and though he had to fight hard to bring his whole party behind him, he killed [the bank]."[10]

In his message on July 10, 1832, vetoing the rechartering of the Bank of the United States, Jackson's comment offered an insight into his philosophy about the cause of poverty in America, although he did not use those words. Instead, he charged: "It is to be regretted that the rich and powerful too often bend the acts of government to their selfish purposes. . . . There are no necessary evils in government. Its evils exist only in its abuses. If it would confine itself to equal protection, and, as Heaven does its rains, shower its favors alike on the high and the low, the rich and the poor, it would be an unqualified blessing."[11]

In his farewell address of March 4, 1837, Jackson warned of the danger of sectional rivalries in the North and South. It read, in part:

> From the extent of our country, its diversified signs of evil are sufficiently apparent to awaken the deepest anxiety in the bosom of the patriot. . . . We behold systematic efforts publicly made to sow the seeds of discord between different parts of the United States and to place party divisions directly upon geographical distinctions; to excite the South against the North and the North against the South, and to force into the controversy the most delicate and exciting topics—topics upon which it is impossible that a large portion of the Union can ever speak without strong emotions.[12]

Arthur Schlesinger put the age of Jackson in perspective when he wrote: "Jackson grew visibly from the day of his inauguration. His leadership gained steadily in confidence and imagination. He grew much stronger after every contact with the people. In the last analysis, there lay the secret of his strength: his deep natural understanding of the people."[13]

But that characterization comes from hindsight. During his presidency, Jackson was not seen as a reformer or as a friend of the Indians or the slaves. He was perceived as a strong personality, but he did not make any substantive progress in the generations-old battle to solve the issue of poverty. At the close of Jackson's presidency, his handpicked heir was the man who served as vice president in his second term, Martin Van Buren.

The ascendency of **MARTIN VAN BUREN** (1837–1841) to the presidency on March 4, 1837, triggered anxiety among the American people in the wake of a severe economic decline in 1836. The voters had supported the fifty-four-year-old Democrat from New York, but the eighth president found himself in a politically uncomfortable situation. Having been selected as Jackson's protégé, politically he could not blame his former leader, especially since Van Buren had been a contributor to Jackson's policies.

According to one account of this transition,

> When Van Buren entered office, it was clear that the nation's economic health had taken a turn for the worse and that the good times of the early 1830s were over. Two months into his presidency, the roof fell in. On May 10, 1837, some important state banks in New York, running out of hard currency reserves, suddenly refused to convert paper money into gold or silver. Other financial institutions throughout the nation quickly followed suit. This financial crisis, the worse yet faced by the young nation—would become known as "the Panic of 1837."[14]

The rapidly deteriorating economy caused loans to dry up, new purchases to fall off, and new businesses and civic construction projects to collapse. Many Americans did not have jobs and went hungry. A real estate panic caused more than 40 percent of America's banks to fail, and people blamed Van Buren.

As for the continuing issue of slavery, in his inaugural speech on March 4, 1837, Van Buren had addressed the issue in the context of the challenges that the nation faced. He took a status quo position—in other words, to preserve slavery. Relying heavily on the tradition of adhering to the Constitution, he recalled in his inaugural that

> the last, perhaps the greatest, of the prominent sources of discord and disaster supposed to lurk in our political condition was the institution of domestic slavery. Our forefathers were deeply impressed with the delicacy of this subject, and they treated it with forbearance so evidently wise that in spite of every sinister foreboding it never until

the present period disturbed the tranquility of our common country. Such a result is sufficient evidence of the justice and the patriotism of their course; it is evidence not to be mistaken that an adherence to it can prevent all embarrassment from this as well as from every other anticipated cause of difficulty or danger.[15]

Continuing Jackson's Indian removal policy, Van Buren supported additional removals after his election in 1836. The federal government forcibly removed the Cherokee people in 1838, a disastrous, cold-blooded operation in which 25 percent of the Cherokees lost their lives. A number of Americans called the removal campaign inhumane and criticized the Van Buren administration's conduct. It was yet another setback for the man who had high hopes of continuing Jackson's popularity but, in the end, failed miserably.

The ninth president of the United States, **WILLIAM HENRY HARRISON** (1841), was a Whig from Ohio. At sixty-eight years old, he was a self-styled aristocrat and the oldest president to be inaugurated up to that time and the only president to have studied medicine. He also proved to be a man who unknowingly tempted fate on the day of his inauguration. He gave a two-hour address on the frigid day of March 4, 1841, standing bareheaded and not wearing a topcoat, scarf, or gloves.

In his 8,445-word inaugural speech—the longest in U.S. history up until that time—he spelled out his agenda, but, tragically, he did not live to accomplish anything. He died on April 4, only one month to the day after taking the oath, and became the first American president to die in office. Harrison wrote the entire speech himself, though soon-to-be Secretary of State Daniel Webster edited it. Meanwhile, the Whigs were rapidly gaining power in Congress, and the public recognized the party as a fresh, new change in American politics. Democrats had dominated the national political scene, but the new Whig Party had started to garner support in Congress. It did not last long, but the Whigs' goals played a key role in creating the modern Republican Party.

Harrison's successor, Vice President **JOHN TYLER** (1841–1845), a Whig from Virginia, immediately became president upon Harrison's death. At fifty-one years old, Tyler was sworn in on April 6, 1841, but without a vice president. Nothing in the Constitution provided for Tyler to succeed Harrison, but the prevailing political powerbrokers of the time went along with his assumption that he would be the tenth president and not serve as an "acting president." It was not until 1967 that Tyler's decision to assume office was written into law with the adoption of the Twenty-fifth Amendment to the Constitution.[16]

On the subject of slavery, one historian described President Tyler's attitude this way:

> As a young man he was less certain of his relationship to the slave institution. . . . Like his father, he was a slave owner all his life. Nevertheless, he opposed a continuation of the African slave trade. As a United States senator in 1832 he fought for legislation to end the actual buying and selling of human beings within the shadow of the Capitol. The sign of this [repulsive activity] made him physically ill. He never attended a slave auction.[17]

In his early years, Tyler was a moderate and an intellectual who read all the newspapers to keep himself informed. He was a firm believer in the view that the United States was the superior country in the world, a view that has come to be known as American exceptionalism. In other words, Tyler thought it was his job as president to promote American values as known abroad. At the same time, however, he was well aware of the obvious contradiction in American society of preaching liberty and justice while, at the same time, embracing slavery. In one debate when he served in the House of Representatives, in fact, Tyler recognized that the issue of slavery "had been represented on all hands as the dark cloud" hanging over the Union. "It would be well," he recommended, "to disperse this cloud." His answer: territorial expansion would be a way to "thin out" and "diffuse" the slave population, and with the exodus of blacks from some of the southern states a process of gradual emancipation could get under way. Of course, "Tyler's logic of diffusion was a tacit admission that the South's peculiar institution was a fatal anomaly in a republic dedicated to liberty and justice." Thus while he recognized slavery as evil, he not only failed to make any attempt to join those who would abolish slavery but also—quite the contrary—"he strongly defended slavery for the remainder of his public life," forced by what he considered political necessity to continue the slave system that he had inherited from his predecessors.[18]

Despite his personal lifelong ambivalence toward slavery, Tyler devoted a great deal of time to defending the institution. As a slave owner who had a social conscience, Tyler clearly exemplified a country's moral aversion to buying and selling slaves while, at the same time, keeping it in place as a tradition. In fact, in 1787 at the Constitutional Convention, Tyler had opposed the Constitution for that reason. As historian Edward P. Crapol noted, "Tyler's aversion to the practice of trading in human flesh was yet another manifestation of his moral qualms about slavery's corrosive impact on America's civic virtue."[19]

Indeed, Tyler reflected the beginning of this new age of reform. He and others shared a passion to remove the impediments to freedom—such things as superstition, the dogma and ritual of the church, and ignorance. Further, as historians Nevins and Commager wrote, "Poverty was an impediment, and the intellectuals joined forces with labor to improve the condition of the dangerous and perishing factories and mills, and to protect helpless women and children from the rush of the Industrial Revolution."[20]

When his first term was up, Tyler decided not to run for reelection in 1844. Instead, his Southern roots and long-standing support of slavery influenced him to join the Confederacy. He died on January 18, 1862, at the age of seventy-one.

Tyler's successor, **JAMES KNOX POLK** (1845–1849), a Democrat from Tennessee, was the eleventh and youngest president up to his election in 1844. He became president at age forty-nine. A loyal Jacksonian Democrat, Polk spent most of his life in politics—including twice elected as Speaker of the House of Representatives—before becoming president.

Unlike that of his two immediate predecessors, Polk's agenda was largely concentrated on foreign policy issues, such as foreign trade expansion. In the domestic arena, slavery was the least of the subjects to which he paid attention. As for Indian tribes and expansionism, in his inaugural address on March 4, 1845, Polk spoke of this long-standing issue by stating confidently:

> In the earlier stages of our national existence the opinion prevailed with some that our system of confederated states could not operate successfully over an extended territory, and serious objections have at different times been made to the enlargement of our boundaries. These objections were earnestly urged when we acquired Louisiana. Experience has shown that they were not well founded. The title of

numerous Indian tribes to vast tracts of country has been *extinguished* [italics added]; new states have been admitted into the Union; new territories have been created and our jurisdiction and laws extended over them. As our population has expanded, the Union has been cemented and strengthened.[21]

Although he was a difficult man to get to know, ironically, he was one of the most accessible of presidents. He saw himself as a servant of the people and was one of the hardest working ever to occupy the White House as a "hands-on president." He exemplified the concept of America's Manifest Destiny, the term coined in 1843, the year before he began his presidency. Manifest Destiny was interpreted at the time as the doctrine that the United States should expand its territory over all of North America.[22]

Polk tried to distance himself from the issue of slavery as much as possible. Still, as author John Seigenthaler wrote in his biography of the president: "Polk was acculturated by a lifelong reliance on slave labor in a racist agrarian society. Reared in a family that owned slaves, he accepted indentured servitude as a way of life."[23]

Accordingly, it can be said with confidence that President Polk did not pay much attention to either cause—slavery or poverty.

ZACHARY TAYLOR, a sixty-four-year-old Whig from Louisiana, the twelfth president of the United States, served only from March 1849 to July 1850. A "hearty, tobacco-chewing Regular Army man with little schooling, no knowledge of law, government or politics, [he] had never cast a vote in his life when the Whigs decided they wanted him as their candidate."[24] His supporters believed his military record as a hero of the Mexican War would give him the advantage. Tragically, however, after taking part in ceremonies at the Washington Monument on a steaming hot July 4, 1850, Taylor—who was reportedly not in the best of health at the time—attended several other Independence Day ceremonies. That evening, he suddenly became ill and developed a severe case of diarrhea. He died only five days later on July 9, 1850.

Taylor was a wealthy slave owner who held properties in the plantation states of Louisiana, Kentucky, and Mississippi. He hardly had the look of a president, but based on his war record and his public appeal, he was one of the most popular figures in America at the time. According to author John S. D. Eisenhower,

Zachary Taylor was a man whose looks deceived those who met him for the first time. One glance at that rough physiognomy could convince the casual viewer that here was a son of a poor family, a man of the soil. The fact was that Zack Taylor, "Old Rough and Ready," was, indeed, a farmer, but a gentleman farmer. Throughout his life, even when he was in the army, he kept ownership of several plantations, tilled by numerous slaves.[25]

Taylor had chosen not to actively campaign, a position that allowed him to avoid party politics, although his supporters went all out for him. The reason for his unusual "stay above the fray" presidential campaign was simply that his supporters relied on Taylor's broad popular appeal. Thus, he ran without making the usual promises (at least in public) as to what he would do if elected president. That tactic, too, was a first in presidential politics.

Election Day, November 7, 1848, some 2,880,572 men (women had not yet gained the right to vote) went to the polls, or 72.7 percent of the eligible voters. In his race with Lewis Cass, Taylor won a plurality of the popular vote.

Taylor made no specific references to slavery or Indians or poverty in his inaugural speech on March 4, 1849. He closed, however, with a homily on a general note of patriotism:

> Let us invoke a continuance of the same protecting care which has led us from small beginnings to the eminence we this day occupy, and let us seek to deserve that continuance by prudence and moderation in our councils, by well-directed attempts to assuage the bitterness which too often marks unavoidable differences of opinion, by the promulgation and practice of just and liberal principles, and by an enlarged patriotism, which shall acknowledge no limits but those of our own widespread Republic.[26]

Meanwhile, Taylor, a slaveholder himself, was personally opposed to the institution in principle. He would not disrupt the Union by trying to abolish slavery in states where it already existed, but he would not allow its expansion into the new territories.

Taylor's sudden, unexpected death on July 9, 1850, catapulted Vice President **MILLARD FILLMORE** (1850–1853), a Whig, into the presidency.

Fillmore took office immediately and did not give an inaugural address. Instead, he sent a written message to Congress praising Taylor and asking both chambers to come together and face the country's problems. In his presidential oath, he pledged to uphold the Constitution, which still supported slavery. Some fifteen years later, the Thirteenth Amendment abolished it.

Once in office, Fillmore proceeded to reverse much of the impact of Taylor's presidency. The twelfth president knew one thing: the nation was involved in a sectional crisis of the greatest magnitude, and he would be the center of attention. According to one historical account, Fillmore ran into trouble at the outset when he said he was opposed to the Compromise of 1850. Under the bill, California would be admitted to the Union as a free state, New Mexico and Utah would be organized as territories without legislation either for or against slavery, a more efficient machinery would be set up for returning fugitive slaves to their masters, the slave trade would be abolished in the District of Columbia, and Texas would be compensated for territory it had previously ceded to New Mexico.[27]

As a response to this turnaround in policy, Fillmore's cabinet resigned en masse to protest his failure to protect the compromise. At that juncture, battle lines formed between those for and against the compromise. Fillmore eventually capitulated after the compromise was modified and divided into five different bills that Fillmore found palatable. He saw their passage as a triumph of interparty cooperation that had kept the Union intact.

Unfortunately, in the end, Fillmore alienated nearly everyone by trying to please everyone. The fallout from the conflicting points of view on slavery left the Whig Party considerably weakened. The compromise split the party in the northern states and contributed heavily to its demise. Nonetheless, writes historian Robert J. Scarry, "he [Fillmore] didn't waiver to party reaction, the media of the day, popularity, and the advice of individuals. His personal courage has not been properly credited by most historians."[28]

As a footnote to the Fillmore years, it is instructive to point out that Harriet Beecher Stowe's book *Uncle Tom's Cabin*, first published on March 20, 1852, was an immediate best seller in the United States and abroad, with more than a million copies sold. It had a major impact on its times. "Its theme—the evils of slavery—exerted tremendous influence on American thought and probably did more to hasten the overthrow of slavery than anything else," observed authors John Durant and Alice Durant.[29]

Summing up, Scarry wrote that, in response to questions from the Erie County Anti-Slavery Society, Fillmore felt that the slave trade was "an unholy traffic in human flesh that must often sunder the tenderest ties of our nature" and that "he was in favor of exercising whatever Constitutional authority it may possess for the suspension of this barbarous traffic." He believed that "gradual emancipation should be a work of time, in which education and moral influences as well as legislative enactment 'must necessarily contrive to raise the slave from his degraded state to that of a freeman.'"[30]

Despite Fillmore's efforts to lessen tensions over slavery, the Civil War appeared inevitable at the end of his term, and he found his own dying party rejected him and denied him the renomination. In his last annual message on December 7, 1852, Fillmore went out in style, reviewing the history of slavery and expressing his fear of a racial war if the antislavery movement did not tone down its rhetoric. Scarry observed, "He thought that, in any case, the elimination of slavery would not prevent a civil war between the races or a civil war between the sections [of the country]."[31]

3

A NATION DIVIDED (1853–1881):

PIERCE, BUCHANAN, LINCOLN, ANDREW JOHNSON, GRANT, HAYES

No men living are more worthy to be trusted than those who toil up from poverty; none less inclined to take or touch aught which they have not honestly earned.

—Abraham Lincoln, first annual message
to Congress, December 3, 1861

At a time of rapidly increasing hostility between the North and South in the years of controversy before the Civil War, **FRANKLIN PIERCE**, a forty-eight-year-old Democrat from New Hampshire, came to office in 1853 as the fourteenth president of the United States (1853–1857). In the run-up to the Civil War, the issue of race began to split the two regions of the country to the point where Pierce seemed incapable of keeping the nation together.

On top of this discord, he had emerged as the candidate in the Democratic Party, which itself was internally fragmented into two politically incompatible factions. Even worse, given his actions when he took office, some observers viewed him as the president who set the nation on the path to the Civil War. All in all, as president, he faced divisions within both his party and his nation. Ironically, the opposition Whig Party was also in disarray.

A handsome, amiable man, Pierce was liked by many politicians on both sides of the aisle. He swiftly rose in the political ranks from Speaker of the House in the New Hampshire state legislature to a bright, young, favored Democratic presidential nominee in a period of twenty years. He was a good public speaker and attracted large crowds wherever he gave a speech.

He was known to be sympathetic to the South. As historian Michael F. Holt described him: "Not only did Pierce hold anti-slavery groups in contempt, but his consistent votes against federal subsidies for internal improvements and lower federal land prices displayed callous indifference to the needs and interests of [people in poverty] in the Midwest. His political vision was narrow, even parochial."[1]

But he had a razor-sharp memory. Accordingly, in his inaugural address on March 4, 1853, Pierce memorized his entire 3,319-word speech, in which he made clear his position on slavery: it was entirely up to the states to determine the fate of slaves. He stated, unambiguously:

> I believe that *involuntary servitude, as it exists in different States of this Confederacy, is recognized by the Constitution* [italics added]. . . . I hold that the laws of 1850, commonly called the "compromise measures," are strictly constitutional and to be unhesitatingly carried into effect. . . . I fervently hope that the [slavery] question is at rest, and that no sectional or ambitious or fanatical excitement may again threaten the durability of our institutions or obscure the light of our prosperity.[2]

Pierce's opening salvo did little to calm the political waters. Instead, had he been a bit more insightful or a good politician—which he was not—he would have realized that the coming U.S. Civil War was destined to become part of the tapestry of history that would occur on his watch.

Well-known historian and author of *The Presidency of Franklin Pierce*, Larry Gara, aptly described Pierce's political leanings:

> To Franklin Pierce the Union was sacred, and he revered the Constitution as the founding fathers had written it. Those who agitated against slavery, he thought, were a threat not only to the concept of private property but to the Union itself. . . . No doubt a majority of Pierce's fellow citizens shared his view that black Americans were unfit for freedom or to participate in a democratic system. Yet even then, some argued against slavery, a few even supporting a multiracial society. They spoke, but most Americans did not listen. All the people really meant "all the white, male people."[3]

Pierce was totally opposed to the abolition of slavery in the states where already existed. He backed Southern positions on their right to take slaves into new territories—particularly Kansas—and supported the Compromise of 1850. On May 30, 1854, the Kansas-Nebraska Act became law, allowing settlers to vote on the issue of slavery in this territory.

This bill established the territories of Kansas and Nebraska and would lead to much of the dissension over slavery that continued after he left office.

On the question of Indians, Pierce dealt with them during his efforts to construct the transcontinental railroads. He had a policy of forced removal at gunpoint, but he provided both army protection for Indians who agreed not to harass or attack settlers and annual cash payments to the various tribes.[4] Yet the North did not adhere to the treaties. The Indians countered, arguing that they were an entirely separate nation and race with separate origins and separate destinies.

If the Indians' pleas ever reached Franklin Pierce, they had little effect on his policy, as he continued to move Indians to reservations and to administer harsh punishment for any tribes that resisted. His administration created a separate Indian Bureau to manage this transition, but it was poorly done.

Pierce's passion for interpreting the Constitution literally, it should be noted, was renowned. He displeased his own Democratic liberal supporters by vetoing several measures that would have enabled the federal government to help states in certain matters. For example, his initial veto was that of a bipartisan bill that would transfer federal dollars to the states to construct and manage asylums for the indigent and thus alleviate a segment of poverty.

In vetoing the bill he said, "If Congress could provide for the indigent insane, why not for the healthy poor as well? The Constitution did not grant authority to make the federal government the great almoner of public charity. The bill would be 'subversive' of the whole theory upon which the Union of these States is founded."[5] The same Congress that had passed the bill for the indigent insane could not summon the votes to override Pierce's veto.

Pierce promised to run a corrupt-free administration, to be a "strict constructionist" of the Constitution, and to prevent the federal government from operating by centralizing all of the government power.[6] Referring to Pierce's domestic policies, Holt, in his book *Franklin Pierce*, added: "Pierce seemed to go out of his way to put the kibosh on other domestic policies that might re-inspirit Democratic Party loyalty."[7]

In examining his record, one can safely conclude that in the course of Pierce's only term, he did little, if anything, to ease poverty in America. Further, as a result of his political miscalculations, he turned out to be the only president in the nineteenth century who tried for—but was not successful in obtaining—renomination by the party to which he was so devoted. His failure even to begin to solve the burning question of slavery left the public with an image of him as indecisive and ineffective—which, indeed, he was.

When the tall and stately **JAMES BUCHANAN** (1857–1861), sixty-five, a Democrat from Pennsylvania, assumed office on March 4, 1857, the fifteenth president stepped right up to the burning issue of slavery and left no doubt where he stood. At his inauguration, while his audience was cooling off on the hot day by consuming twelve hundred gallons of ice cream provided for the onlookers, the formal man who appeared to be aloof to those around him demonstrated that he would follow his predecessor's policy. Buchanan believed it was up to the states—not the federal government or the courts—to decide the issue of slavery.

Buchanan said, "It is the imperative and indispensable duty of the Government of the United States to secure to every resident inhabitant the free and independent expression of his opinion by his vote. This sacred right of each individual must be preserved. That being accomplished, nothing can be fairer than to leave the people of a Territory free from all foreign interference to decide their own destiny for themselves, subject only to the Constitution of the United States."[8]

American voters translated his message to mean, quite simply, that "people of a territory" specifically referred *only* to the white male voters (blacks and women were not eligible to vote). While Buchanan was known to question the legitimacy of slavery privately, no writings reflect any moral indignation or sympathy for slaves on his part. For Buchanan, the issue was a cut and dried; he talked about it dispassionately. One account of his life recorded that he not only favored slavery but also took actions to maintain it. For example, he more than once defended the right of postmasters to censor abolition literature.[9] His close-minded attitude did nothing whatsoever to help slaves out of poverty. Further, Buchanan appeared unable to resolve peacefully the slavery issue. His public speeches were to no avail. In his fourth annual State of the Union message in 1860, the president said:

> How easy it would be for the American people to settle the slavery question forever and to restore peace and harmony to this distracted country! They, and they alone, can do it. All that is necessary to accomplish the object, and all for which the slave States have ever

contended, is to be let alone and permitted to manage their domestic institutions in their own way. As sovereign States, they, and they alone, are responsible before God and the world for slavery existing among them.[10]

In the end, as Buchanan tried not to alienate anyone, he wound up disappointing almost everyone. One reason for his decline in popularity was the recession of 1857, which occurred after the New York City branch of the Ohio Life Insurance and Trust Company failed, rattling consumer confidence and leading to a panic and a run on the banks. More than five thousand banks failed in a year; most of the trouble was confined to the North.

During his term, he had shown signs of leadership, but he was sometimes erratic and inconsistent. To those closest to him and even to the public, Buchanan appeared anxious to exit the White House before what appeared to be an inevitable civil war began.

But he did not get out in time. The eruption of secession during the end of his administration ruined his legacy. He had been warning since the 1830s that the North's encroachments on the South would lead to war, even though he himself was a known ally of the North. The 1860 Republicans triumphed, but before Abraham Lincoln and the new administration took office on March 4, 1861, seven cotton-producing states seceded from the Union and joined together to form the Confederate States. Only a month later the Civil War started on April 12, 1861.

Enter **ABRAHAM LINCOLN** (1861–1865), the tall, quiet-spoken politician-lawyer from Illinois with an impoverished "log cabin" background. "Lincoln knew firsthand the deprivations, the marginal livelihood of the subsistence farmer unable to bring produce to market without dependable roads. He was paid the meager wages of the hired hand,"[11] historian Doris Kearns Goodwin wrote in her book *Team of Rivals: The Political Genius of Abraham Lincoln.*

By this time, Lincoln was an accomplished orator and politician. He served four terms in the Illinois state House of Representatives and one term in the U.S. House of Representatives in Washington. Plain people were drawn to him because most felt that he was one of them. In his previous bid for the Senate in 1858, he had participated in the "great debates" with Illinois Democratic senator Stephen A. Douglas, who was the incumbent. At the state Republican convention in Springfield on June 16, 1858, Lincoln, always courteous and dignified, was elected to be the Illinois Republican candidate for Senate. Following the election he read his historic "House Divided" speech, which he had labored over more than any other previous oration. It read, in part:

> If we could first know where we are, and whither we are tending, we could then better judge what to do, and how to do it. We are now far into the fifth year, since a policy was initiated, with the avowed object, and confident promise, of putting an end to slavery agitation. Under the operation of that policy, that agitation has not only, not ceased, but has constantly augmented. In my opinion, it will not cease, until a crisis shall have been reached, and passed. "A house divided against itself cannot stand." I believe this government cannot endure, permanently half slave and half free. I do not expect the Union to be dissolved—I do not expect the house to fall—but I do expect it will cease to be divided. *It will become all one thing or all the other* [italics added].[12]

Lincoln and Douglas had debated in seven cities in Illinois before Election Day. Lincoln lost the Senate race to the better-known Douglas in 1858, but he came back to upset Douglas and three other contenders in the November 6, 1860, election for the presidency. Lincoln took office as the sixteenth president on March 4, 1861, only two weeks after Jefferson Davis was inaugurated president of the newly formed Confederate States of America at Montgomery, Alabama.

Lincoln's first priority, he made clear in his inaugural address on March 4, 1861, was the preservation of the Union. He stated, in part: "I hold that, in contemplation of universal law and of the Constitution, the Union of these States is perpetual. Perpetuity is implied, if not expressed, in the fundamental law of all national governments. . . . [T]he Union will endure forever—it being impossible to destroy it except by some action not provided for in the instrument itself."[13]

The speech was greeted with mixed reviews; however, the majority of Northern newspapers backed Lincoln's position. Lincoln believed that the Southern states, if left alone, would return to the Union, but his confidence in such an outcome was undone within weeks after his inauguration. All Americans awaited Lincoln's decision about what to do about the rebellion at Fort Sumter, South Carolina, where federal troops had been holding out against the Confederate Army. Fighting had occurred up to the time Lincoln took office, but when he sent supplies to reinforce the Northern troops, the sound of rifle fire on April 12, 1861, touched off the Civil War.

In mid-1962, Lincoln's policy of delegating the war to his generals in the early stages combined with Confederate victories shifted the momentum and shook the Union's will to fight. Lincoln had played his last card, and it was time to change strategy or lose the war. Indeed, that change of tactics would turn out to be historic and dramatic: Lincoln decided to deliver his Emancipation Proclamation, which he believed would be the best way to bolster his cause. That history-making proclamation was the foundation of the generally accepted view that Lincoln fought the war primarily to free the slaves rather than to preserve the Union, as he had originally declared in his inaugural address in 1861.

The Emancipation Proclamation, issued on September 22, 1862, read in part:

> By virtue of the power, and for the purpose aforesaid, I do order and declare that all persons held as slaves within said designated States, and parts of States, are, and henceforward shall be free; and that the Executive government of the United States, including the military and naval authorities thereof, will recognize and maintain the freedom of said persons.
>
> And I hereby enjoin upon the people so declared to be free to abstain from all violence, unless in necessary self-defense; and I recommend to them that, in all cases when allowed, they labor faithfully for reasonable wages.
>
> And I further declare and make known, that such persons of suitable condition, will be received into the armed service of the United States to garrison forts, positions, stations, and other places, and to man vessels of all sorts in said service.
>
> And upon this act, sincerely believed to be an act of justice, warranted by the Constitution, upon military necessity, I invoke the considerate judgment of mankind, and the gracious favor of Almighty God.[14]

Reaction to the proclamation was mixed. Some people were critical of the proclamation for only freeing some of the slaves. Others read it as the beginning of the end of slavery. On January 1, 1863, President Lincoln issued the formal Emancipation Proclamation. With it he officially freed all slaves within the states and the parts of the states that were in rebellion and not in Union hands, but it left one million slaves in Confederate territory still in bondage.

On November 19, 1863, Lincoln gave what arguably could be called his shortest—at two minutes long—and most memorable speech at Gettysburg, Pennsylvania. That address, according to historian George McGovern, "remains his most famous speech, and perhaps the most beloved in American history."[15] It read simply:

> Four score and seven years ago our fathers brought forth on this continent, a new nation, conceived in Liberty, and dedicated to the proposition that all men are created equal.
>
> Now we are engaged in a great civil war, testing whether that nation, or any nation so conceived and so dedicated, can long endure. We are met on a great battle-field of that war. We have come to dedicate a portion of that field, as a final resting place for those who here gave their lives that that nation might live. It is altogether fitting and proper that we should do this.
>
> But, in a larger sense, we can not dedicate—we can not consecrate—we can not hallow this ground. The brave men, living and dead, who struggled here, have consecrated it, far above our poor power to add or detract. The world will little note, nor long remember what we say here, but it can never forget what they did here. It is for us the living, rather, to be dedicated here to the unfinished work which they who fought here have thus far so nobly advanced. It is rather for us to be here dedicated to the great task remaining before us—that from these honored dead we take increased devotion to that cause for which they gave the last full measure of devotion—that we here highly resolve that these dead shall not have died in vain—that this nation, under God, shall have a new birth of freedom—and that government of the people, by the people, for the people, shall not perish from the earth.[16]

That address lifted the spirits of the Union Army, but it also spurred the South to fight on even more fiercely. Finally, on April 18, 1865, the Civil War stopped only nine days after the Confederate Army surrendered. It formally ended on May 10, 1865, when Lincoln's successor, fifty-six-year-old Andrew Johnson, issued a proclamation announcing that hostilities between the North and the South had ceased. Some 617,000 Americans had died in the war, and thousands more were injured.

When Lincoln ran for reelection in 1864, he was politically vulnerable because of the extraordinary number of casualties suffered in the war. His followers stayed with him, and on November 8, 1864, he was elected in a landslide, winning 221 electoral votes to 21 for Gen. George

B. McClellan, the Democratic candidate. Lincoln clearly showed his sense of renewal in his second inaugural address on March 4, 1865, which is inscribed on one wall of the Lincoln Memorial in Washington, D.C.: "With malice toward none, with charity for all, with firmness in the fight as God gives us to see the right, let us strive on to finish the work we are in, to bind up the nation's wounds, to care for him who shall have borne the battle and for his widow and his orphan, to do all which may achieve and cherish a just and a lasting peace among ourselves and with all nations."[17]

It should be mentioned that in addition to his profound commitment to the slaves, Lincoln also demonstrated compassion for the Indians. In his annual message to Congress on December 6, 1864, Lincoln focused on building the transcontinental railroad, the conversion to a national banking system, and the need to reorganize and remodel government bureaucrats to "improve the condition of the Indian."[18]

As he continued to fight for peace and keep the Union together, his life came to a shocking and sudden end on Good Friday, April 14, 1865. John Wilkes Booth, an actor from Maryland who was obsessed with avenging the Confederacy's defeat, assassinated the president at Ford's Theatre in Washington, D.C. Lincoln died the following morning.

Ever since the Civil War, some Americans have been confused about why the war was fought. The simple answer is: to abolish slavery. Allan Nevins and Henry Steele Commager, two scholars of history, captured the nuance of the reasons for the war in their book, *A Short History of the United States*. They explained the dilemma this way:

> Actually, few Americans, North or South, really understood the nature of the peculiar institution [slavery] which one side was so bitterly attacking, the other side so passionately defending. For the most important fact about American slavery was that it was Negro slavery: most of the features that characterized it were connected with race rather than with legal status. The whole institution was designed largely to regulate the relationships of black and white rather than of master and slave, and though the status of the Negro was completely changed by the Civil War and the Thirteenth Amendment [abolishing slavery], the economic and social relationships of Negroes and whites were not greatly changed for another three quarters of a century.[19]

Thus, in perspective, Abraham Lincoln contributed enormously to the goal of alleviating poverty in America by freeing the slaves. While his effort was far from achieving the mission, it was a remarkable accomplishment in his time. He will always be remembered for his twin accomplishments as a transformational president for black Americans: he led the Union into war against the slaveholding Confederate States of America and was solely responsible for both lifting the slaves out of poverty and winning the war. As historian Carl Sandburg has told us:

> In thousands of commentaries Lincoln incarnated two results—Emancipation and the Union. Two causes directed by Lincoln had won the war. Gone was the property status of the Negro, gone the doctrine of secession and states' rights. Black men could now move from where they were miserable to where they are equally miserable—now it was lawful for them to move. Now too for the Negro no longer was it a crime for him to be found reading a book nor was it any longer a crime to teach a Negro to read.[20]

Although some historians have written that Lincoln's initial concern to preserve the Union was the cause of the Civil War, over time there is no doubt that Lincoln's view of slavery in historical perspective was negative from the outset. "Lincoln always believed that if slavery is not wrong, nothing is wrong," according to historian Goodwin.[21]

Perhaps historian Richard Striner wrote the best phrase to sum up Abraham Lincoln as a man: "Lincoln was a rare man, indeed: a fervent idealist endowed with a remarkable gift for strategy. An ethicist, Lincoln was also an artist in the Machiavellian use of power. It was a combination of qualities that made Lincoln's contribution to the antislavery movement so demonstrably necessary."[22]

Postscript: Lincoln was a giant compared to his predecessors. Some historians are not kind to the pre–Civil War presidents. Here is how Nevins and Commager characterized the men who preceded Lincoln: "The most significant thing about the politics of the prewar [Civil War] years was their insignificance. [The] administrations of Pierce and Buchanan, for example, had been dull and incompetent."[23]

Following Lincoln's assassination on April 14, 1865, Vice President **ANDREW JOHNSON** was sworn in as the seventeenth president on the National Union Party line (1865–1869). Like Lincoln, Johnson was in favor of saving the Union, but at the outset—having been sympathetic to the South—he was not a supporter of the Abolitionists' movement.

Johnson had eventually come around to joining Lincoln in backing the slaves' emancipation, but he was not a passionate abolitionist. Lincoln is said to have picked Johnson of Tennessee in 1864 to balance the ticket.

As it turned out, when Johnson took over the presidency, his goal was to return the country to what it had been before the war—a nation dominated by whites. Historian Annette Gordon-Reed writes about how history turned its back on the Abolitionists:

> Were it not so thoroughly steeped in mindless tragedy—the first assassination of an American president, the destruction of the hopes of a people long treated as property who thought they were finally going be able to live in dignity and peace, to the last chance to make the promise of America real to all who lived here—one might be content to cast Andrew Johnson's time in the White House as a form of cosmic joke. . . . But the effects of Johnson's presidency were too profound, too far ranging—reaching into twenty-first-century America—to be considered anything approaching a joke or trick, even one to teach an important lesson.[24]

Incontrovertible evidence in his writings, speeches, and actions demonstrate that Johnson was clearly a racist. As historian Gordon-Reed puts it:

> Johnson's attitude toward blacks, or "niggers," as he termed them in private conversations, was resolutely negative. This fact must be counted as a crucial element of his character that affected his conduct as president, particularly and tragically in the period when he was in office. There is no wonder that Reconstruction under his aegis proceeded in the way it did, it would be impossible to exaggerate how devastating it was to have a man who affirmatively hated black people in charge of a program that was designed to settle the terms of their existence in post–Civil War America.[25]

Johnson was probably the worst politician to have following Lincoln. He was supposed to enforce political and social rights for Southern blacks, but his efforts, if any, were not evident. After Congress stripped Johnson of the Tenure of Office Act—the ability to make appointments and fire cabinet secretaries as the president saw fit—Johnson responded by firing his secretary of war (a clear violation of Congress's desire to put restraints on him), challenging the Congress, and taking a cross-country tour to stir up support. He received little. Subsequently, he was impeached, but a single vote saved him from conviction.

As historian Hans L. Trefousse wrote in his biography of Johnson, "Although he had been through the fire, what Johnson ultimately achieved was more than just an acquittal." Indeed, Trefousse pointed out, "he preserved the South as a white man's country."[26]

Johnson then served the duration of Lincoln's term. He inherited two pieces of historic legislation—two new amendments to the Constitution—that indirectly helped blacks out of poverty in the long run and should have been credited to Lincoln. The Fourteenth Amendment, passed in June 1868, granted citizenship to all people born or naturalized in the United States, and the Fifteenth Amendment, passed in February 1869, guaranteed that no American would be denied the right to vote on the basis of race. Following Reconstruction, in fact, blacks were denied their legal right to vote in many states until a century later when the next great president with an opportunity similar to Lincoln's to make a huge impact on American history and pursue the dream of a nation without poverty—none other than President Lyndon B. Johnson—signed the Voting Rights Act of 1965 into law.

Succeeding Andrew Johnson, **GEN. ULYSSES S. GRANT** (1869–1877), forty-six years old and a Republican from Ohio, was elected in 1868 and became the youngest elected president at that time (Theodore Roosevelt, at age forty-two, was sworn in as president in 1901 and remains the youngest). Seen in his day as a president who was committed to continuing Lincoln's dream of healing the Union, in one way Grant did so even before he took office: he was the first president elected without winning a majority of the white vote. Blacks in the South were allowed to cast ballots for the first time, and roughly 700,000 did, representing 12 percent of the total vote.

In his inaugural address on March 4, 1869, the eighteenth president set forth his fundamental philosophy on suffrage: "The question of suffrage is one which is likely to agitate the public so long as a portion of the citizens of the nation are excluded from its privileges in any State. It seems to me very desirable that this question should be settled now, and I entertain the hope and express the desire that it may be by the ratification of the fifteenth article of amendment to the Constitution."[27]

According to historian William S. McFeely, a Grant biographer, "Unsaid but understood was a commitment to prevent the extermination of the Native Americans. . . . This was the only issue, the only cause, mentioned in the speech in which Grant had a deep personal interest, and he followed his startling and heartening statement by making the most interesting of all his appointments. He named an Indian commissioner of Indian Affairs."[28]

Paradoxically, for a general, Grant was often seen as a quiet man, humble and even shy; however, he projected a much stronger image, reportedly smoking more than twenty cigars a day to keep his adrenaline going. He regarded his presidency as a continuation of his Civil War role, with a goal of settling differences within the Union. He sought a permanent peace between the states and the federal government he led. He entered office hoping to pursue a peaceful policy toward the Indians, in addition to continuing Lincoln's policy of supporting rights for blacks.

Late in Grant's first term, however, corruption scandals by his subordinates in his administration plagued the president. Grant refused to distance himself from his underlings even though he had been unaware of their misdeeds at the time. Despite the scandals, Grant's popularity won him reelection in 1872.

An escalation in Southern violence in a series of states rocked his second term, and the political climate made Grant refrain from sending troops to cope with Indian uprisings. In addition, in 1873 an economic recession in the North—after a series of disasters, such as the Great Chicago Fire and the equine flu epidemic—caused progress in Reconstruction efforts to stall and dealt a blow to the poor seeking jobs.

During these trying years, the Ku Klux Klan raged out of control. Terrorist groups' actions, lynchings, beatings, and burnings undermined the federal government and the president. Grant, working with Congress, essentially launched "a war on terror"—a phrase that would be used in an entirely different and international context again during the presidencies of George W. Bush and Barack Obama in the twenty-first century. Using new powers granted to him by a series of anti-Klan laws, Grant sent federal troops to the Southern hotbeds of violence to round up Klansmen and hold them without trial. He crushed the Klan—for the time being.

In the end Grant is remembered more for his failures than for his achievements, which were few and far between. Although he was well intended when he became president, nothing in the record indicates he was concerned specifically with poverty. Most historians consider

Grant's administration as one of the most failed in American history. They place it at the bottom of the presidential achievement list, along with that of Richard M. Nixon.

The inaugural address by **RUTHERFORD B. HAYES** (1877–1881), a fifty-four-year-old Republican from Ohio, marked a major shift in tone from his predecessor. Hayes revealed at the outset that he was a principled man with a social conscience who cared about the living conditions of all Americans. On March 5, 1877, he delivered a resounding inaugural address to the American people, making a dramatic plea to build a strong Union after the Civil War.

The nineteenth president's speech read, in part:

> The sweeping revolution of the entire labor system of a large portion of our country and the advance of 4,000,000 people from a condition of servitude to that of citizenship, upon an equal footing with their former masters, could not occur without presenting problems of the gravest moment, to be dealt with by the emancipated race, by their former masters, and by the General Government, the author of the act of emancipation. That it was a wise, just, and providential act, fraught with good for all concerned, is not generally conceded throughout the country. That a moral obligation rests upon the National Government to employ its constitutional power and influence to establish the rights of the people it has emancipated, and to protect them in the enjoyment of those rights when they are infringed or assailed, is also generally admitted.
>
> . . . Let me assure my countrymen . . . that it is my earnest desire to regard and promote their truest interest—the interests of the white and of the colored people both and equally—and to put forth my best efforts in behalf of a civil policy which will forever wipe out in our political affairs the color line and the distinction between North and South, to the end that we may have not merely a united North or a united South, but a united country.[29]

It was crystal clear that Hayes wanted to be known as the man who finally reconciled the North and South. To alleviate hard times, he urged the nation to return to the gold standard, to eliminate political corruption, and to rid itself of the remaining hatred among Southerners growing out of the Reconstruction legislation that gave blacks rights they had never had. By the time Hayes assumed the presidency, however, Reconstruction was almost completed. He chose not to run for reelection.

Unfortunately, his vision did not come true. The death of Abraham Lincoln, the impeachment of Andrew Johnson, and the failures of Ulysses S. Grant had weakened the presidency. And Southern whites' residual resentment of blacks was so strong that not until Hayes forced the Southern states to uphold pledges of equal rights did he withdraw troops that he had sent there to keep the peace.

Southern states later failed to live up to their promises, and a stressful situation began as the Democratic Party governed with an iron fist to ensure complete denial of voting rights for blacks. The situation persisted until the civil rights movement of the 1960s erupted. According to one historical source, Hayes "was a patient reformer who attempted what was possible and was optimistic that education of the public would accomplish in the future the present day impossibility. Shortly before he died Hayes concluded, "I am 'a radical in thought (and principle) and a conservative in method (and conduct).'"[30]

Summing up Hayes's tenure, it was clear that he had to go slowly under difficult circumstances. In the environment in which he found himself, it would have been all but impossible for him to even think of eliminating poverty. His presidency did not come at the right time in history to make any sweeping, lasting changes. Furthermore, he pledged to serve only one term.

As historian Harry Barnard put it: "The practical results for his party that Hayes hoped for from the new Southern policy did not materialize. . . . Hayes had to admit that there had emerged precisely what he had hoped his policies would prevent, a 'solid' Democratic South."[31]

4

THE GOLDEN AGE (1881–1897):

GARFIELD, ARTHUR, CLEVELAND, BENJAMIN HARRISON, CLEVELAND

The elevation of the Negro race from slavery to the full rights of citizenship is the most important political change we have known since the adoption of the Constitution of 1787.

—James A. Garfield, inaugural address, March 4, 1881

JAMES GARFIELD (1881), a Republican, was forty-nine years old when he became the twentieth president of the United States. Born in a log cabin, he was the youngest of five children, and the family farm in the country outside of Cleveland, Ohio, earned very little money. After Lincoln, he is said to have been the poorest man ever elected president up to that time.[1]

He was sworn in on March 4, 1881, but, tragically, Charles J. Guiteau—a self-styled politician, theologian, and lawyer—shot him in Washington, D.C., on July 2, 1881. On September 19, 1881, less than seven months after taking office, Garfield died of blood poisoning and was the second of four presidents to be assassinated (following Abraham Lincoln and preceding William McKinley and John F. Kennedy). Garfield's vice president, Chester Arthur, immediately succeeded him.

As a young man, Garfield worked in a variety of jobs, including as a carpenter, a janitor while in college, and then a teacher. Ambitious, he earned a law degree and passed the bar exam in 1861, after which he went into politics and won a seat in the Ohio state legislature based on his being a hero in the Civil War. Garfield won the nomination of the Grand Old Party (GOP) in 1880. In the closest presidential election up to that time, he barely beat Democrat Winfield S. Hancock by a vote of 4,453,295 to Winfield's 4,414,082, or by the razor-thin margin of 48.3 percent to 48.2 percent.[2]

In his inaugural address on March 4, 1881, Garfield left no doubt whatsoever about his strong support of the Negroes. He also made it clear that he never forgot his poor roots. He focused his inaugural speech on the status of the Negro in the South. Vowing to continue the fight for voting rights for the Negroes, he noted that "to violate the freedom and sanctities of the suffrage is more than an evil. It is a crime which, if persisted in, will destroy the Government itself."[3] He also argued that education was the permanent solution to the issue of the Negro's place in society. The new president went on to remind his audience of what had already been accomplished in race relations:

> The elevation of the Negro race from slavery to the full rights of citizenship is the most important political change we have known since the adoption of the Constitution of 1787. . . . It has added immensely to the moral and industrial force of our people. It has liberated the master as well as the slave from a relation which wronged and enfeebled both. It has surrendered to their own guardianship the manhood of more than 5,000,000 people, and has opened to each one of them a career of freedom and usefulness. It has given new inspiration to the power of self-help in both races by making labor more honorable to the one and more necessary to the other. . . .
>   [Negroes] are beginning to enjoy the blessings that gather around the homes of the industrious *poor* [italics added].[4]

It is worth noting that although Garfield was a cautious man, prior to his becoming president, he had publicly supported Negro suffrage in 1865, "believing it the only way to preserve Republican rule and therefore the sanctity of the Union."[5] The South, he once declared, possessed a "bastard civilization." In the course of one rally, he is said to have shouted: "We have seen white men betray the flag and fight to kill the Union, but in all that long dreary war, we never saw a traitor in black skin."[6]

Indeed, as he approached the day when he would take office, Garfield was certain in his own mind that the "cure" for the black issue was in education. Garfield was a crusader of sorts from the outset. He once told a delegation of prominent Southern business leaders that had sought his help in obtaining voting rights for blacks that "genuine equality must come through the native hungering and thirsting for knowledge that the Creator has planted in every child."[7]

With his passion for equality for Negroes and the poor, one wonders what Garfield might have accomplished, had he lived. While he has always been remembered because of his assassination, historians count him among those presidents who wanted to improve the condition of minorities and the poor.

Garfield's successor, fifty-one-year-old **CHESTER A. ARTHUR** (1881–1885), a Republican, was a typical New Yorker. "He enjoyed the good life. He was a bit of a peacock, talked the latest fashion, lived the Gilded Age life."[8] Although the twenty-first president was open-minded in dealing with the Indians, he did not make any effort for extending suffrage to them because the U.S. Supreme Court ruling in the case of *Elk v. Wilkins* (1884) held that Indians could not be counted as American citizens without the government's consent. Further, it said that giving up one's tribal privileges did not constitute grounds for admission to citizenship.

Arthur had a singular presence and immediately drew respect from those who met him for the first time. He stood "six feet two in height, symmetrically built; a head adorned with silken wavy hair, always carefully combed; whiskers of the Burnside variety, invariably trimmed to the perfection point; blue, kindly eyes, straight nose, ruddy cheeks—these and his polished manners gave him the address of a veritable Chesterfield."[9]

In the political arena, he talked about introducing "the Indian tribes to the customs and pursuits of civilized life. Indeed, he looked for a way of gradual absorption into the mass of our citizens."[10] He called for the passing of a "severalty" law, one that would include from twenty to twenty-five years' protection and the extension of federal law to cover Indian reservations. The heatedly debated issue involved the Indian Bureau. On the one hand, Garfield had earlier been quoted as saying, "Their hunting days are over"; but on the other hand, he still wanted to give the Indians "the assurance of permanent title to the soil to till it, and they would gladly till it."[11]

In his annual message of December 6, 1881, Arthur called for federal aid to education, alluding specifically to the need to assist southern Negroes in their pursuit of literacy.[12]

GROVER CLEVELAND (1885–1889), a fifty-five-year-old Democrat from New York, took office on March 4, 1885, a beautiful, sunny day. A man who prided himself in neatness and order, as well as recalling information in an instant, he gave his inaugural address from memory, startling many people in the audience. His speech lasted only fifteen minutes and included little, if anything, substantive in terms of legislation he would propose.

At first, the twenty-second president was all business, but he did make himself available to officeholders and other prominent people. Monday morning was his time to receive members of the public who believed they had business with him. He experienced a somewhat rocky start after showing his displeasure for the press, no doubt the result of the hard treatment the newspapermen had given him during the campaign. He further aggravated his relationship with the press by spurning an invitation to the traditional, formal-dress dinner of the Gridiron Club, an association of the Washington press corps. The reporters who covered the White House organized the annual dinner and invited both the press and the president. The dinner featured good humor, with reporters making fun of the president and vice versa.[13] Prior to Grover Cleveland's absence, no president had dared to miss the dinner for fear of being seen as aloof and indifferent.

Cleveland's first major sign of trouble came when, as Henry F. Graff described in his book *Grover Cleveland,* "pension fever" began to plague Congress. A bill had been introduced in Congress to give a pension to any Union Army veteran who had served for at least ninety days. Never a believer in government welfare, Cleveland set afire a wave of angry action when, as chief executive, he vetoed the bill that congressmen had introduced to help veterans in their home districts. He based his veto on the belief that such assistance was not the province of national government. As he put it: "Though the people support the government, the government should not support the people."[14] This veto, however, turned out to be a mistake of enormous proportions. Yet, Cleveland held to his position: "I do not believe that the power and duty of the general government ought to be extended to the relief of individuals' suffering, which is in no manner properly related to the public service or benefit."[15]

Thus, Cleveland laid the foundation for his own undoing. In retrospect this unpopular veto certainly had such a bad effect on his reputation that it cost him a second consecutive term, although he would return to the White House and serve once again from 1893 to 1897. Little could he imagine that his opponent in the 1892 campaign would be none other than Benjamin Harrison, the president who would succeed him in 1889.

Having made it clear that he, as president, did not believe the government should offer financial assistance to its citizens and even though the disparity between the rich and the poor was obviously growing, it was no surprise that during the 1886 congressional campaign the issues of economics and poverty never arose. Poverty was simply not a political plus. In time, Cleveland recognized that his party expected him to run for reelection, but he himself was "lukewarm for a campaign or even for another term."[16]

A bachelor when he was elected, Cleveland was the first president to be married in the White House. The former New York governor also was known as a solid public servant whose campaign promises had included preventing Congress from granting special privileges to special interests, a theme that would find its place in future presidential campaigns right up to the present. He saw himself as a hands-on leader but not necessarily an innovator when it came to legislation. He was a great speechmaker but did not send many bills to Congress; instead, he tried to make the federal government more efficient by appointing people based on merit rather than on political ties to him or his party. Cleveland's management style was to name qualified cabinet members, delegate authority to them, and use them for advice and counsel.

Cleveland said what he meant and meant what he said. He did not lust for political office, and he never felt he had to make any deals or phony promises to get elected. Like Harry Truman many decades later, he was forthright and plainspoken. In today's political environment he would be considered a conservative-leaning Democrat, or possibly a Libertarian. In describing a bill that would have helped some Texas farmers who had been virtually wiped out by drought, Cleveland solidified his view and stated that the government should not take care of individuals by putting them on relief.[17]

He did uphold treaties with Native American tribes and protected their territory from settlers' expansion. Cleveland's legacy for his first term, however, could best be summed up as a president who accomplished little, if anything, to assist the poor. Nonetheless, almost completely contrary to his reputation, paradoxically he took advantage of being a lame-duck president in his fourth annual message to Congress in December 1888. He both praised the country's economic growth in industry but lamented the inequalities he witnessed:

> We discover that fortunes realized by our manufacturers are no longer solely the reward of sturdy industry and enlightened forethought, but

that they result from the discriminating favor of the Government and are largely built upon the undue exactions from the masses of the people. The gulf between employers and the employed is constantly widening, and classes are rapidly forming, one comprising the very right and powerful, while in another are the toiling poor . . . we discover the existence of trusts, combinations, and monopolies, while the citizen is struggling far in the rear or is trampled to death beneath an iron heel.[18]

There is no question that such sharp language, unusual from Cleveland's lips, connected with his successors in the so-called Progressive Era that soon followed in the early twentieth century.

BENJAMIN HARRISON (1889–1893), a Republican, was known as the Centennial President because he was elected a hundred years after George Washington. His grandfather William Henry Harrison had been president of the United States in 1841. "Harrison," wrote his biographer Graff, "had long been considered something of a dandy and an unbending little man . . . only five feet six inches tall. . . ."[19]

Almost immediately after his election on November 6, 1888, Harrison began to lose the support of those around him because of his glacial, brusque, and formal personality. The twenty-third president alienated almost every political boss in the Republican Party. His administration presided over America's Congress, with a budget of $1 million, and passed the first comprehensive pension legislation for Civil War vets, which turned into a boondoggle.

In his inaugural address on March 4, 1889, Harrison showed his disdain for slavery and the future of the nation:

Shall the prejudices and paralysis of slavery continue to hang upon the skirts of progress? How long will those who rejoice that slavery no longer exists cherish or tolerate the incapacities it put upon their communities? I look hopefully to the continuance of our protective system and to the consequent development of manufacturing and mining enterprises in the States hitherto wholly given to agriculture as a potent influence in the perfect unification of our people. The men who have invested their capital in these enterprises, the farmers who have felt the benefit of their neighborhood, and the men who work in shop or field will not fail to find and to defend a community of interest.[20]

Some of Harrison's legislative initiatives were controversial. For example, one particular measure for ensuring Negroes the right to vote, called the Force Bill, attempted to establish federal supervision of congressional elections in order to prevent the disenfranchisement of southern blacks. He was a visionary when he suggested using federal aid for education; thus, southern whites would no longer be able use literacy tests to prevent blacks from registering to vote in party primaries. Neither bill passed, however. Voting rights, which generated much debate, would continue to be a controversial issue through the present day.

Toward the end of the Harrison administration, the surplus in the treasury began to disappear. The country was in danger of falling into a recession.

In the next election, Grover Cleveland challenged Harrison, the man who had beaten him four years prior. The Republicans renominated Cleveland in 1892, and he went on to win, in effect becoming the first president to serve two nonconsecutive terms in the White House.

GROVER CLEVELAND was the only president to serve twice in two nonsequential terms (1893–1897). He unseated Benjamin Harrison, the man who had defeated him in the previous election, overwhelming Harrison in popular votes by more than 300,000 votes and in electoral votes by 277 to 145.

His second election to the presidency, however, was unproductive. One reason may be because the twenty-fourth president continued to hold the press in disregard. He paid dearly for this political misjudgment, as would another future president, Richard Nixon. In fact, he refused to give the press any space to set up shop in the White House, an act that most certainly raised animosity between them. So removed was Cleveland from the press, in fact, that as he did in his first term as president, he failed again to attend the Gridiron Club's annual dinner.

Another reason for his failure to make any impact in his second term was, at the outset of Cleveland's second administration, the nation entered the most severe economic depression in its history to that point. Called the Panic of 1893, it all but brought the nation to its knees. Another factor in his downslide was his stern, unforgiving character. He made it a point to confront rather than to compromise.[21]

By 1893, years of economic expansion, and especially an overextension of the railroads, backfired. Triggered by the bankruptcy of the

Philadelphia and Reading Railroad, a run on the banks followed, and the public panicked, bringing the economy to a near standstill. Some fifteen thousand businesses shuttered, some five hundred banks closed, and unemployment shot up to 18 percent by the end of 1893.[22]

Labor unrest continued to haunt Cleveland during his second term. In 1894, 150,000 railroad workers nationwide went on strike in support of the Pullman car workers' strike at a company town outside Chicago. Even though the governor of Illinois, John Altgeld, did not want Cleveland to use federal troops to break the strike, the president did so anyway. Many observers wondered whether the nation was on the brink of either anarchy or presidential tyranny. Unhappiness among the populace came in many forms, but perhaps the most noteworthy at the time was an organized army of unemployed workers from the Midwest who marched to Washington, D.C., and demanded that the government provide for public works projects and relief. Though only five hundred men actually arrived, the newspaper gave the event major coverage.

Cleveland, however, opposed the idea of the government sponsoring work projects to relieve the depression. When the Great Depression hit in 1929, however, Herbert Hoover would adopt the policy.

5

THE PROGRESSIVE MOVEMENT (1897–1921):

MCKINLEY, THEODORE ROOSEVELT, TAFT, WILSON

The most vital problem with which this country . . . has to deal, is the problem which has for one side the betterment of social conditions, moral and physical, in large cities. . . .
—Theodore Roosevelt, first annual message, December 3, 1901

The Progressive Era, sometimes called the Age of Reform, was ushered in with the election of Republican **WILLIAM MCKINLEY** (1897–1901). The fifty-four-year-old from Ohio won by more than a half million votes—the greatest electoral margin in twenty-five years—sweeping into office with him a historic reformation of the American political scene. He was sworn in as the nation's twenty-fifth president on March 4, 1897. Meanwhile, it was a stunning defeat for Democrat William Jennings Bryan, who was arguably the most influential politician in the liberal wing of the party. Although he ran for president unsuccessfully in 1896, 1900, and 1908, the flamboyant, fiery, fearless Bryan remained in the national political spotlight and continued to make history for years to come.[1]

In fact, the Democratic Party would make a strong comeback. As historians Allan Nevins and Henry Steel Commager explained in their book *A Short History of the United States*, "The ideas of the Populists and agrarian Democrats were ultimately, without a single important exception, to be written into legislation. They were to change the course of American history."[2]

The economic Panic of 1893 hit the nation hard, increasing the unemployment rate to an alarming 18 percent of the workforce and during a time when immigration was burgeoning. That depression lasted for five years. The 1893 economic slide was the fourth major economic downturn in fifty-six years. Consequently, change was in the air—and it was dramatic.

Scott Myers-Lipton, author of *Social Solutions to Poverty: America's Struggle to Build a Just Society*, described the rise of capitalism and, conversely, the simultaneous increase in poverty at the time: "In the late nineteenth century, industrial capitalism created immense wealth and massive poverty. As a result, the poor and the working class generally lived in substandard housing, lacked basic medical care, and received inadequate education. To make matters worse, the depression of 1893 caused the unemployment rate to soar. Compounding the unemployment problem was the tremendous influx of immigrants."[3]

The period, according to Nevins and Commager,

> was marked by revolt and reforms in almost every department of American life. Old political leaders were ousted and new ones enlisted; political machinery was overhauled and modernized; political practices were subjected to critical scrutiny, and those which failed to square with the ideals of democracy were rejected. Economic institutions and practices—private property, the corporation, the trust, great fortunes—were called before the bar of reason and asked to justify themselves or to change their ways. Social relationships were reconsidered—the impact of the city, immigration, inequalities in wealth, the growth of classes, all came in for critical attention.[4]

The foundation of America's belief in itself had begun to crumble with the 1893 downturn. It started with the collapse of the railroads, which had been overbuilt in the nation's desire to conquer the West. The questionable financing of this economic expansion caused a series of bank failures while, at the same time, there was a run on the gold supply (as compared to silver). Up to then, the nation had functioned under a policy loosely called "bimetallism," based on both gold and silver metals. Historians of the day viewed the Panic of 1893 as the worst depression the United States had ever experienced. It certainly dashed the hopes of millions of entrepreneurial Americans who thought the nation was building up a head of economic expansion that seemingly had no limits.

McKinley was a quiet-spoken leader, who many assumed at the time was being managed by his political cronies. His presidential pronouncements were not dramatic in any way, unlike those of many of his successors—specifically, Theodore Roosevelt, Woodrow Wilson, Franklin D. Roosevelt, John F. Kennedy, and Lyndon B. Johnson. McKinley is, perhaps, best remembered for becoming embroiled in the so-called 100-Day War, in which the United States intervened in the battle between Cuba and Spain. The ensuing peace treaty then gave ownership of Puerto Rico, the Hawaiian Islands, and Guam to the United States. Tragically, he is also remembered for being cut down by an assassin's bullet early in his second term.

On the domestic front, McKinley displayed a proper—but hardly action-oriented—interest in blacks, naming some to lower-level clerical positions in the diplomatic ranks. It is worth noting that he paid lip service to those Americans who detested the then acceptable practice of lynching. In his inaugural address on March 4, 1897, McKinley stated, "Lynchings must not be tolerated in a great and civilized country like the United States; courts, not mobs, must execute the penalties of the law. The preservation of public order, the right of discussion, the integrity of courts, and the orderly administration of justice must continue forever the rock of safety upon which our Government securely rests."[5]

A cautious man by nature, McKinley's rhetoric could be inspiring, but he failed to introduce any legislation that would make lynching illegal at a time when anti-black violence in the South was rampant. Nor did he or his administration display any outward concern for those citizens hopelessly mired in poverty.

Although poverty was not one of McKinley's top priorities, as a former labor lawyer, he embraced labor, playing the patronage card to enhance his reputation with the unions and appointing various labor leaders to positions in his administration. On the whole, however, McKinley offered no substantive legislation or programs to help the nation's poverty-stricken minorities. Instead, he spent much of his time in office on matters of improving trade and tariff issues.

Nonetheless, noted historian Kevin Phillips evaluated McKinley as follows: "By any serious measurement, William McKinley was a major American president. His life is all the more interesting for achieving so much stealthily but honorably. . . ."[6] The press, which treated him well, applauded the president's willingness to open up the White House to anyone who wanted to visit and shake his hand. In the opinion of some historians, though, he came up short when attending to the needs of the poor. Nonetheless, to describe his tenure in office, McKinley's 1900 reelection campaign adopted the slogan "Prosperity, Protection and Progress" for his campaign pamphlets.[7]

McKinley was not given to boasting, but he was proud of his record, especially when it came to progressive ideas for the average working

man. "His self-effacement, even rarer in a president, was also misunder-
stood as weakness," according to Phillips's account.[8] Elected to a second
term in 1900 with the legendary Theodore Roosevelt as his running
mate, McKinley's leadership ended prematurely and tragically on September 6, 1901, on the grounds of the 1901 Pan-American Exposition
in Buffalo, New York, when a deranged assassin shot him twice. McKinley died eight days later.

To many historians, **THEODORE ROOSEVELT** (1901–1909), a Republican who
immediately succeeded McKinley, is seen as the first modern president
because he significantly expanded the influence of the presidency. At
age forty-two, "T.R." was the youngest American president in history.
He had held the vice presidency for less than a year before succeeding
President McKinley immediately after his death on September 14, 1901.

Roosevelt inherited a nation that had grown significantly in many
ways. From 1870 to 1900 the population had almost doubled to 76.1
million people, according to the U.S. Bureau of the Census, as immigrants came to the United States to seek jobs and economic opportunity in the rapidly growing factories. As the nation became increasingly
urban and industrial, it developed many of the disadvantages common
to industrial nations: terrible working conditions, overcrowded slums,
enormous economic disparity between the rich and the poor, and the
beginning of the dominance of big corporations. As soon as he took
office, the twenty-sixth president began to look for solutions to solve
these problems. For a majority of Americans, their quality of life was
suffering, and he knew it.

He was a man of action. For example, when a strike in Pennsylvania
caused an anthracite coal shortage and paralyzed the country in the fall
of 1902, the president interceded. "As winter approached and heating
shortages were imminent," according to one account of his era,

> he started to formulate ideas about how he could use the executive
> office to play a role—even though he did not have any official author-
> ity to negotiate an end to the strike. Roosevelt called both the mine
> owners and the representatives of labor together at the White House.
> When management refused to negotiate, he hatched a plan to force
> the two sides to talk: instead of sending federal troops to break the
> strike and force the miners back to work, TR threatened to use troops

to seize the mines and run them as a federal operation. Faced with Roosevelt's plan, the owners and labor unions agreed to submit their cases to a commission and abide by its recommendations.

Roosevelt called the settlement of the coal strike a "square deal," meaning that everyone gained fairly from the agreement. That term soon became synonymous with Roosevelt's domestic program. The Square Deal worked to balance competing interests to create a fair outcome for all sides: labor and management, consumer and business, developer and conservationist.[9]

Roosevelt was the first president to give his domestic program a name, and succeeding presidents adopted this practice. For example, Woodrow Wilson called his program the New Freedom; Franklin D. Roosevelt, the New Deal; and Harry S. Truman, the Fair Deal. When Teddy Roosevelt subsequently was elected in a landslide in 1904 to a full term as president, the reason for his huge victory was that the people felt that the McKinley government had not lived up to what the Founding Fathers envisioned. McKinley's successor, however, offered a domestic program that emphasized an effort to reform the American workplace. T.R. pushed for legislation that would improve the people's social welfare and vastly increase government regulation of industry.

By 1900, federal as well as state governments had assumed responsibility for caring for the poor and veterans. In that era, "cash payments, medical services, and domiciliary care were all parts of a system that viewed the social welfare of veterans and their families as a special obligation of the society as a whole," according to historians June Axinn and Mark J. Stern in their book *Social Welfare*.[10]

Roosevelt felt that helping to ensure social justice and economic opportunity through government regulation was his responsibility. Known as a "trust buster" because he focused on breaking up big businesses cartels, he liked to quote a favorite proverb: "Speak softly and carry a big stick."[11] It is instructive, incidentally, to read Roosevelt's words during his first annual message delivered on December 3, 1901:

> In my judgment the time has arrived when we should definitely make up our minds to recognize the Indian as an individual and not as a member of a tribe. The General Allotment Act is a mighty pulverizing engine to break up the tribal mass. It acts directly upon the family and the individual. . . . This is the case also with the lands. A stop should be put upon the indiscriminate permission to Indians to lease their allotments. The effort should be steadily to make the Indian work like

any other man on his own ground. The marriage laws of the Indians should be made the same as those of the whites.[12]

Teddy Roosevelt kept up the drumbeat. In his second annual message on December 2, 1902, he addressed the topic of Native Americans. He stated:

> In dealing with the Indians our aim should be their ultimate absorption into the body of our people. But in many cases this absorption must and should be very slow. In portions of the Indian Territory the mixture of blood has gone on at the same time with progress in wealth and education, so that there are plenty of men with varying degrees of purity of Indian blood who are absolutely indistinguishable in point of social, political, and economic ability from their white associates.[13]

Roosevelt also showed a personal and abiding interest in the millions of poor white people—mostly immigrants—living in city slums, especially in New York City. As the former head of the New York Police Board of Commissioners (1895–1897), he had firsthand experience with the squalid, uninhabitable tenements, which he saw as a major weakness in the country's economic system. Teddy Roosevelt often referred to the depths of poverty in overcrowded areas of American cities in his stump speeches and during his travels around the country. His words touched the social consciences of millions of Americans.

As a result, a brand-new profession called social work emerged in the Roosevelt era. Indeed, "Theodore Roosevelt himself, acting on the commonly held conviction that all were personally responsible for the current state of affairs depicted so graphically in muckraking literature [newspapers and magazines of the day], called upon each citizen to contribute to reform through social work."[14] Two similar but separate organizations—charities and settlement houses—carried out this effort. Both played major roles in caring for hundreds of thousands of immigrants who landed on New York's shores. Many were penniless, hungry, exhausted, and with only the clothes on their backs, nowhere to sleep, and nowhere else to turn. Many of the immigrants became the unheralded heroes of young America. They helped settle our country and later became leaders in all walks of American life. They pursued what would become known in later years as the Great American Dream and succeeded. These immigrants were to benefit from the passage of child labor laws. At the turn of the twentieth century, nearly two million children from ages ten through fifteen and almost five million young women older than fifteen years of age were conscripted into the labor force in twenty-eight states. By 1914, after considerable pressure from well-organized social welfare organizations, virtually all of the states in the Union had passed laws "covering working hours and conditions of child labor in factories, mills, and workshops and setting minimum wages for leaving schools."[15]

"T.R., like his father, Theodore Roosevelt Sr.," was said to have had "compassion for the underprivileged."[16] Of all the presidents up to this time, T.R. was undoubtedly the most concerned with the sordid living conditions that were rapidly developing in America's cities, especially where Negroes lived. During his tenure with the police commission, Roosevelt was encouraged by crusading newspaper reporters like Jacob Riis to see for himself the evils of urban squalor. And when Roosevelt became governor (January 1889–December 1900), Riis accompanied him on tours of the city. "Once or twice," Roosevelt wrote in his autobiography, "I went suddenly down to New York City without warning any one and traversed the tenement-house quarters, visiting various sweatshops picked at random. Jacob Riis accompanied me, and as a result of our inspection we got not only an improvement in the law but a still more marked improvement in its administration."[17]

Thus, his loyal supporters were not surprised that when T.R. assumed the presidency, his program to help the poor came to be called the Square Deal. It reflected Roosevelt's vow not to favor any group of Americans but to be fair to all. It also indicated his profound conviction that the federal government should use all of its resources to help achieve equality and social justice.

On matters of race and civil rights, T.R. was not half as aggressive as he was at going after the big corporations or bad landlords. He did not approach the improvement of race relations with the same fervor as he did, for example, his battle against the slums. He was a complex man with seemingly conflicting views on various topics when it came to supporting the masses. His personal attitude toward blacks, for example, might properly be described as torn. As one account candidly stated:

> Theodore Roosevelt reflected the racial attitudes of his time, and his domestic record on race and civil rights was a mixed bag. . . . He believed that African Americans as a race were inferior to whites, but he thought many black individuals were superior to white individuals and should be able to prove their merit. . . . Although he appointed blacks to some patronage positions in the South, he was generally unwilling to fight the political battles necessary to win their appointment.[18]

Nonetheless, Roosevelt moved in the fall of 1901 to improve relations between blacks and whites. He had heard about Booker T. Washington, a self-taught slave who, in 1881, had founded the Tuskegee Institute, a technical school for African Americans. T.R. was a believer in Washington's "accommodation" philosophy toward whites and labeled Washington "the most useful, as well as the most distinguished member of his race in the world."[19] T.R. invited Washington to the White House for private meetings twice in October 1891 and discussed numerous topics, including race relations and education for African Americans in the South. Although well intended, these two visits caused a major uproar when the press learned of them. That a black man had dined with the president and his wife Edith enraged segregationists. Their criticism was heated and personal, and more and more voters became involved.

This controversy came at a time of great population expansion. The 1890 census showed a U.S. population of 62,979,766, or an increase of 25.5 percent since the 1880 census.[20] As noted earlier, the sharp increase came from the flow of immigrants flocking to America, hoping to work in the mushrooming businesses and factories that were turning out new products in a rapidly growing marketplace. Unfortunately, this wave of people faced poor working and living conditions while the nation experienced a complete takeover by big business. At the turn of the twentieth century, however, Americans had begun to look for ways to address some of these issues.

T.R. helped usher in a new, progressive era during which he and other public officials were sensitized to what one famous reporter of his time Lincoln Steffens called "the shame of the cities."[21] Many crusading reform-minded newspaper reporters—including the aforementioned Riis—wrote stories about Roosevelt's many-pronged efforts to improve cities and the nation as a whole.

In fact, Riis also wrote a biography of the president, *Theodore Roosevelt the Citizen*. Published in 1903, it referred to the former police commissioner of New York as a leader who "was stirring New York up as it had not been stirred in many a long day."[22] Riis also vividly described how he worked hand in hand with Roosevelt to rid New York City of its slums and subhuman conditions. Riis's newspaper articles had been a call to action and Roosevelt had responded. This relationship between a newspaper reporter and a powerful public official in New York City was unprecedented. Riis wrote, "Roosevelt wanted to know the city by night, and the true inwardness of some of the problems he was struggling with. . . . One might hear of overcrowding in tenements for years and not grasp the subject as well as he could by a single midnight inspection with the sanitary police. He wanted to understand it all, the smallest with the greatest, and sometimes the information he brought out was unique, to put it mildly."[23]

As a direct result of his travels with Riis, Roosevelt ordered dozens of rotting, tenement houses shut down and demanded that city officials prosecute landlords for their misdeeds. Riis and Roosevelt were an unbeatable team in the history of reform and the ongoing war against poverty. Arguably, Riis may well have been the one man in Teddy Roosevelt's life who influenced him most in matters of social conscience during his long and historic career. Roosevelt indeed credits Riis's writing as the spark that set him in motion. Said Roosevelt:

> His [Riis's] book "How the Other Half Lives" had been to me both an enlightenment and an inspiration for which I felt I could never be too grateful. Soon after it was written I had called at his office to tell him how deeply impressed I was by the book, and that I wished to help him in any practical way to try to make things a little better. I have always had a horror of words that are not translated into deed, of speech that does not result in action—in other words, I believe in realizable ideals and in realizing them, in preaching what can be practiced and then in practicing it. Jacob Riis had drawn an indictment of the things that were wrong, pitifully and dreadfully wrong, with the tenement homes and the tenement lives of our wage-workers. In his book he had pointed out how city government, and especially those connected with the departments of police and health, could aid in remedying some of the wrongs.
>
> . . . I felt that with Jacob Riis's guidance I would be able to put a goodly number of his principles into actual effect. He and I looked at life and its problems from substantially the same standpoint. Our ideals and principles and purposes, and our beliefs as to the methods necessary to realize them, were alike.[24]

Roosevelt added in his book: "The midnight trips that Riis and I took enabled me to see what the Police Department was doing and also gave me the personal insight into some of the problems of city life. It is one thing to listen in perfunctory fashion to tales of overcrowded tenements, and it is quite another actually to see what that overcrowding means, some hot summer night, by even a single inspection during the hours of darkness."[25]

Indeed, Riis opened Roosevelt's eyes to many of the city's ills and accompanied him regularly on tours of the slums during the nights and early hours of the morning. According Riis's book *Theodore Roosevelt, the Citizen,* "He [T.R.] shut the saloons as Police Commissioner, since the law he had sworn to enforce demanded it. And though politicians claimed that he alienated support from the administration he stood for, he taught us a lesson in civic honesty that will yet bear fruit; for while politics are allowed to play hide-and-seek with the majesty of the law, that majesty is a fraud and politics will be unclean."[26]

Riis gave his reason for his admiration of his beloved T.R.: "It has seemed in this generation as if every influence, especially in our big cities, were hostile to the home, and that was one reason why I hailed the coming of this plain man of old-time ideals into our people's life, and wanted him to be as close to it as he could get."[27]

Riis told his readers of the most private conversations he had with the president. "I have said that I speak for myself in these pages; but for once you can take it that I speak for Theodore Roosevelt too," he wrote. In revealing what Roosevelt thinks, Riis noted that the "underlying thought of his oft-expressed philosophy, [is] that the poorest plan for an American to act upon is that of 'some men down,' and the safest that of 'all men up.' For, whether for good or ill, up we go or down, poor or rich, white or black, all of us together in the end, in the things that make for real manhood. And the making of that manhood and the bringing of it to the affairs of life and making it tell there, is the business of the Republic."[28]

Riis summed up his thoughts about Roosevelt this way: "My story stops here. There is nothing in it, as I have shown you Roosevelt and his life, that is beyond the reach or strength of any one who will make the most of himself with determined purpose. . . . It is for that reason above all significant that he should be the young man's President, the type of hero of the generation that is to shape the coming day of our Republic as it is entering upon its world-mission among the nations."[29]

Later Roosevelt paid mutual tribute to Riis, noting that the man who was closest to him throughout his two-year post in the Police Department was Jacob Riis. "My whole life was influenced by my long association with Jacob Riis, whom I am tempted to call the best American I ever knew," he wrote.[30]

Meanwhile, Riis was not alone in catering to Teddy Roosevelt, who enjoyed an outstanding reputation in the media. According to one historical account, "Roosevelt was the first President to use the power of the media to appeal directly to the American people. He understood that his forceful personality, his rambunctious family, and his many opinions made good copy for the press. He also knew that the media was a good way for him to reach out to the people, bypassing political parties and political machines. He used the media as a 'bully pulpit' to influence public opinion."[31]

It had been his leadership of the "Rough Riders," the First U.S. Volunteer Cavalry Regiment, and its performance in the Spanish-American War in 1898 that eventually became part of T.R.'s "tough guy" or "big bully" presidential image. People saw him as a fighter who never quit.

Having joined forces with Jacob Riis, Roosevelt was shrewd enough to cooperate with other journalists of the muckraking era, including Thomas W. Lawson, Henry Demarest Lloyd, Frank Norris, Fremont Older, Charles Edward Russell, Samuel Hopkins Adams, Ray Stannard Baker, Cecil Chesterton, Claud Cockburn, Burton J. Hendrick, Frances Kellor, and John Spargo. Many others also wrote front-page stories about the poor living in slum tenements in their cities, as well as about social abuses in business and other areas of American life, such as the environment—one of T.R.'s most passionate interests.

These stories inspired many women to play an active role in the reform era. They joined a movement that was an offshoot of the progressive spirit and helped create the settlement houses, which sheltered a great many immigrants in communal settings in urban poor neighborhoods. Women who heeded Roosevelt's call to action and became social workers include Lillian Wald, head of the Henry Street Settlement in New York's Lower East Side; Jane Addams, who founded and ran Hull House in 1889 in Chicago; Ida Wells-Barnett, antilynching crusader; Mary McLeod Bethune, education and civil rights activist; Evangeline Booth, Salvation Army leader; Carrie Chapman Catt, women's suffrage leader; Frances Power Cobbe, founder of Ragged Schools; Dorothea Dix, prison reformer; Julia Ward Howe, author, hymn writer, philanthropist, and reformer; and Mary H. Hunt, American temperance reformer and educator.

The downside of the settlement house movement was that some of the reformers inadvertently contributed to racism in society at large because they did not permit African Americans to live in such environments. Historian Myers-Lipton noted: "Some white settlement houses argued that segregated facilities were necessary so that each neighborhood had its own social center; however, in reality they feared that black participation would scare off the white community."[32] Thus, even the privately run institutions to house the poor had their limitations.

The two best-known black leaders of this era—Booker T. Washington and W. E. B. Du Bois—opposed this kind of wanton discrimination, but they held different views on how to accomplish their goals. Washington's approach was to have blacks demonstrate their intelligence to the larger white community as the best way to be accepted as individuals. Meanwhile, Du Bois, who founded the National Association for the Advancement of Colored People, disagreed that people should take the gradual integration approach and sacrifice their social and political equality. Du Bois argued that blacks should put all of their energy into ending discrimination and segregation and into lobbying for the right to vote. Either way, Roosevelt was flexible enough to support the black man's battle for freedom through his many speeches to Congress and the public.

Among Teddy Roosevelt's other achievements was that after the Spanish-American War, he cut the size of federal government almost to its prewar status. Succeeding presidents, with few exceptions, obviously failed to learn from his example.

Toward the end of his second term in the White House, non-profit organizations across the country petitioned Roosevelt to hold a White House conference on child dependency in 1909. Eventually it led to the creation of a federal Children's Bureau in 1912 and the Child Welfare League in 1921. The precedent of federal interest in child welfare led to reconvening the White House conference for many years thereafter.

As for Teddy Roosevelt's retirement years after his successful presidency—which included his receiving the Nobel Peace Prize in 1906 for negotiating an end to the Russo-Japanese War—they were almost as productive as when he served in the Oval Office. Still an idealist, he worked for the Progressive Party's "New Nationalism" effort in 1910. Roosevelt clearly articulated that he favored labor over capital and a strong government to oversee the economy and corporate business, a graduated income tax on people who had large fortunes, and an inheritance tax. This philosophy preceded that of the liberal groups of the 1930s, which, in turn, supported Democratic presidents Harry S. Truman, John F. Kennedy, and Lyndon B. Johnson during the history-making social and civil rights revolution of the 1950s and 1960s. Delivering a campaign speech in Osawtomie, Kansas, on December 6, 2011, the forty-fourth president of the United States, Barack Obama, also alluded to former president Teddy Roosevelt's populist philosophy when he talked about the disappearing middle class.

The twenty-seventh president, **WILLIAM HOWARD TAFT** (1909–1913), was a fifty-one-year-old Republican from Ohio who had served as Teddy

Roosevelt's vice president and right-hand man and became best friends with Roosevelt. But the rotund, six-foot-two, 350-pound Taft, who hardly fit the stereotypical picture of a chief executive, was reluctant to succeed his boss. Partly, he wanted eventually to serve on the United States Supreme Court, for in his mind the lofty job of Supreme Court justice was the highest position to which any man could aspire. Taft was a strict constructionist and believed the Constitution as written held the key to all judicial questions. Another reason he preferred the bench was because he is said to have been put off by the glare of publicity and the press.

However, the pressure from his party was too much, and he accepted the nomination and won office. Taft felt that the president's job was that of a caretaker of the government and not as an initiator of action as Roosevelt had been. Much to T.R.'s astonishment, his handpicked successor began to unravel Roosevelt's programs. Taft, in the end, clearly did not share Roosevelt's philosophy toward minorities or the poor.

Accordingly, in Taft's bid for reelection in 1912, Roosevelt challenged Taft for the nomination. As their relationship soured, it resulted in a bitter split in the Republican Party. Roosevelt ran, instead, on the third-party "Bill Moose" ticket, but the campaign was short of money, as the business interests that had supported him in 1904 either backed the other candidates or stayed neutral. Also handicapping Roosevelt was the fact that he had already served nearly two full terms as president and thus was challenging the unwritten "no third term" rule. In the end, the Taft-Roosevelt dispute paved the way for an unexpected but solid triumph by Woodrow Wilson, the long-shot Democratic candidate.

Taft did achieve his lifelong dream when President Warren G. Harding named him chief justice of the Supreme Court in 1921. Taft was the only man to have served as both president and chief justice.

Following Taft came **WOODROW WILSON** (1913–1921), a Democrat from New Jersey. At fifty-six years of age, he had served as the president of Princeton University and the governor of New Jersey. He was an intellectual who stated his progressive reform philosophy and set the tone for what would be remembered as a thoughtful time of open-mindedness— but not necessarily one of domestic action, at least in the area of poverty. In his first inaugural address on March 4, 1913, the twenty-eighth president laid out some of the goals he believed government should play. After dubbing his administration "The New Freedom," he talked about the nation's great accomplishments but inserted a note of warning: he reminded Americans at his inaugural that our country had not fulfilled all of its potential. He stated:

> There has been something crude and heartless and unfeeling in our haste to succeed and be great. . . . The firm basis of government is justice, not pity. These are matters of justice. There can be no equality or opportunity, the first essential of justice in the body politic, if men and women and children be not shielded in their lives, their very vitality, from the consequences of great industrial and social processes which they can not alter, control, or singly cope with. Society must see to it that it does not itself crush or weaken or damage its own constituent parts. The first duty of law is to keep sound the society it serves. Sanitary laws, pure food laws, and laws determining conditions of labor which individuals are powerless to determine for themselves are intimate parts of the very business of justice and legal efficiency.[33]

Wilson has been described as intelligent, religious, aloof, and academically methodical. In fact, it has been said that Wilson tried to bring a bit of the Ivory Tower to the Oval Office. His first term focused on a domestic agenda. Among his major changes were the creation of the Federal Reserve to manage the U.S. currency system, which, at that time, was badly in need of reform, and his appointment of a Council of National Defense to review and put in place recommendations regarding veterans' benefits, which greatly enhanced those already in existence.

Woodrow Wilson can be considered the first of three outstanding presidents who accomplished a great deal in their first hundred days. In the history of the modern presidency, Wilson, Franklin Delano Roosevelt, and Lyndon B. Johnson stand out for their legislative achievements, the result of a shrewd strategy, cagey maneuvering, and intellectual flexibility. All of these efforts boiled down to deal making, or the God-given ability to make a promise and to make the other fellow keep his.

Hardly a backslapping politician, Wilson gathered the Democratic majority behind him to pass major legislation. He supported the Clayton Antitrust Act, which Congress passed in 1914. It was hailed by farmers and labor because it exempted their organizations from antitrust prosecution under the Sherman Antitrust Act. He also created the Federal Trade Commission, whose board had the power to investigate and publicize corrupt, unfair, and anticompetitive business practices.

Wilson asked Congress to create a separate cabinet-level Department of Labor, and it did so on March 4, 1913. Further displaying his progressive thinking, he nominated the first Jewish justice to the Supreme Court, Louis Brandeis, whose outstanding record as an attorney included fighting in court against the exploitation by big business of women and children workers. Wilson took additional actions to help the less fortunate: he backed improved credit for farmers and a workers' compensation program for federal employees. In 1916 he also pushed through a law to eliminate child labor, but the Supreme Court ruled it unconstitutional in 1918. It was not until Franklin Roosevelt's New Deal program two decades later that Congress passed the Fair Labor Standards Act, which, among other things, placed limits on many forms of child labor.

When American railroad unions threatened to strike in 1916, Wilson signed into law the Adamson Act. The bill set an eight-hour workday for railroad employees and eventually led to shortened workdays for workers in all industries.

When the United States entered World War I, three years after it had started, Wilson was forced to put his domestic agenda on hold and concentrate on mobilizing the nation to win the war. As a result of his leadership, unions agreed not to strike during wartime and union membership increased from 2.7 million to more than 4 million by 1919.

Postscript: Wilson attempted to create a League of Nations, as he called it, after World War I because it reflected his vision for worldwide peace. Although his effort failed, Franklin Roosevelt and Eleanor Roosevelt and later Harry S. Truman after World War II would work successfully to bring his view to life and to establish the United Nations.

6

THE RISE OF BIG BUSINESS (1921–1932):
HARDING, COOLIDGE, HOOVER

The chief business of the American people is business.
—Calvin Coolidge, in a speech to the American Society
of Newspaper Editors, Washington, D.C., January 17, 1925

After the roller coaster years of William McKinley, Theodore Roosevelt, William Howard Taft, and Woodrow Wilson, WARREN HARDING (1921–1923), a fifty-five-year-old Republican from Ohio, campaigned on a pledge to restore normalcy to the nation, which after World War I was yearning for peace at home and abroad. Interestingly, before his nomination and subsequent election to the presidency, Harding gave Americans a clue about how he saw the role of government. In a campaign speech in Boston on May 14, 1920, he declared: "If we can prove a representative popular government under which a citizenship seeks what it may do for the government rather than what the government may do for individuals, we shall do more to make democracy safe for the world than all armed conflict ever recorded."[1]

Harding stressed the concept of moving America back to its previous position, before the shock of World War I. In his inaugural address on March 4, 1921, the twenty-ninth president repeated his call for the people to help their government in a passionate speech: "Service is the supreme commitment of life. I would rejoice to acclaim the era of the Golden Rule and crown it with the autocracy of service. I pledge an administration wherein all the agencies of the Government are called to serve, and ever promote an understanding of Government purely as an expression of the popular will."[2]

It was a prophetic accident of history that Harding's vision of the people serving the government, rather than the government serving the people, foreshadowed John F. Kennedy's celebrated patriotic phrase in his inaugural address four decades later: "And so, my fellow Americans: ask not what your country can do for you—ask what you can do for your country."[3]

While Harding demonstrated his ability to deliver emotional rhetoric, he fell far short on actions to carry out his promises. He made a moving appeal to all Americans to become involved in the body politic.

But it was not to be.

Harding—a handsome, impressive-looking president who appeared as if he had come straight from central casting—grew up in Marion, Ohio. He tried his hand at numerous jobs after college and wound up as his hometown's newspaper editor and one of its most influential people. He eventually went into politics and was elected to the U.S. Senate in 1914. Making it a point to avoid controversy by voting with his party 95 percent of the time, he gathered enough support to announce his candidacy for the GOP nomination for president with Governor Calvin Coolidge of Massachusetts as his running mate. They won handily over the Democratic candidates—Ohio governor James M. Cox as the presidential candidate and thirty-eight-year-old Franklin Delano Roosevelt of New York for vice president.[4]

Most historians see Harding as a caretaker president who, more or less, performed his job as a ceremonial executive, eschewing behind-the-scenes political deal making that had become almost a ritual at the White House prior to his election. Nonetheless, everyone liked and accepted Harding, mostly because he articulated no strong views of his own and was able to bring people together through conciliation.

As Eugene P. Trani and David L. Wilson wrote in *The Presidency of Warren G. Harding,* "Taken together, Harding's outstanding trait was his ability to get along with others and serve as a conciliator of interests. This compulsion to arbitrate diverse views often led him to avoid troublesome questions or to ignore facts that might shatter the unity he sought. He wanted a cabinet which would serve his conception of the presidency. He would arbitrate between the best opinions on an issue. He thus placed a high premium on loyalty."[5]

Unfortunately, Harding's political naïveté in allowing his subordinate cabinet officers to manage with a free reign was his undoing. One particular incident gave his White House a corrupt and ineffective image, even though Harding himself was not involved. Called the Teapot Dome scandal, Harding's secretary of the interior, Albert Fall, was indicted and convicted of taking bribes from prominent private oil producer Henry F. Sinclair for control of the Teapot Dome federal oil reserves in Wyoming in the 1920s.[6] As a result, Congress held hearings. The newspapers published sensational headlines that gave the impression at the time that Harding was mixed up in the affair. According to a former Richard Nixon aide and historian John W. Dean, "None of these investigations, however, implicated Warren Harding in any corrupt activity or wrongdoing."[7]

During his campaign for office, he showed little, if any interest in improving the status of blacks or other minorities. He postured at times in an effort to draw black votes and seemed to arouse hope for their cause, but in the end he was "unwilling to make commitments," according to two of his biographers.[8] He temporarily engendered some optimism among blacks when he met with black leaders shortly after taking office. They "proposed a program to gain full citizenship for blacks. They requested antilynching legislation, investigation of peonage in the South, a national commission to study race relations, black assistant secretaries in the Departments of Labor and Agriculture, an end to occupation of Haiti, and an executive order ending segregation in government service."[9]

In response, Harding sent out mixed messages, revealing his ambivalent attitude about blacks. Not long after he assumed office, Harding asked Congress on April 21, 1921, to "wipe the stain" of lynching away from American life. He also agreed to create a biracial commission to look into this pervasive issue of race relations. Black leader W. E. B. Du Bois labeled Harding's particular phrase of "wipe the stain" as the strongest pronouncement on the race problem that a president ever had made up to that time in a message to Congress.[10]

However, Harding sharply reversed direction in a speech in Birmingham a few months later, on October 26, 1921, when "he cautioned against black people gaining social equality, as it was unattainable."[11] This statement left both blacks and segregationists unhappy.

Harding had a better record when it came to white women's struggle for social, political, and educational equality when he supported the Sheppard-Towner Maternity and Infancy Protection Act of 1921, which gave clout to the legislation that Taft had signed creating the Children's Bureau. In addition, Harding signed a bill—over the objections of the powerful American Medical Society—that enabled states to provide funds for medical care.[12] He also signed the Cable Act of 1922, which guaranteed that American women would no longer lose their citizenship if they married foreign nationals eligible for citizenship.

However, Harding essentially missed a golden opportunity to help working people during his short time in office. His secretary of commerce, Herbert Hoover, wanted to help labor and persuade large companies that still maintained twelve-hour workdays to shorten the workday to eight hours, as Wilson had done before him. Hoover urged Harding to call a high-level meeting at the White House with top business executives. Harding did so but without publicizing it, and his effort to convince the tycoons to go along with his scheme was hardly persuasive. In time, Hoover would win some concessions, and the steel industry and other business eventually capitulated. Hoover demonstrated—seemingly going against his own belief in a hands-off government—"that an aggressive government could bring about substantial social change on a 'voluntary' basis."[13]

Harding served only briefly—from 1921 until he died on August 2, 1923 of natural causes. He accomplished little and certainly brought no substantive solutions to the fundamental issues of poverty and race relations. Despite his oratory at the outset of his term, he failed to follow through or, perhaps, was a victim of his own inability to take any concrete actions, with the possible exception of creating the Bureau of the Budget. Harding's biographers Trani and Wilson concluded in their book "that Harding's presidency was transitional and that he was an ineffective leader who suffered both personal and political scandal. It is not surprising that historians rate Harding a poor president."[14] For one thing, he vetoed the Bonus Bill for World War I veterans.

Coincidentally, John Dean's hometown was Marion, Ohio, as well. In his biography of Harding, he, too, concluded: "Warren G. Harding is best known as America's worst president."[15] Dean, who once lived near Harding and delivered newspapers to his house, qualified his statement by adding: "A compelling case, however, can be made that to reach such a judgment one must ignore much of the relevant information about Harding and his presidency."[16]

When **CALVIN COOLIDGE** (1923–1929), a Republican from Vermont, quite unexpectedly succeeded Harding on August 2, 1923, he was virtually unknown, not having been an active vice president. "Politically, the vice president did not make much of an impression," wrote Robert H. Ferrell in his biography of the thirtieth president. "This may have been because he made no efforts to be a maker of policies."[17]

Coolidge, then fifty-one years old, was a lawyer and former governor of Massachusetts. After finishing Harding's term, Coolidge was elected on the slogan "Keep Cool with Coolidge" and sworn in by Chief Justice William Howard Taft. It marked the first time in history that an ex-president had given the oath of office to a president. From the outset, Coolidge made no bones about his desire to be fiscally conservative.

In his inaugural speech on March 4, 1925, he stated, loudly and clearly, his philosophy of how he intended to run the country's finances. In doing so he revealed his propensity to favor the rich.

> We can not finance the country, we can not improve social conditions, through any system of injustice, even if we attempt to inflict it upon the rich. Those who suffer the most harm will be the poor. This country believes in prosperity. It is absurd to suppose that it is envious of those who are already prosperous. The wise and correct course to follow in taxation and all other economic legislation is not to destroy those who have already secured success but to create conditions under which every one will have a better chance to be successful.[18]

In effect, Coolidge may well have been the first president to launch what would eventually be labeled the "trickle down" policy of economics. He kept a tight rein on the federal budget, but Coolidge's stubborn adherence to ultraconservative economic policies put him in the uncomfortable position of failing to satisfy two of his key GOP constituencies—the veterans and the farmers. He vetoed a bill that would have given pay raises for postal workers and bonuses for World War I veterans, the World War Adjusted Compensation Act. The Veterans Bonus Act of 1924 awarded World War I veterans paid-up insurance policies that were redeemable in twenty years. The Bonus Bill was passed over the president's veto. Coolidge was also shortsighted in killing farm relief bills. These bills would have established a government entity to purchase surplus crops at artificially set prices and then sell the surplus crops when market prices rose. This program could have boosted the slumping farm economy and might have helped lessen the shock or even the severity of the Great Depression.

During the 1924 campaign, Coolidge spoke readily on behalf of big business and his desire to preserve the nation's business culture. "The man who builds a factory builds a temple," he said. "The man who works there, worships there." The president believed firmly in a simple formula for prosperity: "The chief business of the American people is business."[19] Once in office, Coolidge lowered taxes twice. His goal, simply stated, was to keep government small and to make certain big business and the rich continued to benefit from the economy. This bedrock Republican economic philosophy has not changed much in the intervening years and right up to the present.

Coolidge was known as Silent Cal because of his generally quiet demeanor and his propensity to answer questions in as few words as possible. He was the opposite of Harding, who was a tall, dignified-looking man who carried himself with confidence and was an eloquent speaker. Similar to President Bill Clinton more than seventy years later, Harding was so charismatic that he made his audiences feel as though he were speaking directly to each individual on the premises.

That was not the case with Coolidge, who failed to stir many people during his public addresses. A Massachusetts colleague once described his speeches this way: "His words are trenchant, exact, and meaningful and the delivery of them cold."[20] Paradoxically, he was also known for greeting visitors at the White House. In fact, he and his wife, Grace, were said to have entertained more people than any of his predecessors had. In a time of rapid installations of telephones, purchases of radios, stepped-up manufacturing and purchasing of automobiles, and the government's building of roads during the freewheeling Roaring Twenties, Coolidge nonetheless remained conservative in his views and his actions. For example, even though Coolidge reportedly was opposed to Prohibition, which was proposed in 1917, ratified in January 1919, and made the manufacture, sale, and transportation of liquor illegal, he made little or no effort to repeal it. The law was not repealed until 1933. He also managed to live with, but not exactly embrace, passage of the Nineteenth Amendment in 1920 that gave women the right to vote.

He was equally passive when it came to civil rights and civil liberties—two areas of potential reform that badly needed to be addressed if the country was going to achieve any progress in eliminating poverty. Like the majority of his constituents, however, Coolidge believed that the Civil War had addressed these issues, and he saw no need to initiate any changes. His stance reflected, for the most part, his philosophy of governance, which might be summed up this way: "Don't do anything unless you have to. Let's avoid trouble."

Poverty, it can reasonably be argued, was rarely discussed in Coolidge's White House. A slice of evidence in the record, however, illustrates one positive aspect of the Coolidge years: on several occasions he advised Congress to pass an antilynching bill. Other than that effort, however, he kept his opinions on race to himself.[21]

Yet another sign on the horizon of a coming economic crash that Coolidge failed to factor into his planning was the public's underconsumption of manufactured goods.[22] He had spoken out in favor of installment buying, not fully realizing that a mountain of debt might someday come crashing down on the country—as it did. But economists of that era did not see under consumption as a problem. Accordingly, Coolidge should not be too harshly critiqued on this score. Simply put, the American economy was a consumer economy in which few consumed.

It is fair to look at Coolidge's presidency—and keep in mind those of his policies that might have impacted poverty in America—and conclude that while Coolidge presided over record economic prosperity in the midst of plenty, he failed to see the increasing instability of the economy, which was heading rapidly toward poverty. Although it hardly seems possible today, during the Coolidge years, nobody in government or close to the White House saw the Great Depression coming. Quite the contrary, Coolidge himself saw his own tenure in the White House as the height of public service—and he wanted to convey to all Americans that serving one's country was the most important contribution a citizen could make.

When **HERBERT HOOVER** (1929–1933) of Iowa—the first president born west of the Mississippi River—assumed office on March 4, 1929, all was well in America. The fifty-four-year-old Hoover had the credentials to run the country, having served in the Wilson administration as head of the Food Administration in 1914 and as the secretary of commerce for Presidents Harding and Coolidge. As commerce secretary, he had promoted partnerships between government and business under the heading of modernizing the economy.

A somewhat stiff and reserved businessman from a mining company, Hoover stood out, nonetheless, as the epitome of a hardheaded, practical, profit-driven international capitalist. He won the Republican nomination on June 12, 1928, at the Republican National Convention in Kansas City, although he never had held any previous elected office. Ironically, in hindsight, at that convention Hoover became the first American president to be bullish about eliminating poverty in America. At a time when the country enjoyed extraordinary prosperity, Hoover proudly stated:

Unemployment in the sense of distress is widely disappearing. . . . We in America today are nearer to the *final triumph* over *poverty* [italics added] than ever before in the history of any land. The poorhouse is vanishing from among us. We have not yet reached the goal, but given a chance to go forward with the policies of the last eight years, and we shall soon with the help of God be in sight of the day when *poverty will be banished from this nation* [italics added].[23]

In his inaugural address on March 4, 1929, the thirty-first president continued—again, ironically—to emphasize "removing poverty" as one of his major goals. He even mentioned the word "poverty" three times in his text:

In the large view, we have reached a higher degree of comfort and security than ever existed before in the history of the world. Through liberation from widespread *poverty* [italics added] we have reached a higher degree of individual freedom than ever before. . . .

. . . The larger purpose of our economic thought should be to establish more firmly stability and security of business and employment and thereby remove *poverty* [italics added] still further from our borders. . . .

. . . We do know what the attainment of these ideals should be: . . . the direction of economic progress toward prosperity for the further lessening of *poverty* [italics added]. . . .[24]

One can interpret Hoover's references to poverty as a sign of his awareness that the problem existed. Hoover had good reason to be quite confident, but he was also farsighted enough to cover all bases and include those who cared about the poor or even the poor themselves. This astuteness was a side of Hoover that few people credited to him.

The country was riding a wave of unprecedented prosperity. Between 1925 and 1929, the stock market rose 250 percent to staggering new heights. People bought homes, cars, dishwashers—everything they ever wanted. Industry was thriving, the entertainment world was on a tear, and new inventions and discoveries were making the news in medicine, the arts, and in all of the professions.[25] It was a heady time in American history. Yet, paradoxically, during the first four years of Hoover's administration, an unparalleled economic phenomenon developed. Historian Albert U. Romasco explains:

Americans in the Hoover years of the Great Depression, 1929–33, were a people perplexed by plenty. They saw the nation's magnificent productive plant intact, its ability to produce unimpaired. And yet, in a land celebrated for its abundance, the people were plagued by scarcity. This paradox confounded the age-old notion of poverty. America's poverty was not cut in the familiar pattern of the past; it represented a new phenomenon. It was the result of rich resources and not of the niggardliness of nature; the outcome of energy and inventiveness, not of indolence and inefficiency; the product of the world's most advanced industrial nation and not of its most backward one. The situation was one peculiar to the modern world of invention and technology. America's poverty was the poverty of abundance. . . . The economy was cluttered and stalled by its own unmanageable surplus.[26]

Nobody could figure out what to do. Many people in 1929 thought of the economic downturn as just another recession. Let it run its course, said the experienced business hands. About all they could figure out was that America had produced more than anyone wanted. At the time there appeared to be no ready solution to overproduction and under consumption. But Hoover, a great proponent of laissez-faire conservative business principles, never considered having the government intervene. Instead, he first called for the people to take voluntary actions to solve the dilemma. Who was responsible? As it turned out, capitalism itself went on trial; in fact, it resulted in the public harshly judging the leaders—both business and political.

When the economy began to go sour, Hoover stuck to his philosophy. As he had during his campaign, he maintained that the trusted values of rugged individualism would be the key to a recovery. But no matter how often he repeated the same message, it fell on deaf ears, and the economy continued to spiral downward.

Finally, what was called the Great Bull Market of the 1920s came to a thunderous halt. The Great Crash was triggered on Thursday, October 24, 1929, when prices began to plunge, and by Black Tuesday, October 29, $30 billion in securities literally disappeared. The market collapsed. It was the prelude to what soon became known as the Great Depression.

Despite Hoover's public call for voluntary stimulation of the economy with business activity, nothing concrete came of it. Few argued with the president's goals of getting business to right itself by conventional means—that is, through voluntary actions by business. But Hoover's blind spot turned out to be his lack of vision and failure to use the full power and force of the federal government to stop the economic downslide that led to the Great Depression.

Hoover's own distaste for any relief program for the poor only exacerbated the disaster. He rejected calls for more aggressive government actions, such as relief bills or bond sales to fund unemployment benefits, and opposed any handout or dole because, as he stated, the voluntary efforts of the American people were sufficient to solve the crisis. Meanwhile, as he spoke these words, millions of little shanty shacks built out of cartons and tarpaper—dubbed "Hoovervilles" by those who were disgusted with the administration's efforts—were cropping up all across America. The depression also hit Hollywood hard. Some big-name and independent studios located in a shabby area in Hollywood were factiously dubbed "Poverty Row" (including the famous Sunset Boulevard). Inexpensive, independent movies were made there with low budgets, stock footage, and second-rate, over-the-hill actors.

No matter, Hoover seemed more concerned with the historic deficit of nearly $1 billion. He addressed the nation and told Americans that nothing would contribute more to the return of prosperity than to maintain the federal government's sound fiscal position. He further aggravated the situation by calling for substantial tax cuts along with cuts in federal spending—or exactly the opposite of what was needed.

By the end of his term, Hoover had failed to achieve his goal of eradicating poverty because of his own weaknesses and of the federal government's failure to respond to any number of pleas to revive the economy. Perhaps the most telling way to sum up Hoover's tenure as president is simply with these stark statistics: When Herbert Hoover took office, the U.S. unemployment rate was 4.4 percent. When he left office, it was 23.6 percent.[27]

7

THE GREAT DEPRESSION
AND SOCIAL REFORM (1932–1961):
FRANKLIN D. ROOSEVELT, TRUMAN, EISENHOWER

I see one-third of a nation ill-housed, ill-clad, and ill-nourished.
—Franklin D. Roosevelt,
second inaugural address, January 20, 1937

For **FRANKLIN DELANO ROOSEVELT** (1933–1945), a fifty-one-year-old Democrat from New York, the Great Depression that he inherited gave him an opportunity to apply his various talents—many of which he himself probably did not know that he possessed—in time to save a nation. Above all, it was his courage and optimism that carried the day.

The magnetic and smiling Roosevelt, with his jaw jutting out confidently, his cigarette in a long holder and his rimless spectacles reflecting the sun, ushered in a new era that lifted a nation's spirits out of the doldrums. Even before he was elected the thirty-second president on November 8, 1932, he gave his first major radio address on April 7, 1932. In his emotionally moving speeches, he caught the full attention of all Americans. In his now-famous "The Forgotten Man" reference, he drew an analogy between the economic plights at home that year and the beginning of World War I in 1917. He stated, in part:

> Fifteen years ago my public duty called me to an active part in a great national emergency, the World War. Success then was due to a leadership whose vision carried beyond the timorous and futile gesture of sending a tiny army of 150,000 trained soldiers and the regular navy to the aid of our allies. The generalship of that moment conceived of a whole Nation mobilized for war, economic, industrial, social and military resources gathered into a vast unit capable of and actually

in the process of throwing into the scales ten million men equipped with physical needs and sustained by the realization that behind them were the united efforts of 110,000,000 human beings. It was a great plan because it was built from bottom to top and not from top to bottom.

In my calm judgment, the Nation faces today a more grave emergency than in 1917.

. . . These unhappy times call for the building of plans that rest upon the forgotten, the unorganized but the indispensable units of economic power, for plans like those of 1917 that build from the bottom up and not from the top down, that put their faith once more in the *forgotten man* [italics added] at the bottom of the economic pyramid.[1]

FDR's second major speech prior to being elected took place when he was nominated on July 2, 1932, at the Democratic National Convention in Chicago. There he preannounced the theme of his campaign—the New Deal—when he stated, unequivocally:

Throughout the Nation, men and women, forgotten in political philosophy of the Government of the last years look to us here for guidance and for more equitable opportunity to share in the distribution of national wealth.

On the farms, in the large metropolitan areas, in the smaller cities and in the villages, millions of our citizens cherish the hope that their old standards of living and of thought have not gone forever. Those millions cannot and shall not hope in vain.

I pledge you, I pledge myself, to a *new deal* [italics added] for the American people. Let us all here assembled constitute ourselves prophets of a new order of competence and of courage. This is more than a political campaign; it is a call to arms. Give me your help, not to win votes alone, but to win in this crusade to restore America to its own people.[2]

Elected on November 8, 1932, FDR was sworn in on March 4, 1933. The Great Depression had reached its lowest point, and the economy was rapidly heading toward rock bottom.

The gregarious, energetic governor of New York—who had held positions in previous administrations and had unsuccessfully run for vice president in 1920—was elected with 57 percent of the popular vote and 89 percent of the electoral vote.[3] He was a fifth cousin of Theodore Roosevelt's, and the two men shared extraordinary traits: optimism, dynamism, charisma, unbridled energy, and the emotional strength to carry out their promises. However, Franklin was seen as possessing more sophistication, with an ability to use his own forceful personality and charm to make men of differing opinions see his way of thinking.

His persuasive manner was undoubtedly the best attribute he had, in addition to his being an inspiring orator and projecting the image of a strong leader who was determined to lift his nation out of desperate times. He rarely used a frontal approach when he wanted to get something done; instead, he would float ideas among those he most trusted and then seize upon an idea or plan that had already been made public. Consequently, some saw Roosevelt as disingenuous in his approach to politics; others saw him as a brilliant political strategist who knew precisely how to rally political and public support behind his programs.

He gave another memorable speech when he took office. From the outset, Roosevelt "told it like it was." He stated bluntly in his inaugural address on March 4, 1933:

> This great Nation will endure as it has endured, will revive and will prosper. So, first of all, let me assert my firm belief that *the only thing we have to fear is fear itself* [italics added]—nameless, unreasoning, unjustified terror which paralyzes needed efforts to convert retreat into advance. In every dark hour of our national life a leadership of frankness and vigor has met with that understanding and support of the people themselves which is essential to victory. I am convinced that you will again give that support to leadership in these critical days.

Roosevelt put his finger on his main goal ahead, when he continued: "Our primary task is to put people to work. This is no unsolvable problem if we face it wisely and courageously. It can be accomplished in part by direct recruiting by the Government itself, treating the task as we would treat the emergency of a war, but at the same time, through this employment accomplishing greatly needed projects to stimulate and reorganize the use of our natural resources."[4]

However, in case Congress failed to take action, FDR said he would seek broad executive power to wage a war against the emergency, as great as the power that Congress would give him if, indeed, the United States was invaded by a foreign country. That promise, itself, caused many members of Congress to sit up straight and brace for what was to come.

This address, according to historians Allan Nevins and Henry Steele Commager, was a milestone in American history. They noted,

It served formal notice on the nation that there was to be a New Deal. For over a decade now, politicians had played with marked cards, and business had gathered in almost all of the chips. Roosevelt proposed to restore the rules of the democratic game. To many contemporaries the New Deal seemed like a revolution. It aimed to protect against violence from the left or from the right, the essentials of American democracy—to conserve natural and human resources, to preserve the balance of interests under the Constitution, security, and liberty.[5]

The country was at its lowest ebb—on the verge of total economic collapse—when Roosevelt took command. Small business suffered miserably while, ironically, big corporations continued to have satisfactory bottom lines. The latter still had many layoffs so they could maintain their profits—a scenario that unfortunately would occur again early in the twenty-first century when the Great Recession almost brought the nation to its knees at the intersection of the administrations of George W. Bush and Barack Obama in 2008–2009.

At the height of the Great Depression in Roosevelt's era, starting in New York and happening in virtually every major city across the country, so many people were unemployed that bread lines and soup kitchens opened for the poor, many of whom had been solid middle-class, white-collar workers as well as executives before the crash. Their clothes ragged and their faces unshaven, men sold apples and other goods on street corners. America overnight, it seemed, turned into huge masses of poor huddled over barrels with fires lit at night and became wanderers during the day with nothing to live for. It seemed like a bad dream, a nightmare of unfathomable proportions that had brought the greatest and most powerful nation in the world to the edge of economic collapse. Everywhere people were desperate, afraid, even driven to stealing morsels of food from stores and cart vendors. Some were driven to suicide. Hope was all but gone for the average American family.

FDR wasted no time. On his first night as president, he gave Treasury Secretary William Woodin five days to draft a banking bill. And Roosevelt assumed his role as though he were a commander in chief in wartime. On the following day, March 5, he issued two presidential directives—one calling for a special session of Congress and another for halting transaction in gold and announcing a national bank holiday to soften the run on the banks.

And so Roosevelt's multipronged actions in his historic "First Hundred Days" got under way with a flourish and well-publicized actions. No one doubted that he had seized the helm of a big ship and was changing directions in a stormy sea. During the first two weeks, in fact, his orders came so swiftly and urgently that they prompted many in the news media and notable business leaders to speak out in his favor.

Roosevelt took office with the eyes of the world upon him. Nobody was quite certain what kind of a president he would be. As the distinguished historian James Macgregor Burns expressed it:

> All in all it was hardly surprising that observers in 1933 differed so much on Roosevelt's capacities. To some he seemed, quite rightly, lacking in persistence, conviction, and intellectual depth and maturity. Others had seen a different side of the man. To them he had a grasp on Jefferson's deeply humane ends and on Hamilton's creative means; he had Bryan's moral fervor without the Great Commoner's mental flabbiness; he had Wilson's idealism without his inflexibility; he had some of Bob La Follett's and Al Smith's hardheadedness without their hardness and bitterness; and he had much of T.R.'s vigor and verve.[6]

No matter how he was viewed, there was a near-unanimous respect for him because of a giant hurdle he had overcome in life. Tragedy had befallen FDR in 1921 when he contracted polio, an incurable disease that paralyzed his legs. However, with the support of his courageous wife, Eleanor, and his family, FDR regained some use of his legs. This so-called handicap turned out to be almost an asset for the single-minded FDR, who spent a great deal of time and his own money recuperating in a spa in Warm Springs, Georgia. History books record that he rarely, if ever, complained about his condition. Indeed, he asked the Secret Service to help him literally hide it from the public, even though he was forced to carry ten pounds of steel braces on his legs when he walked with the help of aides on either side of him. The White House asked—and the press granted—his request not to be photographed in a wheel chair either in Washington, D.C., or when he went on trips. Obviously, the press was much more compliant in those days.

Historian Doris Kearns Goodwin has said that FDR changed after his initial bout with polio. "He had always taken great pleasure in people, but now they became what one historian has called 'his vital links to life.' Far more intensely than before, he reached out to know them, to understand them, to pick up their emotions, to put himself into their shoes. No longer belonging to his old world in the same way, he came to empathize with the poor and the underprivileged, with people to whom fate had dealt a difficult hand," she wrote in an essay.[7]

His physical handicap certainly did not slow the pace at which he began his work. The time line record of FDR's dazzling New Deal accomplishments and other actions during his presidency, starting in 1933, was historic.[8] In the words of noted historian William E. Leuchtenburg in his *Franklin D. Roosevelt and the New Deal, 1932–1940*, it was "the most extraordinary series of reforms in the nation's history."[9] Moreover, he introduced some of his ideas in talks directly to the people. As historian Burns correctly pointed out, Roosevelt had a special relationship with the people of America through his informal, almost casual radio talks with them: "Roosevelt's most important link with the people was the 'fireside chat.' . . . Roosevelt threw himself into the role of father talking with his great family. He made a conscious effort to visualize the people he was talking to."[10] Leuchtenburg agreed: "He was the first great American voice."[11]

In carrying out his historic New Deal, Roosevelt included dozens of legislative firsts that covered a broad multitude of fields: banking, the economy, the national budget, conservation, the gold standard, federal emergency relief, agriculture, Tennessee Valley Authority, federal securities, homeowners' refinancing, Federal Deposit Insurance, National Recovery Act, civil works, social reform, Works Progress Administration, emergency relief, rural electrification, National Labor Relations Board, Social Security, revenue, Supreme Court reforms, minimum wage, presidential powers, and judicial reform. Finally, he also introduced fiscal and legislative measures to improve the unemployment rate that held back the entire economy. (For more information, see appendix A.)

From an estimated unemployment annual rate of 3.3 percent during 1923–1929, unemployment rose to a peak of 24.9 percent in 1933. After that, economic recovery was extremely slow and unstable. It even sagged considerably in 1937, and people began to call it "Roosevelt's Depression," as a result of a business tax he had levied in a premature attempt to balance the budget. Shortly afterward, FDR—always responding to the circumstances in practical ways—changed course once again and resumed heavy government spending to bolster the economy. Unemployment gradually receded to 14.6 percent in 1940; and soon after the United States entered World War II in 1941, it dropped precipitously to 4.7 percent, according to Census Bureau figures.

The sharp drop in unemployment helped Roosevelt politically. Even though he was in ill health—few Americans were aware of it—FDR won a fourth term in 1944. He went up against New York governor Thomas E. Dewey, garnering 53.4 percent of the vote against Dewey's 45.9 percent. The electoral votes were 432 to 99.[12]

Roosevelt, of course, would continue to reach across the aisle—and the oceans—to come to the aid of Great Britain and other European Allies after Hitler attacked them in World War II. While America was coming out of the long Depression, it was also making preparations for war. As millions of men began serving in Europe and the Far East, the shortage of men at home meant that women filled jobs in factories, stores, and almost anywhere they were needed. It was the wartime economy, most historians agree, that righted the ship of state and enabled America to come out of the long Depression.

Roosevelt turned his full attention to prosecuting the war in Europe and against the Japanese. Little or no talk focused any longer on the economy. Under the enormous strain of having directed and cajoled the United States through the Great Depression and World War II, Roosevelt died suddenly of a cerebral hemorrhage at his home in Warm Springs, Georgia, on April 12, 1945.

Postscript: Like all previous presidents, FDR faced many critics— more perhaps than any other president in history—because of his length of time in office and because some of his controversial New Deal policies shook up the establishment in America's private and public sectors. Some called the FDR period the Second American Revolution. Aside from the Republican opposition, which was to be expected, he was constantly attacked by many leading figures, including two men, in particular, whom he considered bothersome and as distractions from more serious matters.

One was Father Charles Coughlin, a populist Catholic priest and a vocal Roosevelt critic who delivered bitter commentaries. Coughlin began broadcasting a variety of insults aimed at FDR and the New Deal in his weekly radio show in 1930. Coughlin attracted forty million followers—no small achievement in an era when FDR practically monopolized the news—who agreed with his anti–New Deal and anti-Semitic views. Coughlin blamed the Wall Street moneymen for the Depression. His views were so controversial that he campaigned for the nationalization of the entire American banking system.

He is remembered, among other quotes, for this particular view of FDR: "Roosevelt has a poor brand of Russian communism. . . . I think it is significant the leaders among the Communists of the world never once attacked international bankers. Roosevelt will not touch that subject."[13] Coughlin continued to write pamphlets blaming Jews for communism until his death in Bloomfield Hills, Michigan, on October 27, 1979, at the age of eighty-eight.

Yet another, even more formidable critic, Democratic senator Huey
P. Long of Louisiana, was a second major distraction during the New
Deal years. He took an opposite view from Father Coughlin and did not
believe the New Deal was doing enough for the poor. He said that income inequality was the root cause of the Depression. In a radio speech
to the nation delivered on February 23, 1934, in which he coined he
own slogan, "Every Man is King," he stated:

> Now, we have organized a society, and we call it 'Share Our Wealth
> Society,' a society with the motto *Every Man a King* . . . [italics
> added] so there would be no such thing as a man or woman who did
> not have the necessities of life, who would not be dependent upon
> the whims and caprices . . . of the financial martyrs for a living. What
> do we propose by this society? We propose to limit the wealth of big
> men in the country.[14]

His "distribution of wealth" concept may have seemed new at the
time, but it was a warmed-over belief inherited from Socialists in the
United States. The idea has lingered for generations. It would once
again become a political issue in Barack Obama's presidential campaign
in 2008. Obama was confronted by a plumber at a political rally when
the Democratic presidential candidate stated his intention to raise taxes
on those people who earned more than $250,000 a year. Obama was
roundly criticized at that time and thereafter for bringing up a similar redistribution of wealth concept, urging legislation that would tax
wealthy individuals.

Long, meanwhile, was successful at generating hateful feelings toward Roosevelt; however, he himself became the object of a rumored
assassination plot. On September 8, 1935, Long was in the state capitol
in Baton Rouge for a special session of the Louisiana legislature, push-
ing through a number of bills. He was shot at the capitol and died two
days later on September 10, 1935, eleven days after his forty-second
birthday.

FDR has arguably been the subject of more historical records than
any other president. An astounding number of books, magazine stories,
films, documentaries, and commemorative exhibits of documents have
been written on Franklin Delano Roosevelt, as well as hundreds of profiles. Goodwin, perhaps, said it best about her hero when she wrote: "No
factor was more important to Roosevelt's leadership than his confidence
in himself and the American people."[15] That phrase most aptly sums up
why he was able to lead a great nation out of its dark, poverty-stricken

times and into a brand-new world, much of it his own creation, where America would stand proudly once again as a beacon of democracy. Above all, Roosevelt had a tremendous impact on Americans of all colors, rich and poor, and changed what the general public perceived about what was really possible for the government to accomplish. He raised expectations—and then met or surpassed them.

FDR's successor, Vice President **HARRY S. TRUMAN** (1945–1953), the former Democratic senator from Kansas City, Missouri, was sworn in at 7:09 p.m. on April 12, 1945, the day FDR died. The seemingly mild-mannered Truman, at sixty years old, was perceived in many parts of the country as a simple, small-town country boy. He had been put on the ticket with FDR to balance Roosevelt's tilt toward the so-called Eastern Establishment. Truman was a poker- and piano-playing, hail-fellow-well-met, blunt politician. He had a reputation for being a totally loyal Democrat and a product of the Missouri Democratic machine. He related well to the public; the people saw him as a hardworking honest man.

Truman took office as World War II was coming to an end, and he directed its final stages. He made the historic decision to end the war by dropping atomic bombs on Hiroshima and Nagasaki. After Japan surrendered in August 1945, he led a nation that was now coping with the awful challenges of economic depression or world war for the first time in nearly two decades. Truman's main agenda was twofold—to articulate his own vision for the country and to create a plan for converting the domestic wartime economy to a peacetime normalcy.

Four short days after Truman had been sworn in, the thirty-third president made his first speech to a joint session of Congress on April 16, 1945, paying tribute to FDR and urging the nation to remain focused. He dedicated himself to the fight for freedom and the eventual unconditional surrender of Germany and Japan. He went on to state:

> Today, the entire world is looking to America for enlightened leadership to peace and progress. Such a leadership requires vision, courage and tolerance. It can be provided only by a united nation deeply devoted to the highest ideals.
>
> . . . You, the Members of the Congress, surely know how I feel. Only with your help can I hope to complete one of the greatest tasks ever assigned to a public servant. With Divine guidance, and your

help, we will find the new passage to a far better world, a kindly and
friendly world, with just and lasting peace.[16]

Domestically, Truman was determined to keep America on the
same progressive path as the New Deal and labeled his program the
Fair Deal. He supported such liberal initiatives as housing for the poor
and federal assistance for education. He vetoed Republican tax bills
that favored the rich and rejected a Republican effort to raise tariffs on
imported wool, a measure he deemed isolationist. Along with his veto
of the Taft-Hartley Act (a federal law that was enacted in 1947 that
prohibited certain union practices and required improvement in union
disclosures of financial and political dealings) and his sympathy toward
price controls, Truman kept the Republicans from chipping away the
New Deal programs.

Truman also took an unexpectedly bold stand on civil rights. His
1945 proposal to extend the Fair Employment Practices Commission,
which FDR created on June 25, 1941, requiring that companies with
government contracts not discriminate on the basis of race or religion,
did not succeed. It was intended to help blacks and other minorities
obtain jobs in the home front industries after the war and, some pundits
speculated, to woo black voters to the Democratic Party.

By executive order Truman had created the Committee on Civil
Rights. On January 15, 1947, he addressed its fifteen members. He recalled in his memoir *Years of Trial and Hope* that he exclaimed: "'I want
our Bill of Rights implemented in fact. We have been trying to do this
for 150 years. We are making real progress, but we are not progressing
fast enough. This country could very easily be faced with a situation
similar to the one with which it was faced in 1922.' I was referring, of
course, to the revival of terrorism in that year by the Ku Klux Klan."[17]

That summer, Truman displayed his support for blacks when he
became the first president to address the National Association for the
Advancement of Colored People on June 29 at the closing session of its
Thirty-eighth Annual Conference at the Lincoln Memorial. He stated:
"The only limit to an American's achievement should be his ability, his
industry, and his character."[18]

A few months later, his Civil Rights Commission published a report
titled "To Secure These Rights," calling for the elimination of segregation. In 1948, Truman endorsed its findings and called for an end to
racial discrimination in federal hiring practices. Truman was no liberal,

but when it came to civil rights during his presidency, he was strident. "From the early days of my administration," he wrote in his memoir, "I insisted on a workable fair employment practices program and on the enforcement of civil rights as guaranteed by the Constitution."[19] He also issued an executive order to end segregation in the military, an initiative that would be carried out by his immediate successor, President Dwight D. Eisenhower. Although these moves cost Truman the support of many southern whites, the increased support of black voters made up for the political loss.

As he pursued this strategy with increasing skill, Truman stood poised to win Democratic votes. In his 1948 State of the Union address, on January 7, 1948, Truman again called for civil rights legislation, national health insurance, a housing program, and a higher minimum wage—all aimed to reduce poverty.

Significantly, in 1948 Truman also introduced a national health care program—which would have been the first time in American history all Americans would be covered—but it was defeated after a barrage of attacks by the American Medical Association. However, in 1950, a new public assistance program for the permanently and temporarily disabled was attached to the Social Security Act.

After a rip-roaring Democratic National Convention, Truman won the hard-fought nomination of a divided party. Southerners had cast their lot in favor of the segregationist "Dixiecrat," South Carolina senator J. Strom Thurmond, a formidable politician who represented a real problem to Truman. Truman himself recalled an incident at the 1948 Democratic National Convention when a reporter asked Thurmond to clarify his position. The reporter pointed out to Thurmond, "President Truman is only following the platform that Roosevelt advocated [in 1932]."

"I agree," Thurmond replied, "but Truman really means it!"[20]

In the 1948 campaign, Truman ran against what he termed the Republican "do-nothing Congress," even calling it into a special session to enact legislation. He also embraced more fully the cause of black civil rights and issued executive orders desegregating the military and outlawing discrimination in the civil service. His supporters swept the country with the slogan, "Give 'em Hell, Harry!" Truman won a stunning upset victory over his Republican opponent, the same Governor Thomas E. Dewey of New York whom FDR had defeated in 1944.

Inspired by his history-making victory, Truman announced his agenda in early 1949 and outlined his Fair Deal. It covered policies and programs that liberals in the Democratic Party wanted to pursue. It contained economic controls, a housing bill, and national health insurance; sought a repeal of Taft-Hartley, an increase in the minimum wage, and an expansion of the Social Security program; funded development projects modeled on the New Deal's Tennessee Valley Authority; liberalized immigration laws; and broached ambitious civil rights legislation for African Americans. All of these proposals were geared to make a major dent in poverty across the nation.

Unfortunately, a bloc of stubborn Republicans and conservative Democrats stopped the Fair Deal in its tracks. On the positive side, Congress did pass a moderately effective public housing and slum-clearance bill that Truman wanted in 1949. It also increased the minimum wage that same year and significantly expanded Social Security in 1950. However, he could not get everything he wanted from Congress. There was no doubt in the public's mind that Truman had miscalculated the meaning of his victory; indeed, the voters had not given him a mandate to do whatever he wanted. Similarly, the public—after twelve years of Roosevelt—had had enough of the so-called social welfare state. Whatever momentum the New Deal and the Fair Deal had, it evaporated after the summer of 1950, when everyone's attention turned to the Korean War. At the same time, his plans to expand the economy and to create more jobs as a way of lifting people out of poverty lagged badly because of an economic slowdown in 1949, which resulted in widespread fears that the postwar economic boom had exhausted itself.

As the Korean War began to look like a stalemate, the public became warier of spending taxpayers' money on a war that had no end in sight. The war, which began in June 1950, also affected the American economy, which Truman and his advisers believed had to stabilize in order to support the country's involvement in the Korean conflict. With the World War II experience still fresh and the uncertainty about whether the Korean War was going to develop into a larger conflict, the administration hoped that its intervention would keep unemployment, inflation, and prices under control, stabilize wages, and boost military-related industrial production.

In December 1950, Congress passed the Defense Production Act, and Truman issued an executive order creating the Office of Defense Mobilization. The effort proceeded with few hitches: unemployment stayed low; inflation remained in check, albeit for a sharp, one-time surge in the last half of 1950; the hoarding of consumer goods subsided quickly; and military production increased. Still, Americans disliked the government's economic policies, especially those concerning controls on credit. While mobilizing for the war, at the end of 1951, the U.S. steel industry faced a possible shutdown when labor and management could not agree on a new contract. Hoping to avoid a strike and yet stay on good terms with labor, the government tried to mediate the dispute during the first several months of 1952 but failed to make headway.

In April 1952, needing to maintain production, Truman used his presidential authority and seized the steel industry. The steel companies went to court to overturn Truman's action, and in June, the Supreme Court declared the seizure unconstitutional. Private management took back control but was faced with a fifty-three-day strike. Truman had suffered a major political setback.

It was known among the political pundits at the time that Truman did not intend to run for reelection in 1952. Most scholars agree that various troubles influenced his decision, including the Korean War, battles over economic mobilization, the near-hysterical anti-Communist hearings of Senator Joseph R. McCarthy of Wisconsin and the rise of McCarthyism, and the allegations of corruption in his administration.

On March 29, 1952, Truman publicly announced that he would not be a candidate for president, pointing out that he had already served his country long and hard. By the time he left the White House in January 1953, his approval rating had dropped to 31 percent; it had peaked at 87 percent in July 1945.

Looking for a successor, Truman turned to Illinois Governor Adlai E. Stevenson, who expressed interest in running but refused to make a commitment. Stevenson was reportedly a reluctant candidate and he lived up to the description.

Stevenson won the Democratic nomination at the party's convention in July but had to face World War II hero Gen. Dwight D. Eisenhower in the general election. Because Truman campaigned hard for Stevenson, furiously attacking the Republicans and Eisenhower, his relationship with Eisenhower turned bitter.

Eisenhower triumphed in 1952, winning in a landslide and ending twenty consecutive years of Democratic control of the White House. The electoral vote was Eisenhower, 442, Stevenson, 89. Eisenhower won with 55.2 percent of the votes to Stevenson's 44.3 percent.

Postscript: With each passing decade, Harry Truman has continued to grow in stature. While running for the presidency since the Jimmy

Carter years (1976–1980), Democratic and Republican candidates alike have invoked Truman's name when they wished to show, as Truman did, how resilient and tough they were.

DWIGHT DAVID (IKE) EISENHOWER (1953–1961), a Republican of Kansas, was sixty-two years old and the legendary Allied commander of D-Day—a highly respected general beyond reproach—when both parties initially wooed him for the presidential nomination. He accepted the Republican nomination. In his inaugural address on January 20, 1953, the thirty-fourth president took the opportunity to raise several philosophical questions, which, he implied, only the American people themselves could answer. For example, he asked rhetorically, at the outset of his remarks: "How far have we come in man's long pilgrimage from darkness toward the light? Are we nearing the light—a day of freedom and of peace for all mankind? Or are the shadows of another night closing in upon us?"[21]

In terms of civil rights and progress in eradicating poverty, Eisenhower was known as being somewhat passive when it came to addressing the causes of freedom, equality, and eliminating poverty for minorities. In point of fact, the Bureau of the Census only started tracking poverty figures in 1959, but by the time Ike left office in 1961, the poverty rate was at a record high of 21.9 percent. The president faced one huge unresolved race relations issue after World War II—that is, whether African Americans would continue to live in a segregated society.

The 1950s proved to be a paradox. While more Americans were living well, and inflation was kept to a minimum, many black and other citizens of color did not participate in the prosperity that seemed to abound. The poverty rate ballooned during Eisenhower's presidency, and some forty million Americans were poor when Eisenhower left office. Most of the poor were living in the South, although poverty also had increased in the North after African Americans left the South and migrated to big northern cities like Detroit, Chicago, New York, and Cleveland.

Nonetheless, Eisenhower was known to be cautious in his support of civil rights action. Historians tell us that Ike did not believe that legislation and court decisions, in the long run, would change people's minds about how they felt about race. It was a deeply imbedded, centuries-old emotional scar that had become a part of the culture of society since slavery. Moreover, according to Eisenhower's official historian,

Stephen E. Ambrose, "the civil rights movement presented problems he did not understand, nor wish to study, much less to solve. He wanted to put those problems off, leave them to his successor. This was his great weakness as a political leader. His unwillingness to grapple with long-term problems and his inability to see clearly how moral questions were to cost the nation, his party, and his reputation beyond measure."[22]

Ambrose noted that even though Eisenhower had said during his campaign for the presidency that race was not a front-burner issue for him, when he actually occupied the Oval Office, he quickly came to realize that he was president of all the people—including Negro Americans. Accordingly, he announced in his first State of the Union message on February 2, 1953, that he would use the full powers of his office to end segregation in the District of Columbia, the nation's capital. In his message to Congress, he said, in part:

> A cardinal ideal in this heritage we cherish is the equality of rights of all citizens of every race and color and creed. We know that discrimination against minorities persists despite our allegiance to this ideal. Such discrimination—confined to no one section of the Nation—is but the outward testimony to the persistence of distrust and of fear in the hearts of men.
>
> This fact makes all the more vital the fighting of these wrongs by each individual, in every station of life, in his every deed.
>
> Much of the answer lies in the power of fact, fully publicized; of persuasion, honestly pressed; and of conscience, justly aroused. These are methods familiar to our way of life, tested and proven wise.
>
> I propose to use whatever authority exists in the office of the President to end segregation in the District of Columbia, including the Federal Government, and any segregation in the Armed Forces.[23]

Undoubtedly the most significant event in terms of race relations that occurred in the Eisenhower years was the historic *Brown v. Board of Education* decision on May 17, 1954. Led by Chief Justice Earl Warren, whom Eisenhower had appointed in 1953, the Supreme Court unanimously ruled that segregation in the nation's schools was unconstitutional because it violated the Fourteenth Amendment. The court ordered that the schools, which had been operating under the "separate but equal clause" of an 1896 Supreme Court decision in *Plessey v. Ferguson,* be integrated "with all deliberate speed."[24]

Eisenhower's appointment of Warren had come from his own public statement that he was looking for a highly competent lawyer of broad experience, who possessed integrity and an unblemished record. Former

California governor Earl Warren fit the bill. In 1948 he had been the Republican Party's nominee for vice president of the United States on a ticket headed by the popular Thomas E. Dewey, governor of New York. Warren's appointment to the bench was seen as Eisenhower's indirect contribution to racial progress, even though Eisenhower himself, ironically, did not agree with the Brown decision and said so publicly. He believed the only way change could occur was through persuading "the hearts and minds of the American people."[25] In general, most historians agree that Eisenhower's greatest failure as president was his handling of civil rights. Eisenhower did not like dealing with racial issues, but he could not avoid such matters after the Supreme Court ruling in 1954.

Despite his confidence in Warren, Eisenhower privately expressed dismay after the *Brown v. Board of Education* decision, and he was concerned that the southerners might virtually cancel out their public education system and replace it with an all-white private school system. The president expressed the fear that if such a plan were adopted, it would not only handicap Negro children but also would work to the detriment of the poor whites in the South.

Eisenhower failed, however, to try to resolve the generations-old issue. He vacillated, answering questions with "on the one hand, and on the other hand" responses. Ambrose was critical of Eisenhower: "What he had not done was provide leadership, either moral or political. What he wanted—for the problem to go away—he could not have. . . . He was trapped by his own prejudices, a prisoner of his own limited view."[26] William B. Ewald, Jr., who served as a speechwriter to Eisenhower and later assisted the president in preparing his memoirs, offered yet another perspective of Eisenhower's reluctance. Ewald wrote in his book *Eisenhower the President: Crucial Days, 1950–1960,* that "Eisenhower's refusal to affirm the Brown decision stemmed not from his unconcern for civil rights . . . but, ironically, from a quality both the President and Chief Justice Warren shared in abundance—a rigid awareness of a rule imposed by the Constitution."[27]

Another Eisenhower speechwriter, Arthur Larson, was more cutting in his observations about his former boss in his book *Eisenhower: The President Nobody Knew.* He wrote that Eisenhower had told him specifically, "I personally believe the decision [in *Brown v. Board of Education*] was wrong" and that the court should have called for "equal opportunity" instead of ordering desegregation.[28]

During his reelection in 1956, Eisenhower announced a major undertaking that would add many jobs to the economy, namely, the

Interstate Highway System. On June 29, he authorized what became known as one of the greatest public works programs in history.

After his November election victory over Adlai Stevenson, he came face-to-face with yet another uncomfortable racial crisis the following year. On September 3, 1957, Governor Orville Faubus of Arkansas used the National Guard to prevent nine black students from attending Little Rock Central High. Ensuring that the school was, in fact, desegregated, Eisenhower sent in a thousand paratroopers from the 101st Airborne Division to enforce the law. Troops stayed for the entire school year, and in the spring of 1958, Central High had its first African American graduate. But that was not the end of this story. Sadly, in September 1958, Faubus closed public schools to prevent their integration and the president failed to take any action, despite his earlier stand. When Eisenhower completed his second term, only 6 percent of Negro students attended integrated schools. So, in a very real sense, the entire Faubus affair actually backfired on the White House.

Other incidents had arisen that linked poverty and civil rights in the news. Civil rights activist Rosa Parks, for example, who by refusing to give up her seat on a bus on December 1, 1955, in Montgomery, Alabama, touched off the Montgomery Bus Boycott of 1955–1956. It sparked a mass protest movement. Under the leadership of the Reverend Dr. Martin Luther King Jr., blacks in Montgomery organized a boycott of the entire bus system until it was desegregated. Dr. King, by virtue of his public statements and his nonviolent resistance movement, brought about enormous change but slowly and painfully.

The severe recession of 1958–1959 made matters worse: unemployment for black Americans exceeded 12 percent, the number of people out of work in America doubled, and the government deficit was practically out of control. Economic woes dogged Eisenhower's administration. In fact, a full recovery of the economy did not occur until 1962.

Eisenhower's second term was a mixed bag. He succeeded in moving Congress to pass the Civil Rights Act in 1957, which established a Civil Rights Commission to investigate abuses of people's right to vote and was the first civil rights legislation since the Grant administration. As the law was not strictly enforced, it soon became clear that new and stronger legislation would be needed.

During this time, the government deficit skyrocketed from less than $3 billion in 1957–1958 to more than $12.5 billion in 1958–1959. It is on record as the largest peacetime deficit in history up to that time.[29] A full recovery of the economy did not occur until 1962. [30]

In the latter part of Eisenhower's second term and leading into the 1960s, welfare reform became the politically correct position to support. As the White House began to focus on tighter eligibility rules, the federal government loosened its central authority over welfare and handed the states much of the responsibility for the program. A nationwide effort began to reduce the number of people on welfare, a policy that went hand-in-hand with Eisenhower's own personal belief that individuals should take personal responsibility for themselves rather than continuing to look to the government for sustenance. The Republican Party would adopt this political philosophy and continue to uphold it through the present.

Postscript: During Eisenhower's middle-of-the-road approach to civil rights and poverty over an eight-year period, a number of spectacular events focusing on race relations and poverty occurred, but the actual results did not come to partial fruition until many decades later. That gap is why the goal of freeing America from poverty remains elusive from one president to the next. Meanwhile, in his farewell address to the nation on January 17, 1961, Eisenhower warned America of the dangers of the "military-industrial complex" as representing a threat of misplaced power. It was a message that only a highly respected former five-star general could articulate, and it continues to reverberate through Washington's corridors of power.

8

THE WAR ON POVERTY AND
ITS AFTERMATH (1961–1981):

KENNEDY, LYNDON B. JOHNSON, NIXON, FORD, CARTER

> If a free society cannot help the many who are poor, it cannot save the
> few who are rich.
>
> —John F. Kennedy, inaugural address, January 20, 1961

A brief hint of the political passion that **JOHN F. "JACK" KENNEDY (JFK)** had
for improving the quality of life for all Americans appears in his speech
formally announcing his candidacy for president. He chose an audience of three hundred supporters in the Senate Caucus Room on Sat-
urday, January 2, 1960. He purposely picked a weekend following the
New Year's holiday—usually a slow news period—because he knew he
would receive major press coverage. In his brief announcement, he said
he wanted to ensure "more vital life for our people."[1]

At mid-year, in accepting the nomination as the Democratic candidate for president on July 15, 1960, at the convention in Los Angeles, Kennedy first broached the topic of helping the poor. He also put
forward publicly the concept of his "New Frontier" and made his first
official claim to try to rid America of poverty. As he told his Democratic
convention audience, his plan would follow Franklin Roosevelt's New
Deal but with one critical difference:

> Franklin Roosevelt's New Deal promised security and succor to those
> in need. But the New Frontier of which I speak is not a set of prom-
> ises; it is a set of challenges. It sums up not what I intend to offer the
> American people, but what I intend to ask of them. It appeals to their
> pride, not to their pocketbook—it holds out the promise of more
> sacrifice instead of more security.

> . . . The New Frontier is here, whether we seek it or not. Beyond
> that frontier are the uncharted areas of science and space, [and] *un-*
> *solved problems of . . . poverty* [italics added]. . . .[2]

Indeed, as a congressman and a senator, young Jack Kennedy re-
fined his repertoire of political domestic interests. He waged a long,
hard primary battle against some heavyweight contenders: Senate majority leader Lyndon B. Johnson from Texas, former governor Adlai Stevenson of Illinois, and Senator Hubert Humphrey from Minnesota—by
the time he was nominated for president on the Democratic ticket, he
had surrounded himself with a cadre of tightly knit New Frontiersmen
with brains, imagination, and vision.

In the ensuing thousand days after he was sworn in as the thirty-fifth
president (1961–1963), events unfolded and presented him with the opportunity to distinguish himself in way in which he had never dreamed.
While he will always be remembered for his inspiring quote in his January 20, 1961, inauguration speech, "Ask not what your country can do
for you—ask what you can do for your country,"[3] not even he could
have predicted that he would soon make history as the man who laid
the foundation for what would become known as the War on Poverty. In
1961, Census Bureau figures showed the total U.S. population was 183.7
million people, of whom 21.7 percent were below the poverty line.

The vigorous-looking, forty-three-year-old Massachusetts Democrat specifically mentioned the word "poverty" three times in his inaugural address. He subsequently made it abundantly clear to his inner
circle of advisers that he wished to shake up the government establishment, to find a way to combine existing government programs with
some innovative concepts, and to wage a dynamic attack on poverty in
America.

In his address, he stated: "Now the trumpet summons us again—
not as a call to bear arms, though arms we need—not as a call to battle,
though embattled we are—but a call to bear the burden of a long twilight struggle, year in and year out, 'rejoicing in hope, patient in tribula-
tion'—a struggle against the common enemies of man: tyranny, *poverty*
[italics added], disease and war itself."

Three months after he moved into the White House, Kennedy suffered a major military and political setback in the Bay of Pigs, Cuba. On
April 17, 1961, the Cuban Army quickly killed or captured U.S.-trained
volunteer exiles who invaded the tiny island in a failed attempt to overthrow Fidel Castro. Kennedy changed his focus and on September 12,

1961, boldly announced that he had set a goal of landing a man on the moon by the end of the decade.

On October 16, 1962, during a Cold War showdown with the Soviet Union, Kennedy redeemed himself of the Bay of Pigs fiasco by ordering a blockade of Cuba. For two weeks, the Cuban Missile Crisis brought the world closer to nuclear war than ever before or since. After thirteen days of excruciating negotiations and worldwide tension, Kennedy successfully ended the crisis when Soviet premier Nikita Khrushchev finally agreed to remove the missiles from Cuba. JFK achieved this feat by using personal diplomacy to avoid a cataclysmic nuclear war.

Before long, the explosive issue of civil rights and race relations came to the surface. The civil rights movement began to make front-page news in the early 1960s with blacks and whites alike staging sit-ins and with the "freedom riders" traveling across the Deep South. The issue came to a head in the fall of 1962, when a Negro student named James Meredith tried to enroll in the University of Mississippi, sparking massive and violent protests against his admission. Local police beat and pushed back the protesters. To stop the violence, Kennedy sent in some twenty-three thousand federal troops to restore order.

Again, the following spring, two black students enrolled in the University of Alabama, and JFK used the National Guard to ensure their protection. At first he was a reluctant player in the movement, for fear of alienating southern Democrats. It took a horrendous battle in the streets of Birmingham, Alabama, in May—during which the police viciously used cattle prods, police dogs, and fire hoses against demonstrators—to motivate Kennedy to deliver a historic speech on June 11, 1963, calling civil rights a "moral crisis."

In his speech marking his first decisive action on civil rights, Kennedy shook the southern political establishment and the consciences of millions of Americans. He stated unequivocally: "One hundred years of delay have passed since President Lincoln freed the slaves, yet their heirs, their grandsons, are not fully free. They are not yet freed from the bonds of injustice. They are not yet freed from social and economic oppression. And this Nation, for all its hopes and all its boasts, will not be fully free until all its citizens are free."[4]

According to Kennedy's senior aide Arthur M. Schlesinger Jr., "It puzzled Kennedy that the poor were not angrier and more politically demanding. 'In England,' he said one day in the spring of 1963, 'the unemployment rate goes to two percent, and they march on Parliament. Here it moves up toward six, and no one seems to mind.'"[5]

Throughout 1963, in fact, Kennedy and his team cobbled together a civil rights bill (which later Congress would filibuster but finally pass under the leadership of President Lyndon Johnson in 1964). Meanwhile, as the election of 1964 approached, JFK discussed making a large-scale antipoverty program the centerpiece of his reelection campaign. This plan would later be expanded by his successor, Lyndon Johnson, into the full-fledged War on Poverty. The time was right.

The mood in the country was open to an antipoverty program. As R. Sargent Shriver, Kennedy's brother-in-law and the man who would head up the War on Poverty, put it at the time:

> We were a generation of people who had been in World War II, so when a War Against Poverty was launched, it was typical of all of us at that time to think of this war, the War Against Poverty, in terms just like the war against Hitler. We were accustomed to thinking in terms of the United States being able to do big things. America bestrode the world like a Colossus. There was nothing in the world equal to the United States of America.[6]

It is historically accurate to trace the birth of the War on Poverty to Kennedy himself rather than immediately conjuring up Lyndon Johnson's name, as most political observers do. As historian Frank Stricker wrote in his book, *Why America Lost the War on Poverty—and How to Win It*:

> It was President John Kennedy who planted the seeds of the War on Poverty. When he took office in January 1961, Kennedy indicated that he would concentrate on foreign affairs, not domestic problems. But he had won the election partly on a promise to fight recession and bring down unemployment. If that effort was successful, poverty rates would fall, too. Also, during the presidential campaign he had been shocked by conditions in [Appalachia] West Virginia, and he pledged that within sixty days of taking office he would ask Congress for aid to people of that state.[7]

Kennedy's trips during his presidential campaign to talk the poverty-stricken families of Appalachia had made a deep impression him, according to one of his top aides, Kenneth O'Donnell. In his book, *Jack Kennedy: Elusive Hero,* TV commentator Chris Matthews reports that O'Donnell said, "Here, right in our midst, was a great mass of people totally ignored, yet they didn't complain as he talked to them. They didn't like it; they weren't lazy, they were just people who've been in poverty so long they didn't know any way out."[8]

Pierre Salinger, Kennedy's astute press secretary, reflected O'Donnell's view. "I believe West Virginia brought a real transformation of John F. Kennedy as a person," he said. "He came into contact, really for the first time, with poverty. He saw what had happened as a result of technological changes in coal mines. He saw hundreds of people sitting around the city with nothing to do. It affected him very deeply. It really, in my opinion, changed his whole outlook on life."[9]

Yet, Kennedy began cautiously. Not only was he a son of privilege and class, but he was self-conscious about his "privileged" Boston accent when talking with workingmen in the mines of Pennsylvania and on the docks of Chicago's waterfront. His only "real life" experience was commanding PT-109 during World War II, from which he emerged a hero. His 1960 victory over Richard M. Nixon had been by the thinnest of margins, capturing 112,827 votes nationwide, or in percentage terms among all recorded votes of 68,832,482, Kennedy received a 49.72 percent vote over Nixon's 49.55 percent.[10]

Despite his lack of a mandate, pushed by his top aides—especially his brother Robert F. Kennedy, whom he had appointed attorney general—Kennedy agreed that he would seek legislation to outlaw segregation in federally regulated housing. He also planned to launch other initiatives to help the poor, such as a higher minimum wage, federal aid to low-income housing and education, and even hospital insurance for retirees. He was also credited with the Equal Pay Act of 1963, which addressed disparities in wages based on gender and helped single mothers.

Having ushered in a period of goodwill, Kennedy was successful in having Congress take up three initiatives: an all-encompassing effort to reform welfare and move recipients of welfare to work; a program known as the Area Redevelopment Act to link structural unemployment to poverty, thus enabling depressed areas to apply for grants and loans to improve public facilities and to attract new business; and an effort to retrain workers through passage of the Manpower Development Act to counter the trend toward job losses resulting from automation.[11] As Kennedy's men prepared to carry out his wishes, they became equally concerned with the rising unemployment throughout the country and the rapidly growing demand for jobs. Accordingly, the civil rights movement became a catalyst for carrying out the War on Poverty.

The struggle for racial equality and its accompanying emphasis on poverty as a root cause of racism and stereotyping among whites led to a plethora of books and stories in the mass media about the subject of poverty. Arguably, by far the most influential and widely read work in this flurry of books was written by Michael Harrington, a political activist and member of the Socialist Party. His book *The Other America: Poverty in the United States,* published in 1962, for the first time emphasized in plain language the extraordinary fate of the poor who lived in their own internal world engulfed in "a culture of poverty," a highly descriptive phrase which has since become part of the lexicon of anything written about poverty. The term has been credited to Oscar Lewis, an anthropologist, as a result of his studies of the urban poor in Mexico and Puerto Rico. It refers to a lifestyle of dependency that is passed on from one generation to the next.

The Other America was well received by the reviewers. Kennedy's Task Force brought the book to his attention and recommended it as a blueprint for the War on Poverty. Journalist Richard Reeves reported: "[Kennedy] was impressed with Harrington's statistics. He wanted to do the right thing—when the nation was ready for it. Bigotry was irrational. Poverty was a problem that could be managed. Best of all, it was framed as a new problem. He intended to do something about it—when he was sure of re-election."[12]

In the early fall of 1963, Kennedy approved an all-encompassing program to battle poverty. The day after Kennedy's assassination while campaigning in Dallas, Texas, on November 22, 1963, Johnson—obviously anxious to honor the memory of the fallen president—approved the plan and ordered his staff to move "full speed ahead."[13] In short order, Johnson asked Sargent Shriver, director of the Peace Corps, to put the finishing touches on the plan and implement it.

It should be noted that while Kennedy deserves credit for laying the groundwork for the War on Poverty, his domestic record—as many historians point out—was severely limited by the short time he served. He was seen as a cautious leader on civil rights, despite his having issued executive orders and federal lawsuits against segregation in the South. As historian Robert Dallek observed in his book *An Unfinished Life: John F. Kennedy, 1917–1963,* "He was slow to recognize the extent of the social revolution fostered by Martin Luther King and African Americans, and he repeatedly deferred to southern sensitivities on racial matters, including appointments of segregationist judges in southern federal districts. It took crises in Mississippi and particularly Alabama to persuade him to put a landmark civil rights bill before Congress in June 1963, and even then he was willing to weaken its provisions to win approval from an unreceptive Congress."[14]

Ironically, Kennedy had written in his Pulitzer Prize–winning book *Profiles of Courage*, published in 1956: "Great crises produce great men, and great deeds of courage."[15] In retrospect, undoubtedly Kennedy was, in fact, an extraordinary profile in courage himself. His term in office was tragically cut short, and this leader unquestionably would have gone on to accomplish a great deal more than he did. As it is, his very presence inspired tens of millions of Americans to volunteer for public service, to look at their country and the world with a more optimistic attitude, and to believe that one person can indeed make a difference.

LYNDON B. JOHNSON (LBJ), fifty-five years old, was a son of Texas who grew up poor. He knew the ravages of poverty firsthand and was more comfortable than his predecessor had been in dealing with the poor. For that matter LBJ was also much more adept at deal making with members of Congress, having served as a member of the House of Representatives and as the powerful Senate majority leader.

In point of fact, the thirty-sixth president (1963–1969) had been familiar with poverty through his entire life. As historian Doris Kearns Goodwin pointed out in her book *Lyndon Johnson and the American Dream*, "When Johnson spoke of poverty, and he spoke, he claimed 'from experience,' the experience of a boy who knew what it was like to go hungry, the experience of a boy who saw sickness and disease day after day."[16]

An attack on poverty appealed to Lyndon Johnson as a platform for his 1964 campaign, just as Kennedy had thought it would be his signature reelection theme. As historian Robert Dallek wrote in his book *Flawed Giant: Lyndon Johnson and His Times*, "Johnson had a keen sense of identification with the needy. Throughout his life he had suffered from feelings of emptiness, which he answered with constant activity. 'I never think about politics more than 18 hours a day,' he once joked."[17]

In his first State of the Union message, Johnson called for an unconditional War on Poverty and the creation of a Great Society. He stated to a joint session of the Congress on January 8, 1964: "Let us carry forward the plans and programs of John Fitzgerald Kennedy—not because of our sorrow or sympathy, but because they are right. In his memory, today, I especially ask all members . . . in this election year, to put your country ahead of your party, and to always debate principles; never debate personalities."[18]

In response to the Johnson administration's policies, the federal government's role in domestic policy hugely expanded in connection with the War on Poverty (see appendix B). Johnson was so adept at courting the relevant constituencies interested in poverty that he shaped a strong political consensus among leaders of those groups long before a bill came up for vote in 1964. On March 16, 1964, Johnson sent a special message to Congress asking for a Declaration of War on Poverty so he could go about pursuing his Great Society program.

Congress passed major civil rights acts: the Economic Opportunity Act (1964), which established the new government body that would administer the War on Poverty, the Office of Economic Opportunity; and two important education acts in 1965. In addition, it passed legislation that created the landmark Medicare and Medicaid bills, two of the cornerstones of the New Frontier that are still considered intrinsic to the government's "safety net" today. As an interesting aside, it is worth noting that where LBJ signed the Medicare bill into law on July 30, 1965—in the Truman Library in Independence, Missouri—he presented to Truman the very first Medicare (and his wife, Bess, the second) in recognition of Truman's previous efforts to pass a national health insurance program when Truman was in office.[19] Johnson also signed bills that established Operation Head Start, the Job Corps, Volunteers in Service to America (known as VISTA), and many more.

Johnson publicly gave credit to John Kennedy for formatting the outline for the War on Poverty, but Johnson knew that once the money had been spent and the programs were successful, he—Lyndon Baines Johnson—would get the full credit for one of the most significant accomplishments of any president in American history. And what made him so confident—certainly he played the ultimate president-politician in public—was his knowledge that from all of his years of experience he had acquired through hard work, the slyness of a great poker player, and a unique ability to persuade members of the Congress through exchanging favors for votes, he alone could pull it off. As he once told Goodwin:

> There is but one way for a president to deal with Congress and that is continuously, incessantly, and without interruption. If it's really going to work, the relationship between the President and the Congress has got to be almost incestuous. He's got to know them even better than they know themselves. And then, on the basis of this knowledge, he's got to build a system that stretches from cradle to the grave, from the moment a bill is introduced to the moment it is officially enrolled as the law of the land.[20]

In the end, after billions of dollars were allocated and spent, the Great Society programs—ballyhooed as they were—failed to end poverty in America. The War on Poverty did make a difference; the percentage of Americans living below the poverty level dropped from 21 percent when Johnson took office in 1963 to 12.8 percent in 1968 when he stepped aside. Waste and political corruption in some of the antipoverty programs on the local level across America, however, stifled any major changes in the day-to-day lives of millions of poor people.[21]

Although the Great Society program helped to protect civil rights and to expand social programs, critics charged that antipoverty programs were ineffective and wasteful. The massive amount of money poured into the Vietnam War, as well as the costs of the antipoverty programs, overwhelmed any chance that all of Johnson's domestic initiatives would be successful. The economic costs were estimated at nearly $7 trillion a year.[22]

Highly praised historian David McCullough described Johnson's contribution this way:

> But the real measure of a leader is what he gets done, the size of the problems he faces. Before Lyndon Johnson, we were essentially a segregated society. Inequality among black Americans in the South was set in law. Before Lyndon Johnson, there was no Head Start program, no Medicare—so much that we take for granted—and before Lyndon Johnson, very few Americans had even heard of Vietnam. He is a story, a very American story and, in all, a tragedy in the real sense. He's the central character in a struggle of moral importance ending in ruin.[23]

Meanwhile, Johnson sent more and more troops to Vietnam, a conflict that would eventually claim the lives of fifty-eight thousand Americans and three million Vietnamese. As the war ground on, with no end in sight, Johnson found himself increasingly under fire from the Right and the Left. Johnson's presidency—and especially his War on Poverty—began to suffer badly with each new setback in the stalemated war in Vietnam. By the beginning of 1968, with Vietnam occupying most of his time and energy, Johnson struggled with the decision about whether he should run for president in 1968. He became the target of numerous newspaper and magazine articles because the Vietnam War had become so unpopular with the public. Perhaps the biggest blow to Johnson's possible run for the presidency came on March 12, 1968, when Senator Eugene McCarthy, a Democrat from Minnesota, won 42.2 percent of the primary vote in New Hampshire to Johnson's 49.4 percent, well below the two-thirds pollsters had predicted for LBJ.

Only two weeks later, on Sunday, March 31, 1968, Johnson, at the end of a speech on Vietnam, stunned the political world when he claimed he did not want "the presidency to become involved in the partisan divisions that are developing in this political year." He concluded, "Accordingly, I shall not seek, and I will not accept, the nomination of my party for another term as your president."[24]

Leaders of both parties and even members of Johnson's own team supported this major breakthrough in the race for the Democratic nomination. Robert F. Kennedy, the former attorney general to Presidents Kennedy and Johnson and the then current senator from New York, had presidential ambitions of his own and called Johnson's withdrawal "truly magnanimous." He moved his campaign into high gear and announced his candidacy for president in Washington, D.C., on March 16, 1968, declaring that the crises in American cities, on the farms, and in our ghettos had all been met with indifference or programs that had not worked. His main theme was to rid the country of poverty. In that regard, he traveled to Appalachia in West Virginia and personally visited with poverty-stricken families. The media coverage put Robert Kennedy on the map. His campaign, however, was brought to a tragic end on June 6, 1968, when he was assassinated in a California hotel kitchen. In five short years, the nation had mourned three leaders who addressed civil rights and poverty: JFK, Martin Luther King, and Robert Kennedy.

It is significant, I think, to recall an interview Robert Kennedy had with a reporter before the Democratic Party Convention during the summer of 1968. According to William vanden Heuvel, a close aide to Kennedy and author of *On His Own*, a newsman had asked Kennedy how he would like to be remembered. It was a curiously prophetic question as the newsman had no idea, of course, of how little time Kennedy had left. Kennedy had replied, "I hope it will be because I made some contribution to those who are less well off. . . . I would like to feel that I did something to lessen their suffering."[25]

RICHARD M. NIXON (1969–1974), fifty-six years old, was a Republican who had made one of the most astounding political comebacks in American presidential history after barely losing to John Kennedy in 1960 and to Edmund G. (Pat) Brown for governor of California in 1962. The thirty-seventh president was hardly a liberal. He called himself a "pragmatic" politician who knew how to get things done. Known as the "law and order" president, he was not especially interested in social welfare issues. The cagey and politically savvy new president did not mention the word "poverty" once in his inaugural address on January 20, 1969.

He appealed to those millions of Democrats who had backed Hubert Humphrey, however, by throwing out a few well-placed morsels of compassion for the poor and allusions to social welfare issues when he borrowed a page out of Kennedy's 1960 "Ask not what your country can do for you" inaugural speech when he stated:

> Our greatest need now is to reach beyond government, and to enlist the legions of the concerned and committed.
>
> What has to be done, has to be done by government and people together or it will not be done at all. The lesson of past agony is that without the people we can do nothing; with the people we can do everything.
>
> . . . No man can be fully free while his neighbor is not. To go forward at all is to go forward together.
>
> This means black and white together, as one nation, not two. The laws have caught up with our conscience. What remains is to give life to what is in the law: to ensure at last that as all are born equal in dignity before God, all are born equal in dignity before man.
>
> . . . With those who are willing to join, let us cooperate to reduce the burden of arms, to strengthen the structure of peace, to lift up the poor and hungry.[26]

Nixon's triumph over Humphrey was by the thinnest of margins—43 percent to 42.7 percent—with Governor George Wallace of Alabama, who had campaigned as a third-party candidate, garnering 13.5 percent. Nixon's victory notwithstanding, a great many Americans still had major reservations about Nixon, who had boasted during his campaign that he had a "secret" peace plan to end the war in Vietnam.

During his first term, which was plagued with anti–Vietnam War protests across the country, Nixon tried an experiment to help the poor, but it backfired. Even a well-meaning, innovative, first-term reform of the Family Assistance Program—which provided a minimum income for all families with dependent children—left Americans in worse condition. It was, in effect, a revenue-sharing plan with state and local governments, but it became so burdened with bureaucracy and red tape that it failed. Further, federal cutbacks and freezes in funds left localities worse off than they were before the plan.[27]

At the same time, the political environment soured as the war caused the national debt to hit a new high, cities and states went deeper into debt, and public services, such as health, welfare, education, and transportation, suffered. Taxation was yet another issue, with the wealthiest 1 percent of the people paying taxes at a lower rate than did all other

Americans—a development that would be seen again in the George W. Bush and Barack Obama administrations in later years.

With a resounding landslide victory over his Democratic Party challenger, George McGovern, in 1972, Nixon began to turn back many of the Great Society programs that his predecessor Lyndon Johnson had enacted into law. "Nixon's spectacular popular majority of 17 million (60.7 percent of the vote) in 1972," according to historians Allan Nevins and Henry Steele Commager in their book *A Short History of the United States*, "emboldened him to shed all political inhibitions in his second term. He began to impound monies appropriated by Congress for such social programs as education, social service, urban and ecological problems."[28]

Nixon dealt yet more setbacks to the progressive social reform policies. He "liquidated" the Office of Economic Opportunity, "perhaps the centerpiece of the Great Society program; withdrew support from the fair busing enforcement program; proposed cutbacks in programs for students, farmers, veterans, unemployed, and the mentally ill; ended assistance to consumer protection and to environmentalist proposals; fought strip-mining regulations; vetoed an anti-water pollution bill to which the administration had been pledged. And when this bill was passed over his veto, he impounded the congressional appropriation for it."[29] Nixon also made no effort to have the Justice Department enforce the civil rights laws.

The severity of his actions proved beyond any reasonable doubt what Nixon was really made of and who he really represented. As journalist and author Elizabeth Drew stated in her book *Richard M. Nixon*: "Nixon appealed to the great number of Americans who resented and feared the cultural and social upheavals of the time. He stood with them against liberals, the East Coast intellectuals, big government, and racial minorities."[30]

Nixon often spoke of "the silent majority"—a term that became synonymous with Nixon's vast following, as he saw it, and remained with him throughout his career. In addition to his failure to pursue civil rights vigorously, Nixon also dragged his heels when it came to school desegregation. He opposed busing, which the U.S. Supreme Court's landmark *Brown v. Board of Education* decision had required, to wipe out the effects of the "separate but equal" law that had preceded it.

His Supplemental Security Income proposal has helped families in need, however, and his signing the Occupational Safety and Health Administration and Environmental Protection Agency into law has helped protect workers and families. In fairness, Nixon—a man whose complex mind few people could ever divine—was receptive to an extraordinarily creative idea to reform welfare, one of the issues on which he had campaigned. Like many political accidents of fate, the creative, "outside of the box" thinking of Daniel Patrick Moynihan, a liberal-minded Harvard professor serving as Nixon's urban affairs adviser, conceived the task of welfare reform. He diagnosed the "pathology" of what he called "benign neglect" that caused families to remain on welfare from one generation to the next. Moynihan blamed the government itself for building public housing projects, the tenants of which burned them down because they turned out to be ghettos for the poor, and for ensuring the continuation of poverty through the generations.

Moynihan's revolutionary theory of benign neglect as the fundamental cause of poverty took hold, much to the astonishment of the Democratic liberals who had been Moynihan's colleagues for years. Nixon formulated a program that included work requirements for welfare recipients to make the plan economically feasible. Further, the new program was meant to increase welfare recipients' sense of self-worth. Spending on domestic social programs actually increased during Nixon's tenure, but by 1973 Nixon found a way to withhold funds for programs he did not sanction. The Supreme Court would soon overrule him in 1974, the year in which he faced near impeachment over the Watergate cover-up and resigned in shame. His sturdy vice president, Gerald Ford, succeeded him as commander in chief on July 9, 1974.

The sixty-year-old **GERALD R. FORD** (1974–1977), a Republican from Michigan, was a modest, straight-talking former congressman who was well liked by virtually every member of Congress. He assumed leadership of a nation at a time when the country's economy was deteriorating and unemployment was at 12.3 percent. In the wake of the infamous Watergate scandal, the thirty-eighth president pardoned his predecessor in a controversial action. The crux of his inaugural speech was summed up in one line of his speech: "My fellow Americans, our long national nightmare is over."[31]

But it was not, really. Ford's pardon of Nixon on September 8, 1974, touched off a mass protest across the nation and from members of Congress. So many questions were raised about the story-behind-the-story of the pardon that, in a nationally televised appearance on

October 17, 1974, Ford was forced to deny publicly having promised a pardon in exchange for Nixon's stepping aside. Another negative cloud that hung over his first few months in office was his commitment to keep the majority of Nixon's cabinet in place, thus continuing Nixon's conservative social policies.

Meanwhile, Ford reached out to the so-called liberal wing of his party and named former New York governor Nelson A. Rockefeller as his vice president and head of the Domestic Council, a position in which Rockefeller wanted to play a major role in creating domestic policies. As it turned out, the moderate Rockefeller clashed with other Ford aides and was not able to move a significant social agenda forward.

Further, Ford faced large Democratic majorities in Congress, as well as some Republican factions whose goals were to reassert themselves in the policymaking process. His biggest challenge, aside from the politics of Nixon's resignation, was the economy. During his first year, Ford had to tackle the triple threats of inflation, unemployment, and an energy crisis brought on by a crucial oil shortage.[32]

In addition, "during Ford's brief presidency, both inflation and unemployment rose to heights not seen in the post–World War II years. . . . Crude oil prices skyrocketed to ten times their pre–1973 levels and gas prices doubled at the pump—conditions which, combined with severe oil shortages, made for a gloomy economic environment," according to the Miller Center's analysis of Ford's record.[33]

As Ford focused on inflation, he was accused of ignoring the unemployed. Unemployment had grown from 5.4 percent in August 1974 to 6.5 percent in November, and White House economists expected that number to reach 7 percent. In December, Ford conceded that the economy was in recession with economic production falling and unemployment rising. By 1976, the economy showed signs of recovery as inflation, the consumer price index, and unemployment numbers dipped.[34]

But Ford faced greater problems than the economy. School busing to integrate public schools found its place on the front burner. Ford favored integrated schools and had attended one himself in Michigan. But for blatant political reasons, Ford opposed busing, "largely because he believed the federal government had an obligation only to end 'de jure' (by law) segregation rather than 'de facto' (by circumstance) segregation."[35]

Perhaps one of Ford's most notable political miscalculations that directly affected the poverty-stricken areas of New York City came as the city teetered on brink of bankruptcy in the spring of 1975. The city exceeded its income in trying to provide social services for a population about the size of Sweden's. Throughout that spring and summer, city officials solicited financial aid from the federal government, but it countered that it already supplied a quarter of the city's budget. Despite Rockefeller's advice, Ford never seriously considered intervening. On October 29, 1975, Ford publicly said he would not give federal assistance to bail out the city. The next day, the *New York Daily News* reported Ford's position with a bold headline that read FORD TO CITY—DROP DEAD.[36] Ford did end up signing legislation that provided loans to New York City but only after the city agreed to take austerity measures. Ford's tenure as president came to an end in 1976 when Jimmy Carter, a peanut farmer from Plains, Georgia, won the Democratic nomination and beat him in the national election.

Postscript: Gerald Ford's own assessment of his time in office was positive—and rightfully so. He was convinced in his own mind that his administration changed the mood of the nation for the better, especially after the cynicism of Watergate. At a meeting of scholars and journalists studying the Ford administration at Hofstra University in Long Island, New York, in 1989, the former president recalled the bicentennial celebration event on July 4, 1976, when he was president:

> What I remember most about the super Fourth of July was the sight of Americans hugging each and shouting for joy. I can still see those thousands of smiling faces with thousands of flags waving friendly greetings. . . . I can still hear the Liberty Bell toll, echoes by church bells across this beautiful land. It was a long day, and just before my head hit the pillow that night, I said to myself: "Well, Jerry, I guess we've healed America. We haven't done too badly whatever the verdict [against Jimmy Carter] in November."[37]

JIMMY CARTER (1977–1981), the fifty-two-year-old former governor of Georgia and the thirty-ninth president of the United States, literally burst upon the national political scene as a Washington "outsider" who was only a "peanut farmer." His simple catchphrase when he began campaigning was: "My name is Jimmy Carter and I am running for president." He was a populist Democrat who built a grassroots political organization from the bottom up and represented a refreshing change in the wake of the Nixon-Ford era of "dark" politics. Known as an honest man who sometimes served as a lay preacher in his hometown of Plains, Georgia, he pledged to run his administration with honesty and transparency in government.

On January 20, 1977, Chief Justice Warren Burger administered the oath of office on the Bible that George Washington had used in his first inauguration. In his inauguration speech Carter subtly but nonetheless plainly laid the groundwork for a philosophy that the American people eventually would reject: that America has its limits and we must recognize that fact. He declared: "We have learned that 'more' is not necessarily 'better,' that even our great Nation has its recognized limits, and that we can neither answer all questions nor solve all problems. We cannot afford to do everything, nor can we afford to lack boldness as we meet the future. So, together, in a spirit of individual sacrifice for the common good, we must simply do our best."[38]

That theme would come back to haunt him a few years later when he held a summit meeting in 1979 during what the media was calling a period of malaise. It became apparent that Carter could not move the country forward without considerable sacrifices, and the public was not moved. Knowing that he did not possess all the answers to the rising problems in the nation—whose people, according to public opinion polls, were unhappy in general—Carter called a meeting of opinion leaders at Camp David on July 15, 1979. Out of that weekend session came many ideas on how to improve the country's progress.

After the summit meeting, he addressed the nation in a televised speech on July 15 that was viewed by millions of Americans. He intended to rally and buoy the spirits of the people, but critics labeled it Carter's "malaise speech." In his speech, Carter asked Americans to join him in adapting to a new age of limits, but the concept was foreign to them. America had always been a nation that simply grew and grew and grew. Most citizens could not abide having their president tell them there had to be limits. It was not in the American DNA, they thought. Moreover, Carter also scolded the public for being too fixated on themselves and their personal material desires: "The erosion of our confidence in the future is threatening to destroy the social and the political fabric of America. . . . In a nation that was proud of hard work, strong families, close-knit communities and our faith in God, too many of us now tend to worship self-indulgence and consumption. Human identity is no longer defined by what one does but by what one owns."[39]

Press reports indicated that people didn't want to be told they were the cause of the malaise. Carter "worsened his image problem by giving the . . . speech, in which he described a lack of confidence in America's purpose and its future."[40] Some political observers noted at the time that the address was more like a sermon than a political speech. A majority of the public rejected the president's theory.

Meanwhile, Carter was seeking a solution to the energy crisis, which had resulted in Americans waiting impatiently at the pumps in long lines of cars all across the country. The price of oil skyrocketed, making it hard for especially the poor to use their cars in their daily work and caused prices on delivered goods, such as groceries, to increase as well.

Yet another unnerving event occurred on Carter's watch. In October 1979, Islamic militants stormed the American Embassy in Iran, keeping fifty-two Americans as hostages for 444 days and severely weakening Carter's image. The 1980 election was held on the one-year anniversary of the hostage taking. Carter lost in a landslide to an upbeat, former popular actor and California governor, Ronald Reagan, who had an engaging new conservative message in 1980.

In his best moments, Carter's combination of religious idealism with the tenacity of purpose yielded spectacular results. None was more important than the 1978 Camp David Accords, which Carter personally brokered between Egyptian president Anwar El Sadat and Israeli prime minister Menacham Begin. Carter took on the role as peacemaker in the Middle East. He also signed into law the Department of Education in 1979 and in January 1980 signed a law bailing out Chrysler, saving 200,000-plus jobs

Postscript: With the passing of time, Jimmy Carter is held in much higher esteem in the United States and around the world than he did in 1980. In 1982 in partnership with Emory University, the president and former first lady Rosalynn Carter established the Carter Center, whose mission is to work for human rights and the alleviation of human suffering. It also "seeks to prevent and resolve conflicts, enhance freedom and democracy, and improve world health."[41] He and his wife were tireless volunteers for Habitat for Humanity as well, building homes for people in need. Carter has also served in the role of unbiased monitor in many national elections of nations around the world. He was awarded the Nobel Prize for Peace in 2002.

9

THE EMERGENCE OF GLOBALIZATION (1981–2012):

REAGAN, GEORGE H. W. BUSH, CLINTON, GEORGE W. BUSH, OBAMA

Let's be the generation that ends poverty in America.
—Barack Obama, announcement of candidacy for president,
Springfield, Illinois, February 10, 2007

When **RONALD REAGAN**, a former California governor, was sworn in as the fortieth president (1981–1989) on January 20, 1981, at the age of sixty-nine, he was the oldest man ever to be elected president of the United States. The popular Republican politician—who had been an outspoken Democrat for FDR during the Depression years—easily defeated Jimmy Carter. Reagan garnered 50.75 percent of the vote to Carter's 41.01 percent and 489 electoral votes against Carter's 49, and John Anderson, who ran as an independent, received 6.7 percent of the vote.

In his inaugural address, he set the tone for his administration, stating optimistically his twin themes of self-reliance and small government but never once mentioning the word "poverty." In his opening speech he instead fired his first salvo against "big government." It read, in part:

> The economic ills we suffer have come upon us over several decades. They will not go away in days, weeks, or months, but they will go away. . . .
>
> In this present crisis, government is not the solution to our problem; *government is the problem* [italics added]. From time to time we've been tempted to believe that society has become too complex to be managed by self-rule, that government by an elite group is superior to government for, by, and of the people. Well, if no one among us is capable of governing himself, then who among us has the capacity to

govern someone else? All of us together, in and out of government, must bear the burden.[1]

From the outset, Reagan had the ability to translate complex subjects into everyday language. Some say he oversimplified. Others say he had the talent to digest the complexities and process them into easy-to-understand terms. In any case, he had the advice and counsel of many Republicans who had served in previous White Houses. Reagan's first priority from the day he stepped into the Oval Office was the economy. He faced double-digit inflation, high unemployment, and a prime interest rate of 21.5 percent, the highest since the Civil War.

Reagan split his economic initiatives into two major components—tax reductions and spending cuts, which he played up as the centerpiece of his effort to bring the country in line with what it could afford. This philosophy, which became known as "Reaganomics," was not new, and the Republicans in Congress have since repeated it. Reagan's goal, according to critical Democrats, was to slash many of Lyndon Johnson's Great Society government programs while leaving Franklin Roosevelt's major social programs—Social Security, for example—intact for the time being. For many observers at the time, Reaganomics was seen as a code word for a supply-side doctrine of lower taxes and added incentives to produce productivity.[2]

Ronald Reagan may not have been sensitive to the people who lived in poverty when he first took office, but he knew that, politically, he should not frighten the seniors of America—many of whom had voted for him as a sixty-nine-year-old senior himself. But he was criticized for lacking compassion for the underprivileged when he called for cutting government programs that helped the poor. Democrats charged that would put the poor at even greater risk than they had been before.

Reagan quickly recognized that the economy needed his attention. Before a joint session of Congress on February 18, 1981, he announced his Program for Economic Recovery after only twenty-nine days in office. Edmund Morris, in his book *Dutch: A Memoir of Ronald Reagan*, labeled it "the most galvanizing executive initiative since Franklin D. Roosevelt's proclamation of the New Deal."[3] Reagan's austerity budget added up to a full $695 billion, cutting eighty-three major programs. He included a 30 percent tax cut for individuals over the next three years, presuming that less revenue now (1981) would mean more revenue later, "while poor people and artists suffered. . . ."[4] Not long after Reagan survived an assassination attempt by a crazed gunman outside a Washington hotel on March 30, 1981, he walked into the halls of

Congress as jaunty as ever on April 28, 1981, to deliver a speech to resounding applause. Whether it was sympathy for his surviving an assassination attempt or genuine enthusiasm for his economic program (it could have been both), Congress's reaction was palpable. Even before Reagan started to deliver his talk, wrote Edmund Morris, "All members [of Congress] rose as required but their respect on this occasion verged on reverence—and also signaled a near-helpless capitulation to the message they knew he was bringing."[5]

In his joint speech to Congress calling for 100 percent support for his Program for Economic Recovery, Reagan recognized the economic crisis and the plight of the poor. He said, in part:

> There are still almost 8 million unemployed. The average worker's hourly earnings after adjusting for inflation are lower today than they were 6 months ago, and there have been over 6,000 business failures.
>   . . . Tonight, I renew my call for us to work as a team, to join in cooperation so that we find answers which will begin to solve all our economic problems and not just some of them. The economic recovery package that I've outlined to you over the past weeks is, I deeply believe, the only answer that we have left.
>   Reducing the growth of spending, cutting marginal tax rates, providing relief from overregulation, and following a noninflationary and predictable monetary policy are interwoven measures which will ensure that we have addressed each of the severe dislocations which threaten our economic future. These policies will make our economy stronger. . . .[6]

Reagan received bipartisan support. As Speaker of the House Thomas Phillip "Tip" O'Neill, Jr., philosophically reminded reporters, Congress was ultimately responsible to the American people, "and the will of the people is to go along with the President."[7]

Reagan was a firm believer in what is known as supply-side economics. He was thoroughly convinced that his economic program of combined tax and budget cuts would expand the tax base and lead to a balanced budget. Of course, it did not turn out that way. The lost tax revenues coupled with increased higher spending—much of it from both Democrats and Republicans in Congress who tacked their pet projects onto the budget—sent the deficit rocketing skyward. Furthermore, Reagan wrote in his diary in December 1981 that he was personally suffering from the economic crisis. "We who are going to balance the budget face the highest budget deficit ever," he wrote. "And yet, percentagewise, it will be smaller in relation to G.N.P. We have reduced

Carter's seventeen percent spending increase to nine percent. The recession has added to costs and reduced revenues, however, so even with that reduction in gvt. [*sic*] size, we have a large deficit."[8]

Adding to Reagan's economic woes, by November of his second year in office, the economy had gone into the dumps. "The U.S. economy recorded its worst decline since the Depression," wrote journalist Lou Cannon in his book *President Reagan: The Role of a Lifetime.* By November 1982 more than nine million Americans were officially unemployed, a figure that would rise dramatically to 11.5 million by January 1983.[9]

One of Reagan's favorite expressions was, "It's morning, again, in America," taken from a television ad in his 1984 reelection campaign. At the Republican National Convention in Dallas on August 23, 1984, Reagan referred to America as "that shining city on the hill" in his acceptance speech for the nomination for a second term. For tens of millions of citizens across the country, however, it was clearly not "morning" in America again. Reagan was undoubtedly aware of the disparity of income between the poor and the rich, but his optimism, at least publicly, was a fundamental part of his political persona. He was a steadfast believer in "the marketplace," which is premised on the theory that everyone in America should benefit from the country as a whole growing richer.

As Reagan was completing his first term, the political pundits went to work on the man who they had previously dubbed the "Teflon president." Criticism of his administration began to stick. Some questioned whether he could win another term. Cannon described the scene: people set up tent cities called "Reagan ranches," reminiscent of the shantytowns and Hoovervilles of the Great Depression, near the White House.[10] Finally, the country fell into a recession and Reagan's popularity rating dipped to a low of 41 percent.

In these difficult times, critics compared Reagan to Herbert Hoover.[11] Democrats charged that he was trying to balance the budget "on the backs of the poor."[12]

Lou Cannon provided special insight into how Reagan thought: "Reagan could convince himself of nearly anything, but the key to his conduct was not semantic self-deception but an unshakable conviction that everything would turn out well."[13] With such a consistently optimistic outlook, it would almost be too much to expect that Ronald Reagan would worry about the slums or the poor people of America.

Unfortunately, in his zeal to "stay the course" and keep a rosy outlook, he overlooked bad signs in the economy. Arguably, the problems he faced—a recession that culminated in 1981–1982 and unemployment rates that soared into double digits—were worse than what President Barack Obama would face in 2009. Also hurting Reagan, the Washington establishment at the time argued that inflation was now endemic to the American economy and could not be slowed without serious consequences.

An additional crisis popped up early in the administration with dire warnings from Director of the Office of Management and Budget David Stockman. A nonconformist who often expressed his own blunt opinions, Stockman had irked the administration by writing a report—not intended for release to the public—for the president titled "Avoiding an Economic Dunkirk." "Things could go very badly during the first year, resulting in incalculable erosion of GOP momentum, unity and public confidence," Stockman had predicted.[14] Meanwhile, news reports in the media carried stories that said many Americans were slipping through the safety net, especially the helpless poor.

Ronald Reagan, nonetheless, inspired many Americans. They admired him as a patriot and as a symbol of American power at home and abroad. He stood six-foot-one, ramrod straight; weighed about 185 pounds; and was trim and fit with a full head of dark hair. With his rugged facial features, he resembled advertising's Marlboro Man. Reagan's image as a movie actor hero somehow carried over into his role as president. His persona was strengthened considerably when he urged Soviet leader Mikhail Gorbachev to "tear down this wall" during his now-famous Cold War address from the Brandenburg Gate in Berlin on June 12, 1987.

In addition, Reagan "was slow to join the battle against AIDS."[15] And the poverty level, which was 13 percent when he entered the Oval Office, remained about the same when he left. In between, it rose to 15.2 percent in 1983 at the height of the recession.[16] As for welfare, having coined the phrase "welfare queen" when he was governor of California and attacking welfare, Reagan made no effort to disguise his disdain for people who did not and, in his view, would not work. He mocked the welfare system, which he correctly stated encouraged generation after generation of welfare families. As governor of California, Reagan had opposed efforts to increase cost-of-living payments to recipients. In 1971, he had been successful in persuading then president Richard M. Nixon not to stand in the way of a pilot program in California requiring able-bodied welfare recipients to work as a condition of receiving aid. The program had mixed success but established Reagan as the champion of "workfare."[17]

While Reagan's overall image was positive, he was concerned with the public's negative perception of his views on race relations. He had a generally poor record on race relations, and he even opposed establishing the Martin Luther King holiday. As he wrote in his autobiography, *Ronald Reagan: An American Life*, "In Washington, I argued that any quota system based on race, religion, or color is immoral. Because of these policies many black leaders claimed that if I wasn't a bigot, at the very least I was unsympathetic to the aspirations of blacks and other minorities. Neither claim was true, and I think the record shows that."[18]

Postscript: Reagan was such an effective leader in terms of reaching the people with his mastery of the television media—no doubt from his days as an actor—that he became known as "the Great Communicator" of his conservative philosophy, and he worked so well with the Democrats and Republicans that his practical politics prevailed. He is best remembered for changing course during his first term in 1983 in a bipartisan deal with Speaker O'Neill that preserved Social Security for a generation, defying "liberal" or "conservative" labels.[19] As one commentator concluded: "He casts a long shadow."[20] On the other hand, Reagan did break the airline pilots' union strike in August 1981, support a lawsuit against the IRS to overturn its policy of denying tax breaks to segregated private schools, fail to support the Equal Rights Amendment, and widen the gap between the rich and the poor, tripling the deficit.

All in all, Reagan left the Union in fairly good shape; however, he made little progress in fighting poverty and a coming recession. His successor, George H. W. Bush, had served Reagan well as a steady-as-you-go vice president for eight years. Ironically, some five years after he left office, Reagan unmistakably expressed his honest opinion of the antipoverty program in a *New York Times* story in 1993 when he stated: "We fought a war on poverty, 'and poverty won.'"[21] Perhaps his son Ron Reagan in his book *My Father at 100* wrote the most fitting epitaph about the president. when he succinctly summed up his father's legacy: "Ronald Reagan, who was the most dynamic American political figure of the late twentieth century, whose name remains at the center of policy debates to this day, was an emissary from our nation's past."[22]

GEORGE H. W. BUSH, a Republican from Texas but a New Englander (Massachusetts) by birth, was sixty-four years old when he was elected the forty-first president (1989–1993). He was arguably one of the men best prepared to assume the presidency by virtue of his distinguished background of varied public service. Having served as Reagan's vice president for eight years, he had previously been a member of the U.S. House of Representatives (1967–1971), U.S. ambassador to the United Nations (1971–1972), and director of the Central Intelligence Agency (1976–1977). He was known as a cooperative, able public servant but not especially outspoken on major issues.

He had shown flashes of being able to whip a crowd into an enthusiastic frenzy. For example, when Bush was nominated for the presidency at the Republican National Convention on August 18, 1988, he uttered that famous line of the convention and most important sound bite of perhaps his entire four years as president: "Read my lips: no new taxes."

Historian Herbert S. Parmet, writing in his book *George Bush: The Life of a Lone Star Yankee* was flabbergasted by the promise.

> Such words, incredible to critics, fell on ears that were as convinced as he of the failure of the past Democratic social programs. Society, as they saw it, was no better off for them, and a lot more impoverished, both in the public and private sectors. The poor were poorer, and there were more of them. Cities were rotting and crime infested, filled with people increasingly becoming more irresponsible about themselves and their families . . . and all too easily subordinating any personal initiative to antisocial behavior and the government beneficence.[23]

The impact of the "no new taxes" election promise was considerable, and many supporters of Bush were delighted with his performance. "Bush believes it helped him win the 1988 election," wrote one commentator of Bush's appearance.[24] That pledge would come back to haunt him, as Bush was forced to raise some taxes as part of a budget agreement with the Democratic Congress. To soften the blow, he called them "tax revenue increases."

After he was sworn in on January 20, 1989, Bush—tall, lean, and alert—still lacked the instant charisma of his predecessor, but in his own way he displayed more of an outward social conscience than did Ronald Reagan. In his inaugural address, Bush emphasized the issues of homelessness, drug addiction, and crime. He also advocated volunteerism and community involvement, pledging to support "a Thousand Points of Light, of all the community organizations that are spread like stars throughout the Nation, doing good."[25]

Overall, his invitation to the American people to join hands with government in solving the nation's problems was vaguely reminiscent of

John F. Kennedy's admonition "ask not what your country can do for you," yet Bush did not institute any follow-through programs. In addition, no particular groundswell developed with individuals volunteering to assist the government.

As the first man elected to succeed a president of the same party since Herbert Hoover did in 1929, Bush was more vigorous than he had been in a long time, undoubtedly trying to shake off his popular image as being a "wimp." Some members of the media viewed Bush as having been too loyal to Reagan, and, journalist George Will once described Bush as "Reagan's lapdog."[26]

In his inauguration speech, Bush shed any such description. He aroused the huge crowd by urging Americans to show compassion for the poor. Bush vividly described the social issues the nation faced: "My friends, we have work to do. There are homeless, lost and roaming. There are the children who have nothing, no love, no normalcy. There are those who cannot free themselves of enslavement to whatever addiction—drugs, welfare, the demoralization that rules the slums. There is crime to be conquered, the rough crime of the streets."[27]

One can easily conclude that Bush was a good man with good intentions. In his inaugural speech, he also expressed the hope that he would govern a "kinder and gentler" nation. Bush came to office in a smooth, efficient transition.

Unlike Kennedy and Reagan, both of whom had far-reaching agendas, Bush offered a relatively modest plan for the country. Being the well-organized logistician that he was, he tried to run an orderly and not especially exciting administration. In truth, aside from managing a short but well-conceived war against Iraq's Saddam Hussein, his administration's activities reflected his own noncontroversial personality. Meanwhile, he did little to lift the spirits of the poor, who spent four more years in poverty without an appreciable helping hand from the White House.

However, he did sign two important bills into law in 1990 that potentially had a positive impact on the poor. First, he authorized the Americans with Disabilities Act on July 26. The bipartisan bill, which banned discrimination based on disability in employment, public accommodations, and transportation, is seen as one of Bush's major accomplishments. The second significant bill he succeeded in passing was the Clean Air Act, which focused on three aspects of clean air: reducing urban smog, curbing acid rain, and eliminating industrial emissions of toxic chemicals. It was widely known that Bush was a staunch environmentalist, and he achieved this success by working with the business community—instead of fighting with them—so that the American people in general would benefit. Again, Congress passed the bill with bipartisan support and the president signed the Clean Air Act on November 15, 1990. Bush also supported the Equal Rights Amendment, food stamps, and Planned Parenthood, and he opposed a constitutional ban on abortion. Despite his own public statements, he was a moderate, indeed, in many areas.

But Bush could hardly have done much to transform the poor of the nation in four brief years. Accordingly, when he left office, the feeling in the country that there was still an enormous amount of work that needed to be done to escape from the 1991 recession. Defeating Bush as he sought reelection in 1992, Bill Clinton repeated the exhortation of his aide James Carville: "It's the economy, stupid."[28]

Postscript: It is essential to emphasize that, although he did not make much progress in fighting poverty, George H. W. Bush was known as "a very human leader . . . [who] would nonetheless serve and govern with humility. . . . And without his brief moment in power, neither of the iconic presidents before or after him—Ronald Reagan or Bill Clinton—would have enjoyed the same measure of success," wrote historian Timothy Naftali.[29]

WILLIAM JEFFERSON (BILL) CLINTON (1993–2001), forty-six years old and a Democrat from Arkansas, was sworn in as the forty-second president on January 20, 1993. He defeated incumbent George H. W. Bush, in part, because of the poor state of the economy and because a third-party candidate, independent Ross Perot, took a good chunk of the vote away from Bush. Clinton and his vice-presidential nominee, Senator Al Gore of Tennessee, won 43.0 percent of the vote to Bush's 37.4 percent and Perot's 18.9 percent. When Clinton took office, the U.S. population had numbered more than 250 million people.

Clinton, whose lifelong ambition was to be president, ran as "the Man from Hope," Arkansas, using the name of his birthplace as a slogan in his campaign. Clinton focused like a laser beam almost exclusively on economic issues, concentrating on ways to overcome the slow growth of the American economy. He also sought to energize the Democratic Party by emphasizing his interest in issues facing the middle class: government spending to stimulate the economy, more stringent crime laws, jobs for poverty-stricken welfare recipients, and tax reform to spread the wealth among the many instead of the rich.

Clinton also played on traditional Democratic values, supporting such issues as curtailing military expenditures to promote domestic social programs, gun control, legalized abortion, environmental protection, equal employment and educational opportunity, national health insurance (at the time, nearly sixty million Americans, a majority of them poor, did not have health insurance), and gay rights. He was, in a phrase, a hybrid liberal who combined traditional values with groundbreaking middle-of-the-road programs that would reform the "safety net" that had long been a heavy burden on taxpayers since the FDR years.

He was, in fact, a "New Democrat" who held out the hope that he could both unify the country and put it back on a stable economic track. At the same time, he campaigned as a devotee of the Reverend Dr. Martin Luther King's philosophy of nonviolence and as a dedicated supporter of the civil rights revolution. Historian Nigel Hamilton put the Clinton campaign in proper perspective when he wrote in his book *Bill Clinton: An American Journey:* "The contrast with President Bush— who had won the 1988 election in part by taking as a running mate an unknown younger man who would avoid the geriatric pall that had clouded the Reagan administration in its final days, but who kept his . . . vice president [Dan Quayle] at arm's length—was palpable."[30] The young, vigorous, upbeat, fresh faces of Clinton and his running mate Gore were a welcome change after eight years of Reagan and Bush. By 1992 many saw the latter as two "old" men with conservative ideas who had been in power long enough.

The election of November 3, 1992, moreover, was a momentous event that excited so many Americans that a record 104 million turned out in a country of 230 million voters—a 10 percent increase over the previous presidential election. The public was clearly clamoring for change. Even before Clinton took the oath of office, he quietly made it his business to take a firsthand look at poverty in Washington, D.C., the city in which he would live for the next four to eight years. He explored the city during the transition period before he took office. As he wrote in his book *My Life:*

> From the White House I drove two miles into north Washington, to a neighborhood beset by *poverty* [italics added], unemployment, drugs, and crime. On Georgia Avenue, I got out of the car and walked for a block, shaking hands and talking to merchants and other citizens about their problems and what I could do to help. Eight people had been killed the previous year within a mile of where I stopped. I got food from a Chinese takeout where the worker operated behind

bulletproof glass for safety. Parents of school-aged children said they were frightened because so many of their kids' classmates brought guns to school. The people who lived in Washington's inner city were often forgotten by Congress and the White House, despite the fact that the federal government still retained substantial control over the city's affairs. I wanted the city's residents to know I cared about their problems and wanted to be a good neighbor.[31]

When Clinton was sworn in on January 20, 1993, in his inaugural speech he set the country in an entirely different direction and asked Americans to think of the unfortunate among us:

> Today we celebrate the mystery of American renewal. This ceremony is held in the depth of winter. But, by the words we speak and the faces we show the world, we force the spring, a spring reborn in the world's oldest democracy, that brings forth the vision and courage to reinvent America. When our founders boldly declared America's Independence to the world and our purposes to the Almighty, they knew that America, to endure, would have to change. . . . Each generation of Americans must define what it means to be an American.[32]

Clinton's inaugural address, it is important to recall, also drew comparisons with John F. Kennedy's twenty-two years earlier. Clinton himself helped convey that comparison by harking back in theme to Kennedy's call for Americans to help their country and by repeating that government alone could not create the nation people wanted. Addressing the public at large, he said: "You, too, must play your part in our renewal. I challenge a new generation of young Americans to a season of service. . . . There is so much to be done. . . .

". . . From this joyful mountaintop of celebration, we hear a call to service in the valley. We have heard the trumpets. We have changed the guard. And now, each in our own way, and with God's help, we must answer the call."[33]

It is worth recalling for history's sake that the day before his inauguration—on January 19, 1993—Clinton invited the Kennedy family to accompany him when he visited the graves of both John F. Kennedy and Robert F. Kennedy in Arlington National Cemetery. Scholars David E. Proctor and Kurt Ritter wrote,

> This was a media event and was shown on the evening news programs of both ABC and NBC that night. The next day, the news media found that Clinton's inaugural style echoed Kennedy's inaugural. [TV

political analyst] Jeff Greenfield reported on the ABC evening news that the tone, substance, and themes of Clinton's address were modeled on Kennedy's speech—a point that was reinforced as the news program showed a series of comparative excerpts from both speeches. The impact of such coverage was to call attention to [Clinton's] relative youthfulness, to the circumstances that (like Kennedy) Clinton represented the rise of a new generation to political power, and to the transfer of power from the Republican Party to the Democratic Party.[34]

It was unmistakable: Clinton had long admired John F. Kennedy. Clinton's friends had arranged to release a photo of Kennedy shaking hands with the sixteen-year-old Clinton from Hot Springs High School, Arkansas, in the White House's Rose Garden on July 24, 1963. Clinton had been in Washington, D.C., as one of two delegates from Arkansas to the American Legion Boys Nation Convention.

Clinton was no Jack Kennedy, but the sense of hope and promise that he brought with him to the Oval Office was, indeed, similar to the excitement that Jack Kennedy generated. Clinton was well aware of the voters' high expectations of him. There was no doubt whatsoever that his arrival meant the changing of the guard. From the outset, Clinton raised the hopes of millions of people living in abject poverty. For the first time since Lyndon B. Johnson in the 1960s, a president had put the word "poverty" back into mainstream politics.

Clinton wasted no time reviving the call to help those in poverty. In a speech before a joint session of Congress on February 17, 1993, he was emphatic in his concentration on "poverty," often using the word in the speech, as well as in many other major speeches he gave during his two terms in office. Clinton said: "To those who care for our sick, who tend our children, who do our most difficult and tiring jobs, the new direction I propose will make this solemn, simple commitment: By expanding the refundable earned-income tax credit, we will make history. We will reward the work of millions of working poor Americans by realizing the principle that if you work 40 hours a week and you've got a child in the house, you will *no longer be in poverty* [italics added]."[35]

During his first term, while working with a Republican Congress, Clinton successfully put into law measures to reform social welfare in America and to enhance aid to poor people and seniors needing medical care. Clinton encouraged the economy to grow slowly and was able to help it recover more quickly. Business earnings increased, creating new jobs and enabling the poor to survive the economic crisis.

Clinton had a number of initiatives in his first term, some successful, some not. On the one hand, his effort to create a universal health insurance plan, delegated to his wife, Hillary Rodham Clinton, failed because the president's unelected spouse and her task force worked behind closed doors and developed a program that was so complicated and bulky Congress hardly understood it, let alone the public. Creating it in secret turned out to be a major political blunder and cost both Clintons' considerable political prestige.

On the other hand, Clinton created a National Economic Council and announced an ambitious program to reverse twelve years of what he called "trickle-down economics." He created "empowerment zones" in poor communities and introduced a welfare reform measure that would put more responsibility on poor people to find jobs and break the cycle of poverty. But approaching the topic of welfare was always sticky in politics—and Clinton knew it.

One social historian, Michael B. Katz, author of *In the Shadow of the Poorhouse: A Social History of Welfare in America*, expressed it this way:

> Welfare had become the lightning rod for Americans' anxieties over their work, incomes, families, and futures. Poor, young black mothers increasingly took the blame for violence, crime, and drugs; for the taxes on overburdened workers; for the rot eating its way through the American dream. In truth, single mothers faced enormous problems and the welfare system did little to help them toward independence and security. In all sorts of ways, welfare needed reform. . . . For politicians, however, "welfare" served other purposes. Anti-welfare rhetoric propelled candidates into office as it deflected attention from the politicians' failure to confront racism and the structural sources of poverty, widening inequality, and falling wages.[36]

Clinton also introduced the Elementary and Secondary Education Act, which ended the process of giving poor children what Clinton called a "watered-down" curriculum. At the time, Clinton said that too often children from poor families were placed in special education classes, not because they were unable to learn, but because they had fallen behind in inferior schools and "had too little support at home."[37] In addition, Clinton was able to get bipartisan support from Congress to enact Head Start reform in education and to create the National Service Program. Clinton called the education package "one of the most important achievements of my first two years in office."[38]

Despite his various government initiatives to help the poor and near-poor, public grumblings—mostly from Republicans—that government was becoming too intrusive in people's daily lives continued. This theme was not new, but with Clinton's announcement of each new program, congressional resistance to government hardened. Finally, to keep his efforts in perspective, Clinton announced on his weekly radio show on January 27, 1996, that "the era of big government is over." However, he added a cautionary note for those who might think he was changing course on helping those in need, by adding that America "can't go back to a time when our citizens were just left to fend for themselves." This statement drove a stake in the ground that would be remembered for years to come.[39]

On August 26, 1996, Clinton signed what he termed a "landmark" welfare reform bill known in the maze of the bureaucracy as the Personal Responsibility and Work Opportunity and Reconciliation Act. It passed with the support of majorities of both parties. Under the act, the federal government gives to the states annual lump sums to assist the poor. In turn, the states must adhere to certain criteria to ensure that those receiving aid are being encouraged to move from welfare to work. The bill also made legal immigrants ineligible for welfare during their first five years in the country.

Despite some drawbacks, Clinton signed the bill because, as he put it, "it was the best chance America would have for a long time to change the incentives in the welfare system from dependence to empowerment through work." The administration then organized the Welfare to Work Partnership and signed up employers who would commit to hiring welfare recipients. "Eventually," Clinton wrote with pride, "twenty thousand companies in the partnership would hire more than one million people off welfare."[40]

Washington journalist Sidney Blumenthal attributed a more cynical political motive to Clinton's desire to cut down the welfare population. "One publicly unstated factor in the President's decision was his belief that the welfare reform law would remove race as an issue from the upcoming [presidential] campaign [in 1996] and beyond," he wrote in his book *The Clinton Wars.*[41]

One highly complementary view of this piece of legislation, meanwhile, comes from historian John Iceland, author of *Poverty in America: A Handbook,* who put this act into historic perspective: "This was a dramatic and controversial measure that brought an end to six decades of federal social policy guaranteeing at least a minimum level of aid to those in poverty."[42]

What did all of Clinton's effort on welfare reform do for the country and the poor? Overall, by the time Clinton left office in 2001, according to Clinton, welfare rolls had been cut from 14.1 million to 5.8 million—a 60 percent decrease.[43] The bottom line on poverty? The percentage of families and individuals below the poverty level dropped from 14.8 when Clinton took office down to 11.3 when he left. Although the decrease was hardly enough to make a major dent in poverty, it represented the largest six-year drop in poverty in nearly thirty years. "Signing the welfare reform bill," Clinton wrote in *My Life*, "was one of the most important decisions of my presidency. I had spent most of my career trying to move people from welfare to work, and ending welfare 'as we know it,' had been a central promise of my 1992 campaign."[44]

Yet another topic that Clinton tackled that most previous presidents had not was race relations. He also appointed several African Americans, both men and women, to leading posts in his administration. And author Toni Morrison called him "our first black president." Clinton appointed the distinguished black scholar John Hope Franklin to head a seven-member commission to come up with recommendations about how to build "One America" in the twenty-first century. Eighteen months later, the advisory board completed a set of recommendations primarily focused on policy initiatives in civil rights enforcement, education, economic security and workforce development, community integration, and the administration of justice. The advisory board also called for a meaningful long-term strategy to advance race relations in the twenty-first century. While the intentions were good, little action resulted from it. Clinton's critics called it a politically motivated scheme to soothe the feelings of blacks and other minorities.

In the end, the Clinton record is impressive. His administration's most outstanding achievements in the area of helping the poor included leading the longest economic expansion in American history. The country added more than twenty-two million new jobs, or more than were created in the previous twelve years, and saw the lowest unemployment in thirty years, dropping from more than 7 percent in 1993 to 4 percent in November 2000. Unemployment for African Americans and Hispanics fell to the lowest rates on record, and the rate for women was the lowest in more than forty years. The administration raised education standards, increased school choice, and doubled education and training investment. The country enjoyed the lowest crime rate in twenty-six years, and more than 100,000 police were added to the nation's streets as part of the 1994 Crime Bill. Aiding twenty million Americans, the Family and Medical Leave Act helped parents succeed at work and at home.

In addition, the Clinton administration achieved the smallest welfare rolls in thirty-two years. The president, having pledged "to end welfare as we know it" during his campaign, signaled his heart was in the right place. He certainly was a first-rate salesman of his programs.

Clinton left the White House with a stained record after an infamous Whitewater real estate investigation and the probe into his affair with White House intern Monica Lewinsky wound up with his being the second president to be impeached. But Clinton himself put his two terms in perspective this way:

> Although I would always regret what I had done wrong, I will go to my grave being proud of what I had fought for in the impeachment battle, my last great showdown with the forces I had opposed all of my life—those who had defended the old order of racial discrimination and segregation in the South and played on the insecurities and fears of the white working class in which I grew up; who had opposed the women's movement, the environmental movement, the gay-rights movement, and other efforts to expand our national community as assaults on the natural order; who believed government should be run for the benefit of powerful, entrenched interests and favored tax cuts for the wealthy over health care and better education for children.[45]

GEORGE W. BUSH, at fifty-four years old, was a former Republican governor of Texas when he became the forty-third president of the United States (2001–2009) after narrowly defeating Vice President Al Gore. In the bitter, drawn-out 2000 election, although Bush won the electoral margin of 271 votes to 266, Gore won the popular vote 50,999,897 to 50,456,002. The U.S. Supreme Court ruled 5–4 in Bush's favor, making the final decision.

The presidential election of 2000 was hotly contested from the outset, with numerous candidates in both parties vying for their party's nomination. Among the Democrats was North Carolina Democratic senator John Edwards who, during the course of the primaries, actually broke precedence and ran his entire campaign almost exclusively on the issue of poverty. Although he failed to win the nomination, he won a place on the ticket with Vice President Al Gore on the basis of his populist appeal to the underdog.[46]

Bush and Vice President Dick Cheney appealed to a different kind of voter. Author Kevin Phillips offered this perspective on Bush: "Bush was the first president to clearly represent the kind of low-tax, low-service, high-economic-stratification brand of Southern economic conservatism, since the little-remembered Zachary Taylor of Louisiana won the election of 1848."[47]

In his inaugural address on January 20, 2001, Bush offered some clues about his philosophy of government and how he intended to govern. To his credit, he recognized the disparity between rich and poor in America and expressed his concern this way: "While many of our citizens prosper, others doubt the promise, even the justice, of our own country. The ambitions of some Americans are limited by failing schools and hidden prejudice and the circumstances of their birth. And sometimes our differences run so deep, it seems we share a continent, but not a country."

Bush referred once to the word "poverty" in this context: "America, at its best, is compassionate. In the quiet of American conscience, we know that deep, persistent *poverty* [italics added] is unworthy of our nation's promise.

". . . I will live and lead by these principles: to advance my convictions with civility, to pursue the public interest with courage, to speak for greater justice and compassion, to call for responsibility and try to live it as well."[48]

In his domestic programs he did make some effort to help the poor, directly or indirectly, under the banner of "compassionate conservatism." His father, George H. W. Bush, had originated the phrase in 1986, and the younger Bush resurrected it in his campaign of 2000 as his own favorite campaign slogan. In any case, George W. Bush frequently used it as a backdrop to many of the programs and events he initiated. His first major thrust was in the area of education. He was promoting the topic on September 11, 2001, in a Florida elementary school as the nation suffered a terrorist attack that would make a huge impact on his presidency and draw the country into war. Some three thousand people were killed on that fateful morning when two planes plowed into the World Trade towers in New York City, demolishing them, and two other planes hijacked by terrorists slammed into the Pentagon and into a hillside in Pennsylvania. Al Qaeda was held responsible for the attacks. Bush subsequently ballyhooed an educational reform known as the No Child Left Behind Act, which passed with bipartisan support. The Clinton administration originally created the framework, which had promoted Clinton's concept of school accountability in a report titled "Goals 2000" for eight years, and Clinton had mentioned it in his 1999 State of the Union address as a breakthrough in education reform.

Bush picked up the cue enthusiastically and moved this program forward. Bush signed the No Child Left Behind bill on January 8, 2002. It called for nationwide testing with the results linked to federal government funds. Democrats expressed reservations about the bill because, they said, it was not sufficiently funded. Although it originally had the full public support of Senator Edward M. Kennedy, he, too, later criticized the lack of funding. Further criticism came from Senator John Kerry, the Democratic candidate for president in 2004, who pointed to the legislation as a failure also because of the funding issue.

In a hard-hitting speech on September 2, 2004, in Palm Beach, Florida, Bush noted the gains he had achieved by the No Child Left Behind law. It has since been modified and amended to meet the objections of the teachers as well as politicians, who felt it was not helping students in poverty-stricken areas where schools were closed because of low performances. He also prominently mentioned it in his 2004 address to the Republican National Convention, pointing out that by previously accepting low scholastic achievement by minority students as the norm, the United States had been engaging in the "the soft bigotry of low expectations."[49]

Bush, however, gave himself high marks on the program. In January 2008, he selected a successful school, the Horace Greeley Elementary School, to visit in Chicago while marking the sixth anniversary of No Child Left Behind. Bush wrote in his book, *Decision Points:* "That the school, named for the nineteenth century abolitionist, was seventy percent Hispanic and ninety-two percent poor. It had outperformed most public schools in Chicago. . . ." It was uplifting, he wrote, "to see a school full of low-income minority students thrive. . . . At the end of my visit, I told students, parents, and the press what I had long believed: No Child Left Behind is a piece of civil rights legislation."[50]

Bush also passed the now-infamous "Bush tax cuts" that reduced rates on the wealthy and, at the time, appeared not to endanger the revenue surplus that Clinton had left Bush. As it turned out, of course, those tax cuts—and the costs of two unfunded wars—eventually became a major issue for the Obama administration, which inherited the beginning of by far the worst and longest recession in U.S. history since the Great Depression.

Yet another Bush program, while controversial, was his Office of Faith-Based and Community Initiatives. At the outset of his term in 2000, Bush lined up Republicans in Congress to pass legislation that would enable the government to fund various religious organizations on a tax-exempt basis so they could do more for the poor and the needy.

Critics claimed that this move was infringed on the separation of church and state in the Constitution. Still, the program had some success, especially among African Americans and other minorities whom it helped. In fact, it also gave Bush a lift in political support between 2000 and his reelection campaign in 2004. According to a CNN exit poll, Bush's support from African Americans increased during his presidency from 9 percent of the black vote in 2000 to 11 percent in 2004. Bush also encouraged the private and public sectors to hire more qualified minorities. One could speculate that a possible reason for the uptick in votes was that African Americans tend to be churchgoers and may have been influenced by the faith-based program.

This program, most political observers interpreted at the time, was an outgrowth of George W. Bush's profound belief in God. He proclaimed himself a deeply religious man and frequently mentioned God in his speeches as the guiding force in his life. The extent to which Bush believed in God was revealed during an interview on CBS *60 Minutes* program on December 5, 2007. Correspondent Mike Wallace interviewed Bob Woodward, who had written about the Bush presidency, and asked him about the lead-up to launching the 2003 war in Iraq. Wallace asked: "Did Mr. Bush ask his father for any advice?" Replied Woodward: "I asked the president about this. And President Bush said, 'Well, no,' and then he got defensive about it. Then he said something that really struck me. He said of his father, 'He is the wrong father to appeal to for advice. The wrong father to go to, to appeal to in terms of strength.' And then he said, 'There's a higher Father that I appeal to.'"[51]

One quality of Bush's personality is that he was sensitive to criticism on racial issues. In *Decision Points,* Bush recalls the barrage of criticism he received because of the government's failure to prepare properly for Hurricane Katrina on the Gulf Coast in 2005, when many thousands of people—a great majority of them African Americans—were hit hard and lost their homes. The unfolding story of how the first responders at all levels of government badly bungled their actions during and after the hurricane remains on the minds of Americans—especially black Americans—as much as the storm and its aftermath have. That disaster went down in history as the most destructive catastrophe in America. The blacks' reaction was bitter. Civil rights leader Jesse Jackson compared the New Orleans Convention Center (to which thousands of victims fled) as "the hull of a slave ship." A member of the Black Congressional Caucus claimed that if the storm victims had been "white, middle-class Americans they would have received more help. . . ."[52]

Bush responded to those comments in his book:

> Five years later, I can barely write those words without feeling dis-
> gusted. I am deeply insulted by the suggestions that we allowed Amer-
> ican citizens to suffer because they were black. As I told the press at
> the time, "The storm didn't discriminate, and neither will the recovery
> effort. When those Coast Guard choppers, many of whom were first
> on the scene, were pulling people off of roofs, they didn't check the
> color of a person's skin. The more I thought about it the angrier I felt.
> I was raised to believe that racism is one of the greatest evils in society."

And so it went. Perception often is far different than the truth. George
W. Bush found that out the hard way. "I told Laura [his wife] at the
time that it was the worst moment of my presidency. I feel the same way
today" [in 2010].[53]

Obviously, he was not seen as sympathetic to minorities, especially
blacks, and partly as a result he accomplished little in the way of reducing poverty across the nation. To say that he was sidetracked and dis-
tracted by two wars he initiated himself would be an understatement.
Nonetheless, the historical record, at this point, does not reflect any
credit upon this particular president when it came to poverty—even
despite his programs and his administration providing $400 million in
loans to restore the campuses of and renew recruiting efforts at historically black colleges and universities in the Gulf Coast region. In addition, he showed the "compassionate conservative" side of himself when
he proposed a surprisingly balanced immigration program in a speech
on May 15, 2006, which was all-encompassing and included both
building a fence on the border and offering a pathway to citizenship.
Unfortunately, his own party leaders virtually ignored it.

Postscript: Bush's record in terms of what he did to eliminate poverty was quite unremarkable. It should be noted that the percentage
of people living below the poverty level during his two terms actually
rose from 11.3 to 13.2.[54] For the Bush family legacy, he succeeded in
accomplishing that rarest of American political events: a father and son
who both served as president of the United States. Only John Adams
and his son John Quincy Adams served in that capacity before the
Bushes arrived.

As for George W. Bush's legacy, a National Public Radio program
that aired on January 7, 2009, described it this way: "President Bush
leaves office as one of the least popular presidents ever, but he says it's
up to history to judge him. Bush likes to recall that Harry Truman was

widely reviled when he left the White House 56 years ago but decades later became an icon of strength in adversity."[55]

A more recent assessment of the George W. Bush years in terms of the economy came from a Nobel laureate, economist Joseph E. Stiglitz, who stated in *Vanity Fair* magazine that, as a result of the crippling legacy of Bush's stewardship of the economy, he saw "a generation-long struggle to recoup."[56] These harsh words from one of the nation's most respected economists appear to be quite prophetic so far.

Enter **BARACK OBAMA** (2009–Present), an outspoken, forty-seven-year-old charismatic junior senator from Illinois who wanted to heal a divided nation. Clearly he was an intellectual and at times evoked with his moving prose the cerebral Democrat Adlai Stevenson, a former Illinois governor, who had lost the 1952 and 1956 presidential elections to Dwight D. Eisenhower. Obama was, indeed, a law professor, author of two books, and a conciliator who had worked as an effective community organizer in the poor neighborhoods of Chicago and—against all odds—had catapulted himself into the spotlight of the Democratic Party and, in fact, the entire nation. During the campaign, in which he stressed his catchy "Yes, We Can" theme of hope and change in his oratory, his body language was passionate and energetic. He poured his heart out with an idealistic vision of uniting our badly torn republic, and voters were enticed. Above all, he stressed civility in politics and a fundamental desire for bipartisanship in Washington. He won a history-making election over Arizona senator John McCain by a margin of 52.9 percent to 45.6 percent of the vote and became America's first black president.

A lifelong advocate for the poor, Obama—as a young graduate of Columbia University and Harvard Law School—brushed aside lucrative job offers from prestigious law firms and moved to the South Side of Chicago to work as a community organizer. He worked with Chicago residents, churches, and local government officials to set up job-training programs for the unemployed and after-school programs for kids. He was genuinely concerned with the plight of the poor. The civil rights movement inspired him and his goal of working at the grassroots level.

He first rose to prominence with a rousing speech as the largely unknown keynote speaker at the National Democratic Convention in Boston on July 27, 2004. There, his voice booming, he struck a chord and roused an audience of attendees with this simple but elegant phrase:

"There is not a black America and white America and Latino America and Asian America—there's the United States of America."[57]

Elected as the junior senator from his state in November 2004, he made it his business to listen and learn. Obama's election to the Senate instantly placed him as the highest-ranking African American office-holder in the country. In a twist of fate, one of the previous occupants of his assigned desk on the Senate floor had been Robert F. Kennedy. At the outset, Obama generated considerable interest with his two bestselling books—*Dreams from My Father: A Story of Race and Inheritance* and *The Audacity of Hope: Thoughts on Reclaiming the American Dream*—making him a long-shot contender for the Democratic presidential nomination in 2008. As an active senator for three years, he had voted with his party 95 percent of the time. Then came his blockbuster political decision to run for president.

He announced his campaign for the presidency on a freezing cold day, February 10, 2007, before the backdrop of the Old State Capitol in Springfield, Illinois. In that kickoff speech, Obama declared that the founders had devised a system of government that that can be changed. Referring to the Great Depression as an example, he cited the example of how America put people back to work and lifted millions out of poverty. He spoke in lofty terms from the same site that Abraham Lincoln had begun his 1858 Senate campaign. "The metaphor that day," wrote David Remnick, author of *The Bridge: The Life and Rise of Barack Obama,* "was Lincoln—the man with scant experience and potential greatness facing a nation on the brink."[58] It was obviously no coincidence that Obama selected that particular location for his announcement. After a grueling four-and-a-half-month primary contest against Hillary Clinton and other Democratic candidates, Obama finally prevailed and won the nomination.

In Denver on August 28, 2008, Obama accepted the nomination at the Democratic National Convention. Obama's speech outlined the issues of his general election campaign, pledging, among other things, to "cut taxes for ninety-five percent of all working families" and "to provide affordable, accessible health care for every single American." After citing the sad state of affairs in which America found itself, Obama specifically called attention to the overriding issue of poverty and unemployment in America by using the word "poverty" three times in the course of his acceptance speech:[59]

America, we are better than these last eight years. We are a better country than this.

> . . . We are more compassionate than a government that lets veterans sleep on our streets and families slide into *poverty* [italics added]; that sits on its hands while a major American city drowns before our eyes. For over two decades, he's [John McCain] subscribed to that old, discredited Republican philosophy—give more and more to those with the most and hope that prosperity trickles down to everyone else. In Washington, they call this the Ownership Society, but what it really means is—you're on your own. Out of work? Tough luck. No health care? The market will fix it. Born into *poverty* [italics added]? Pull yourself up by your own bootstraps—even if you don't have boots. You're on your own. . . . I will build new partnerships to defeat the threats of the 21st century: terrorism and nuclear proliferation; *poverty* [italics added] and genocide; climate change and disease.

During his campaign for president in 2008—managed by his cool-headed alter-go, Democratic operative David Plouffe and his politically savvy senior political adviser David Axlerod—Obama pledged to lead a new federal approach to revitalize communities stricken by the economic crisis, as well as communities that were hurting before it began. His "Yes, We Can!" motto became a call to action and attracted millions of Americans—young and old, black, Hispanic, and white—to vote for him. One of the highlights—and a controversial moment—of his campaign came during a fiery exchange candidate Obama had with man in a crowd whom the media tabbed as "Joe the plumber," or Samuel Joseph Wurzelbacher, on October 12, 2008, three days before the final presidential debate. Obama met residents in Wurzelbacher's Holland, Ohio, neighborhood. The national media immediately publicized Wurzelbacher's taking issue at an outdoor rally with then-candidate Obama's plan to let the Bush tax cuts expire for those making $250,000 or more. Obama replied by suggesting that if the wealth were spread around, it would be good for everybody.

While Obama did not specifically mention the word "poverty" in his inaugural address on January 20, 2009, he recognized the economic crisis that Americans faced. He stated, in part:

> Our economy is badly weakened, a consequence of greed and irresponsibility on the part of some, but also our collective failure to make hard choices and prepare the nation for a new age. Homes have been lost; jobs shed; businesses shuttered. Our health care is too costly; our schools fail too many; and each day brings further evidence that the ways we use energy strengthen our adversaries and threaten our planet.

These are the indicators of crisis, subject to data and statistics. Less measurable but no less profound is a sapping of confidence across our land—a nagging fear that America's decline is inevitable, that the next generation must lower its sights.

Today I say to you that the challenges we face are real. They are serious and they are many. They will not be met easily or in a short span of time. But know this, America—they will be met.[60]

With such an unusually bullish beginning, Obama opened his presidency with the nation's expectations so unrealistically high on inauguration day that they were bound to be disappointed. It took less than a year before some people began to become disillusioned with their new president. "By the time the [first] year was over," wrote Remnick, "his [Obama's] visions of post-partisan comity had given way to reality of prolonged battle with the congressional Republicans and conservative Democrats. . . . It was hard to imagine that any president would have remained popular for a long time in terrible unemployment, record deficits, and political rancor."[61]

After Obama's first year, the highly respected historian Michael Beschloss sized up Obama's performance in a PBS television interview on December 30, 2009. Asked if Obama's health care bill would be seen as a "big deal" in history, Beschloss responded:

Well, Medicare was passed in 1965, but if it didn't work it would probably have been repealed pretty quickly and harmed Lyndon Johnson's legacy. With health care affecting so many people's lives, it will be considered a big achievement for Barack Obama. When it came to the financial markets crashing, the people were angry. An enormous number of Americans were thrown out of jobs. They looked at Wall Street and saw those huge bonuses [No doubt the spark that set off the Occupy Wall Street protests across the country]. That was an awful lot for people to swallow.

Nonetheless, Beschloss was bullish on Obama. He added: "Obama has shown he is a multi-tasker par excellence. If you think of what he did in his first year, in terms of legislative accomplishments he is within the range of FDR in 1932 and LBJ in 1965, and an awful lot was on the line. . . . He can say, 'I have done everything I could to keep this nation safe from terrorism,' that is an accomplishment in itself."[62]

Distinguished historian Doris Kearns Goodwin gave an online essay in *The Daily Beast* on January 19, 2010, and said that Obama's first year was, in fact, better than John F. Kennedy's. She asserted:

If you look at John F. Kennedy's first year from the outside, it was a disaster. . . .

The most important thing Obama had to confront was the historic collapse of the economy and the financial system, the likes of which had not been seen since 1929. In 1929, because of the insufficient and mistaken steps taken, the economy continued to decline and ended up in the Great Depression. I think most economists would agree that between the combination of stimulus and bailout steps, the economy is on the road to recovery. That alone would be an historic marker of success in Obama's first year.

Even with the need to prevent economic collapse, Obama has been able to move forward with progressive domestic goals. What has been overlooked is that the stimulus bill includes substantial investments in energy, education [Obama launched his "Race to the Top" program for public schools under Education Secretary Arnie Duncan in an attempt to improve the quality of education in America by awarding sizeable financial grants to those public schools that came up with new and create ways to improve the quality of students results in the classrooms], infrastructure, and *antipoverty measures* [italics added], adding up to the largest social investments since LBJ's Great Society.[63]

Continuing the discussion about Obama's accomplishments on another interview program on December 21, 2011, Goodwin added: "I think there are accomplishments that will last in history—breaking down Al Qaeda and finally getting Osama bin Laden. What's happening in Libya he helped inspire, passing the health care law, [repealing] 'don't ask, don't tell,' education, financial reform." She continued, "None of that is being absorbed right now because people are not happy with the economy. So it's almost going to have to wait five, ten years for people to look back and see those accomplishments."[64]Among them, financial reform was introduced in the Dodd-Frank bill (Senator Christopher Dodd and Representative Barney Frank, both Democrats), which created a sound economic foundation to grow jobs, protect consumers, rein in Wall Street and big bonuses, and end bailouts and "too big to fail" banks and other financial institutions.

Yet another well-respected journalist, Katrina vanden Heuvel, publisher and editor of *The Nation* magazine, reminded us after Obama's first year in office, that

Barack Obama was elected president at a time defined by hope and fear in equal measure. . . .

The night Obama was elected, relief was felt around the world. There was a widespread feeling that the United States had turned its back on eight years of destructive, swaggering unilateralism and was re-embracing the global community. In many ways, the election was a referendum on an extremist conservatism that has guided (and deformed) American politics and society since the 1980s. The spectacular failures of the Bush administration and the shifts in public opinion on the economy and the Iraq War presented a mandate for bold action and a historic opportunity for a progressive governing agenda.

A year later, it's clear we are a long way from building a new order and transforming the prevailing paradigm of American politics. That will take more than one election. It requires continued mobilization, strategic creativity and, yes, audacity on the part of independent thinkers, activists and organizers. The structural obstacles to change are considerable, but at least we now have the political space to push for far-reaching reforms.

. . . Yes, his economic recovery plan was too small and too deferential to the Republican Party and tax cuts. But it has kept the economy from falling into the abyss, and it includes more new net public investment in anti-poverty measures than any program since Lyndon Johnson's Great Society.[65]

During his first two years, in fact, Obama's accomplishments were largely unheralded because of the intransigence of the Republicans in Congress. Nonetheless, his legislative and executive accomplishments resulted in a bill designed to reform Wall Street practices and to end taxpayer bailouts, new home sales saw their biggest jump in forty-seven years, manufacturing grew by the most since 2004, orders rose for most durable goods, consumer confidence rose, and start-up activity in business was higher than it had been during the dot-com boom. Also, Obama overhauled the food safety system, advanced women's rights in the workplace, expanded access to medical care and provided subsidies for people who couldn't afford it, expanded the Children's Health Insurance Program, fixed the preexisting conditions travesty (and rescissions) in health insurance, overhauled the credit card industry to make it much more consumer-friendly, passed legislation regulating the financial sector, and created the Consumer Financial Protection Bureau.

Obama time and time again stressed the income inequality gap—the "great divide," as it was labeled—and asked Congress to help him enable everyone in America to compete with the same rules in the same game on "an even playing field." In his 2012 State of the Union message on January 24, 2012, Obama stated, in part:

> The defining issue of our time is how to keep that promise [of the American dream] alive. No challenge is more urgent. No debate is more important. We can either settle for a country where a shrinking number of people do really well, while a growing number of Americans barely get by. Or we can restore an economy where everyone gets a fair shot, and everyone does their fair share, and everyone plays by the same set of rules. What's at stake aren't Democratic values or Republican values, but American values. We have to reclaim them
>
> . . . Let's never forget: Millions of Americans who work hard and play by the rules every day deserve Government and a financial system that do the same. It's time to apply the same rules from top to bottom. No bailouts, no handouts, and no copouts. An America built to last insists on responsibility from everybody.
>
> . . . I'm a Democrat. But I believe what Republican Abraham Lincoln believed: That Government should do for people only what they cannot do better by themselves, and no more.[66]

Some pundits wrote that the president in this message had decided to duck the poverty issue, mistakenly believing that a "rising tide will lift all boats." And both he and the Republican candidates chose silence on the imperfectly correlated issue of race.

In 2012, Obama was the object of scorn—bitter and some plainly dishonest—from virtually all of the candidates for the Republican nomination for president. Mitt Romney accused him of making the recession worse or trying to turn America into a "European state." Further, Romney accused Obama of being a threat to the "mortal soul of America" as well as attempting to bring about a fundamental transformation of American society into a socialist welfare state. Newt Gingrich, in a veiled attempt to bring racism into the campaign, accused Obama of being "the most effective food stamp president in history." Gingrich's mistaken assumption was that most people on food stamps were black or Hispanic. He also accused Obama of governing from the "radical left" and of undermining capitalism with his plea for more income equality. As they continued, the personal and policy slurs against the president seemingly knew no boundaries.

The facts, which Obama's team had difficulty getting out to the public because it was so overwhelmed by negative attacks, were quite the opposite. Putting events in perspective, as soon as he took office

Obama continued the huge $835 billion bailout of the banks that Bush had begun and, in addition, initiated a bailout of the auto industry. "In retrospect," wrote journalist Andrew Sullivan in *Newsweek* in January 2012, these initiatives "were far more successful than anyone has yet fully given Obama the credit for."[67] Unemployment, which at one point peaked to 10.2 percent at the height of the recession, began a downward trend. At this writing, it was still declining with some ups and downs but was still too high for anyone's comfort, let alone those millions of men and women still out of work after Obama's nearly four years in office. Not to mention that dozens of senior executives at bailed out banks were still awarding themselves multi-million-dollar bonuses even while ordinary citizens could not beg, borrow, or buy mortgages. People were furious—and rightly so.

Taking the long view, Nicholas D. Kristof, a columnist for the *New York Times*, observed in early February 2012: "Persistent poverty is America's great moral challenge, but it's far more than that. As a practical matter, we can't solve educational problems, health care costs, government spending or economic competitiveness as long as a chunk of our population is locked in an underclass."[68] In other words, economic disparity is beginning to trump race as the key cause of poverty, and whites are as susceptible of falling below the poverty line as blacks and other minorities are.

Kristof cited Charles Murray's book titled *Coming Apart: The State of White America, 1960–2010*, which highlighted the social aspects of the crisis among unskilled white workers. "Murray is correct in noting that it is troubling that growing numbers of working-class men drop out of the labor force," wrote Brooks. "The proportion of men of prime working age with only a high school education who say they are 'out of the labor force' has quadrupled since 1968, to 12 percent."[69]

Kristof wrote that he fears the nation is facing "a crisis in which a chunk of working-class America risks being calcified into an underclass, marked by drugs, despair, family decline, high incarceration rates and a diminishing role of jobs and education as escalators of upward mobility." Kristof nailed the answer to how to begin to solve the poverty crisis when he wrote: "We need a national conversation about these dimensions of poverty. . . .

". . . So let's get real. A crisis is developing in the white working class, a byproduct of growing inequality in America. The pathologies are achingly real. But the solution isn't finger-wagging, or averting our eyes—but opportunity."[70]

Further evidence indicates that the income equality gap has become the dominant determinant factor between educational success and race. Stanford University sociologist Sean F. Reardon published a report in the *New York Times* in early 2012 that stated that "the gap in standardized tests scores between affluent and low-income students had grown by about 40 percent since the 1960s, and is now double the testing gap between blacks and whites. . . . The changes are tectonic, a result of social and economic processes unfolding over many decades." [71]

Perhaps the most all-encompassing record of Obama's first three and a half years in office (as of this writing) is found in Michael Grabell's book, *Money Well Spent? The Truth Behind the Trillion-Dollar Stimulus, the Biggest Economic Recovery Plan in History.* Grabell starts his treatise with this observation:

> The American Recovery and Reinvestment Act [ARRA] was the largest economic recovery plan in history. Better known as "the stimulus," the $825 billion package [It was also referred to as the $787 billion stimulus] passed in February 2009, a month after Obama took office] included a mixture of tax cuts, safety net spending, and long-term investments in renewable energy, education, and infrastructure. Adjusted for inflation, it was nearly five times more expensive than the Works Progress Administration (WPA), credited with easing if not helping to end the Great Depression. The stimulus cost more than it did to fight the Iraq War from 2003 to 2010. It was bigger than the Louisiana Purchase, the Manhattan Project, the moon race, and the Marshall Plan to rebuild Europe after World War II. When the various extensions of stimulus provisions are taken into account, the recovery program cost well over a trillion dollars. [72]

February 16, 2012, marked the third-year anniversary of President Obama's $787 billion economic stimulus package, but it turned out to be a mixed milestone. The unemployment rate held steady above 8 percent for thirty-six months, the longest period since World War II. In fact, according to the Bureau of Labor Statistics, the 8.3 percent unemployment rate was precisely where it stood three years before when the ARRA legislation was signed into law. The previous record for above 8 percent unemployment was twenty months, which transpired in the early 1980s.

As Grabell put it: "A common theme in the news coverage was that the White House bungled the message on the stimulus." [73]

Reporting on the political "buzz" that the stimulus package created, Grabell said it represented the government's largest investment in the country in its history. It comprised tax cuts, food stamps, unemployment checks, and education and health care money that halted the decline in state budgets. Following that, a stream of "shovel ready" infrastructure projects were launched, trying to get the economy rolling again. Investments in new energy sources, such as solar power, electric automobiles, wind farms, and other new and innovative businesses—even a novel "Cash for Clunkers" vehicle trade-in program and a $8,000 tax credit for first-time home buyers were added—were marginally successful.

But the stimulus did not turn out the way it was planned. In fact, while the administration made plenty of announcements, they did not appear to be part of a larger, cohesive plan, and the general public received no clear vision of Obama's plans for the future. His critics charged that perhaps Obama's most grievous error was in not getting his priorities in proper order. They saw him putting all of his goodwill into getting a massive health bill passed, while other actions—the jobs crisis, the care of battle-scarred veterans coming home from the wars in Iraq and Afghanistan, or a workable solution to the still-burning quandary of how to fix immigration, for example—were set aside or put into slow motion.

No matter how you look at it, Obama's first gigantic effort—similar to Franklin Roosevelt's in 1933—brought jeers instead of cheers. Despite all that it achieved, Grabell observes that,

> the Recovery Act did not bring about a strong sustainable recovery. [The Obama administration announced in March 2009 that the website http://www.recovery.gov would list all of the projects in the nation that had resulted from the stimulus package.] More than four years since the start of the recession, the economy remained horrendous. Businesses were reluctant to hire. Foreclosed homes sat empty. Infrastructure was still crumbling. With nearly all the money spent, the unemployment rate was 9 percent. Including those who had settled for part-time jobs or given up, it was more than 16 percent. The middle class and the working poor were increasingly unable to make ends meet. And nothing political leaders tried seemed to get us out of the ditch.[74]

Obama had a case to make, of course, but nobody in the White House—including the hard-nosed, outspoken Vice President Joe Biden—could get the attention of the mass media. At the same time, the White House was being besieged by criticisms from the Republicans in Congress, especially the Tea Party, and by the various candidates vying for the GOP nomination for president. All of them steadily blasted Obama with half-truths and downright lies. It was as if Sir Galahad's sword had lost its magic touch and was unable to fend off the ferocity and intensity of attacks upon him.

Grabell put it this way:

> For all its promise, the federal stimulus package became one of the most reviled pieces of legislation in recent memory. Conservatives branded it a flop and a porkfest, a radical takeover of the economy that discouraged businesses from investing and that would saddle our grandchildren with crippling debt. Liberals cried that the stimulus was too small, a flimsy and visionless cave-in to Republicans as part of a foolish foray for bipartisan support. With such polemics dominating the TV, radio, and Twitter, it's been difficult for ordinary Americans to know what to make of what the government did with the taxpayer's dime. Where did all the money go? Was the stimulus too big or too small? Did it pull us back from the brink or push us deeper into the abyss? Somewhere in between these simplified extremes lies the truth.[75]

In the end, Obama literally wasted much of his political capital in his failed bipartisan effort to get his health plan, or "Obamacare" as it became known, finally passed. It chewed up a great deal more time and energy than he or his administration expected. Any chance he might have had to push through programs on energy, infrastructure, and even a full-scale education reform program—all of which might have helped the economy to recover faster in the short term—were not possible afterward.

Obama, it seemed, was stifled by the GOP and drifted a long way from his dreams as stated in *Audacity of Hope,* dreams of developing high-bandwidth wireless service, a modern interstate highway system, a high-speed transcontinental railroad, a self-sufficient nation no longer dependent on "Arab oil" with alternative energy resources, and—perhaps his fondest dream—a nation that was united in spirit and in purpose with a bipartisan political agenda that worked.

"But to get there," wrote Michael Grabell, "Obama would have to overcome a political and economic environment that had changed substantially since he was introduced to America on that warm November night in Chicago's Grant Park," on November 5, 2008, when he gave his rousing victory speech as President-elect of the United States.[76]

As Grabell concluded, "In this new era, audacity had met reality."[77]

Postscript: This book went to press soon after the 2012 presidential election. If there was one thing almost every political pundit agreed on after the final vote was tallied, it was this: At the beginning of his second term, President Barack Obama must embark on a new, bipartisan course in an all-out effort to create jobs, revive the economy, and address the entitlement programs in an unprecedented, all-court press to bring the runaway national deficit under control. Eradication of poverty has become a national emergency.

APPENDIX A

FRANKLIN D. ROOSEVELT AND THE NEW DEAL

President Roosevelt's program to combat the Great Depression included dozens of legislative firsts that covered a multitude of fields: banking, the economy, the national budget, conservation, the gold standard, federal emergency relief, agriculture, Tennessee Valley Authority, federal securities, homeowners' refinancing, Federal Deposit Insurance, National Recover Act, civil works, social reform, Works Progress Administration, emergency relief, rural electrification, National Labor Relations Board, Social Security, Supreme Court reform, minimum wage, judicial reform, unemployment, and much more.

Following are the New Deal's highlights:

WEDNESDAY, MARCH 4, 1933: FDR was sworn in as president, assuring the nation that "the only thing we have to fear is fear itself."

MARCH 9, 1933: Congress convened in special session and began the First Hundred Days, which ran to June 16 and produced a record number of bills. Some pundits at the time called them "alphabet soup" because all the agencies involved were given acronyms.

Also on this date, FDR's Emergency Banking Relief Act gave discretionary powers to the president over the banking system.

MARCH 12, 1933: FDR broadcast his first "fireside chat" to communicate directly with the America people via radio. In this instance, FDR reassured the nation that its banks were safe for business. This method of talking to the people was an epiphany for FDR.

MARCH 20, 1933: The Government Economy Act enacted budget-balancing measures, including a 15 percent reduction in federal salaries.

MARCH 22, 1933: At FDR's request, Congress effectively ended Prohibition, legalizing the sale of wine and of beer with an alcohol content of up to 3.2 percent.

MARCH 31, 1933: The Civilian Conservation Corps was established to provide 250,000 jobless young men work in parks and public lands.

APRIL 19, 1933: FDR took the United States off the gold standard, lowering the value of the dollar abroad (to stimulate exports) and increasing prices at home.

MAY 12, 1933: The Federal Emergency Relief Act (FERA) gave federal grants to the states to operate their relief programs and ease their budgetary problems. FERA chief Harry L. Hopkins, Roosevelt's close, longtime aide, directed it.

Also on this date, the Agricultural Adjustment Act established parity prices for farm products, along with incentives and subsidies to limit production. It also sought to provide farmers with greater borrowing capacity, and the subsidies to farmers were passed on to consumers in the form of processing tax returns. The money came from an exclusive tax on businesses that processed farm products.

MAY 18, 1933: FDR created the Tennessee Valley Authority to construct dams and hydroelectric plants to assist the region.

MAY 27, 1933: Congress passed the Federal Securities Act, intending to bring transparency to stock transactions.

JUNE 13, 1933: The Homeowners Refinancing Act was passed for refinancing home mortgages and farm debts and eventually assisted in a million mortgages.

JUNE 16, 1933: The Glass-Steagall Banking Act created the Federal Deposit Insurance Corporation to secure bank deposits up to $5,000, and the act separated functions of deposit and investment banks.

Also on this date, FDR signed the National Industrial Recovery Act, the signature piece of legislation of the First New Deal that Roosevelt hoped would lift the industrial economy out of the Depression. FDR named Harold Ickes to head the National Recovery Administration, with the charge to create jobs for the unemployed.

NOVEMBER 8, 1933: FDR unveiled the Civil Works Administration, an emergency unemployment relief program, and appointed Hopkins director.

DECEMBER 5, 1933: The Twenty-first Amendment repealing the Eighteenth Amendment (Prohibition) was ratified.

FEBRUARY 2, 1934: FDR created the Export-Import Bank.

JUNE 6, 1934: FDR created the Securities and Exchange Commission (SEC) to oversee the stock market. It was designed to restore investor confidence in our capital markets by providing investors and the markets with more reliable information and clear rules of honest dealing. FDR named businessman and Wall Street executive Joseph P. Kennedy head of the SEC.

JUNE 19, 1934: Roosevelt created the National Labor Relations Board.

JUNE 28, 1934: Congress created the Federal Housing Administration to insure loans for construction and repairs of homes.

JANUARY 4, 1935: FDR outlined additional program of social reform to be enacted as his Second New Deal, aimed more directly at assisting labor and farmers.

APRIL 8, 1935: Congress passed the Emergency Relief Appropriations Act, which allocated $5 billion for the work relief projects administrated through the new Works Progress Administration. Established to create jobs, as an alternative to earlier direct relief of unemployed, the WPA would ultimately employ eight million Americans. FDR appointed Harry Hopkins chief administrator of the WPA.

MAY 11, 1935: Congress passed the Rural Electrification Administration to extend power to those American farms that still lacked electricity.

JUNE 26, 1935: The National Youth Administration was created to provide relief assistance to young people, including college tuition assistance.

JULY 5, 1935: The National Labor Relations Act, or "Wagner Act," passed. It encouraged union organizing and limited employer countermeasures.

AUGUST 14, 1935: FDR signed the Social Security Act, the signature piece of legislation of the entire New Deal Era. It set up a pension system that permanently changed the relationship between the American people, their government, and the free market.

AUGUST 30, 1935: Congress passed the Revenue Act of 1935 (Wealth Tax Act), which included an inheritance tax, a gift tax, and a provision for taxing incomes greater than $1 million at 70 percent. Lower incomes were subject to varying rates, instead of the earlier flat rate of 13 percent.

JANUARY 6, 1936: The Supreme Court invalidated the Agricultural Adjustment Act in *United States v. Butler.*

FEBRUARY 5, 1937: FDR informed Congress of his plan to enlarge the membership of the Supreme Court by adding an additional justice for every sitting justice older than age seventy. Public and congressional opposition stopped FDR's plan in its tracks, although subsequent court rulings upholding parts of the New Deal may have been influenced by the threat. This battle marked the beginning of the end of FDR's command of Congress.

MARCH 1, 1937: Congress passed the Supreme Court Retirement Act, which permitted Supreme Court Justices to retire at seventy with full pay.

MARCH 29, 1937: In *West Coast Hotel v. Parrish*, the U.S. Supreme Court upheld a Washington State minimum wage law, ensuring that government interventions into the economy would no longer be overturned as unconstitutional.

APRIL 12, 1937: In a series of decisions, the Supreme Court rules the National Labor Relations Act is constitutional. Roosevelt reconsiders move to reorganize the court.

MAY 24, 1937: The Supreme Court ruled that the Social Security Act is constitutional. Roosevelt no longer had any impetus to change the court's composition.

JUNE 1938: FDR signed the Emergency Relief Appropriations Act, an extension of his previous efforts to deal with recession.

JUNE 22, 1938: Congress passed the Chandler Act as an amendment to the Federal Bankruptcy Act of 1898 and set forth procedures for settling debt through liquidation.

AUGUST 26, 1938: Roosevelt signed the Judicial Procedure Reform Act, a compromise on his original reorganization plan.

APPENDIX B
LYNDON B. JOHNSON AND THE WAR ON POVERTY LEGISLATION

Following is a list of the major pieces of legislation that comprised President Lyndon B. Johnson's War on Poverty and were integral to his "Great Society" program:

MARCH 22, 1964: The Economic Opportunity Act (EOA) of 1964 was the centerpiece of the War on Poverty, which in turn was a major thrust of the Johnson administration's Great Society legislative agenda. The EOA provided for job training, adult education, and loans to small businesses to attack the roots of unemployment and poverty. Congress passed the act on August 20, 1964.

JANUARY 1, 1965: The Volunteers in Service to America program, created by the EOA, increased employment opportunities for conscientious people who felt they could contribute to the War on Poverty and help poor Americans.

MARCH 20, 1965: Johnson created the Department of Housing and Urban Development as a cabinet-level department to develop and execute policies on housing.

MARCH 28, 1965: Johnson established the National Foundations of the Arts and Humanities to promote progress and scholarship in the humanities and the arts in the United States.

MARCH 20, 1965: The Elementary and Secondary Education Act of 1965 emphasized equal access to education and established high standards and accountability. The law authorized federally funded education programs administered by the states. The act was passed on April 11, 1965. A former teacher himself, LBJ had witnessed poverty's impact on his students and believed that equal access to education was vital to a child's ability to lead a productive life.

JULY 30, 1965: Johnson signed into law the Medicare program, which provides low-cost hospitalization and medical insurance for the nation's elderly.

OCTOBER 3, 1965: The Immigration Act of 1965 abolished the National Origins Formula, which had been in place in the United States since the Immigration Act of 1924. Proposed by Representative Emanuel Celler of New York, cosponsored by Senator Philip Hart of Michigan and heavily supported by Senator Edward M. Kennedy of Massachusetts, it liberalized U.S. policy toward non-European immigrants.

OCTOBER 18, 1965: The Water Quality Act, commonly known as the Clean Water Act, established the goals of eliminating releases of high amounts of toxic substances into water, eliminating additional water pollution by 1985, and ensuring that surface waters would meet standards necessary for human sports and recreation by 1983.

MARCH 19, 1966: The National Traffic and Motor Vehicle Safety Act was enacted to empower the federal government to set and administer new safety standards for motor vehicles and road traffic safety.

MARCH 20, 1966: The Clean Water Restoration Act drew a considerable amount of opposition from some manufacturers, many of whom have been assessed large fines for violating it.

NOVEMBER 7, 1967: Johnson signed the Public Broadcasting Act, which created programming to supplement the broadcast networks.

APPENDIX C
AMERICAN POVERTY: EXPERTS ON THE RECORD

Following are comments from experts on poverty in various fields in the United States. To begin, Peter Edelman of the Georgetown University Law Center, Washington, D.C., put the entire issue into proper perspective in an article he wrote for *The Clearinghouse Review, Journal of Poverty Law and Policy*, in its May–June 2007 issue.

Did we ever have a real war on poverty in the United States?

When Ronald Reagan famously said, "We fought a war on poverty and poverty won," was either part of his statement correct?

Could a federal program end domestic poverty all by itself?

The answers are: no, no, no, and yes but it wouldn't be a good idea.

First, we have never had in place the combination of public policies—let alone the even larger combination of public policies and private actions—that would have the maximum impact toward ending poverty in the United States.

Second, poverty did not "win." Governmental policies relating to poverty are vastly better than they were in 1932 and are impressively successful in keeping tens of millions of people out of poverty.

Third, we could afford to give everybody with an income below the poverty line enough money to get out of poverty (putting aside whether the current measure is the right one), but that would be a bad idea.

Why? Because merely writing checks for everyone in need is bad public policy. For most nondisabled adults of working age, work (outside of the home) is better than welfare. Some may dispute the point, but it is a widely held national value.[1]

—PETER EDELMAN
Author and Professor of Law,
Georgetown University Law Center, Washington, D.C.

It was Michael Harrington's powerful examination of poverty published in 1962, *The Other America*, that moved President Kennedy to begin taking the steps that culminated in President Johnson's War on Poverty. Perhaps there is another Harrington out there. . . . There are always a lot of headlines about poverty the day that the data comes out. But then those headlines fade, and the problem hasn't gone away. What we need is a sustained focus by the media and our elected officials, and we need advocacy groups and grassroots activists to keep making that push. Call it a war on poverty, call it expanding the middle class, call it promoting economic security. Call it whatever you want, but start making the connections between the plight of the middle class and lower-income Americans, and get involved.[2]

—KATRINA VANDEN HEUVEL
Publisher and editor, *The Nation*

So what is the solution to the poverty of so many of America's working people? . . .

Today, the answer seems both more modest and more challenging: if we want to reduce poverty, we have to stop doing the things that make people poor and keep them that way. Stop underpaying people for the jobs they do. Stop treating working people as potential criminals and let them have the right to organize for better wages and working conditions.

Stop the institutional harassment of those who turn to the government for help or find themselves destitute in the streets. Maybe, as so many Americans seem to believe today, we can't afford the kinds of public programs that would genuinely alleviate poverty—though I would argue otherwise. But at least we should decide, as a bare minimum principle, to stop kicking people when they're down.[3]

—BARBARA EHRENREICH,
Feminist, political activist, and author

[The Census Bureau] report documents the vast human damage being inflicted by a weak economy. It also documents the ways in which safety-net programs have at least mitigated that damage—notably, uninsurance among children has actually fallen thanks to the State Children's Health Insurance Program (SCHIP) and Medicaid, unemployment insurance has literally kept millions above the poverty line, and the early features of the Affordable Care Act have helped hundreds of thousands of young adults retain insurance. . . .

But what struck me is the extent to which the suffering didn't begin with the slump—many measures of pain were rising right through the "Bush boom," and have merely continued that rise.[4]

—PAUL KRUGMAN,
Professor of economics and international affairs, Princeton University,
and columnist for the *New York Times*

The current answer to American poverty is through policies of economic expansion, as Paul Krugman describes in his *New York Times* columns. The current Republican assault on the last 100 years of the social contract is exactly the wrong prescription. FDR and LBJ had the right ideas and the right spirit for dealing with poverty.[5]

—ROBERT DALLEK
Historian, author, and professor of history, Stanford University

Poverty in the Unites States is far higher than in many other developed nations. At the turn of the 21st century, the United States ranked 24th among 25 countries when measuring the share of the population below 50 percent of median income. But the solutions to this problem are not out of reach. In communities across the nation, policymakers, business people, people of faith, and concerned citizens are coming together. The commitment of these groups and CAP's recommendations will all help move the nation closer to ending poverty.[6]

—MARK GREENBERG,
Author and director of the Task Force on Poverty,
Center for American Progress (CAP),
Washington, D.C.

Americans have been watching protests against oppressive regimes that concentrate massive wealth in the hands of an elite few. Yet in our own democracy, 1 percent of the people take nearly a quarter of the nation's income—an inequality even the wealthy will come to regret.

The top 1 percent may have the best houses, educations, and lifestyles, but their fate is bound up with how the other ninety-nine percent live.

It's no use pretending that what has obviously happened has not in fact happened. The upper 1 percent of Americans are now taking in nearly a quarter of the nation's income every year. In terms of wealth rather than income, the top 1 percent control 40 percent. Their lot in life has improved considerably. . . . All the growth in recent decades— and more—has gone to those at the top. . . . Among our closest counterparts are Russia with its oligarchs and Iran. While many of the old centers of inequality in Latin America, such as Brazil, have been striving in recent years, rather successfully, *to improve the plight of the poor and reduce gaps in income, America has allowed inequality to grow* [italics added].[7]

—JOSEPH E. STIGLITZ,
Author, economist, and professor
of economics at Columbia University

Unemployment is not necessarily a deal breaker for a president: 1936—Franklin Roosevelt ran for reelection with an unemployment rate of about 16 percent. He was able to make the case that he was pulling the country out of the Great Depression and also that his opponent, Alf Landon, if elected, would return the country to the policies that had caused the Great Depression. Ronald Reagan did sort of the same thing in 1984 with an unemployment rate that was also high, saying that Walter Mondale, who was Jimmy Carters's vice president, would bring back the policies that had caused the recession of 1980. But just as there are no iron laws in politics, not every precedent always holds.[8]

—MICHAEL BESCHLOSS,
Author, political analyst, presidential historian,
and visiting scholar, Harvard University

There are two new rituals about the yearly census reports on poverty in America. One is that the census figures show more Americans continue to sink into poverty. The poverty rate this year jumped to the highest level in nearly two decades. Those hardest hit remain the same. Blacks and Hispanics were nearly twice as likely as whites to be poor. But racial distinctions aside, the census figures showed that there were a lot of poor whites too, and what's become an increasingly even more common trend [is that] many of those who tumbled into the poverty column are those who at one time were by all measures considered middle class.

The other ritual is that the news of rising poverty makes headlines one day. And the next it is forgotten. This year [2011] is no different. Not one of the GOP presidential candidates made mention of the poverty rate jump. The White House was equally mum on the report. Poverty remains the taboo word on the campaign stump, among lawmakers, the media, and the general public. It remains even a taboo word among many of the poor.

. . . The ritual census figures that show that the number of poor continue to grow with little end in sight to the rise hasn't budged the nation to do anything about their plight. Poverty is the forbidden word that sadly is doomed for now to remain America's taboo word.[9]

—EARL OFARI HUTCHINSON,
Journalist, author, and cohost of the *Al Sharpton Show,*
American Urban Radio Network

[Poverty is] a huge and complicated issue, and what I've made clear in this book [*The Time of Our Lives*] is that we all got into this together and we're not going to get out of it unless we all work together. That goes to the core of a lot of the anxiety in this country is that the middle class not only has lost its way, but it's slipping back into another economic strata.

We have more people on food stamps, for example, more children who are living in cars in the Southeast and in other places. That's a terrible commentary on a great and wealthy nation like the United States.

It doesn't mean you just write a check and hand it out, but we have to find new ways to create those economic opportunities and jobs for the people who lost the manufacturing base, for example.

Forty percent of our economy now, 40 percent of our GDP is made up of financial services. They don't make anything. What they do is they create instruments for churning money. Even people on Wall Street understand you've got to get back to making some things and providing jobs for people who want to be able to use their hands and their legs as well as their minds to build this country again.[10]

—TOM BROKAW,
Author and former *NBC Nightly News* anchor

The poor have no lobbyists to do their work. It's time for the religious community to march again for justice, to end poverty, end injustice, end homelessness in our country.[11]

—JOHN LEWIS,
Congressman, Fifth District, Georgia
Former aide to Rev. Dr. Martin Luther King Jr., Civil Rights archivist

The message here is that it is time to examine the differences between black families on either side of the divide for clues about how to address an increasingly entrenched inequality. We can't afford to wait any longer to address the causes of persistent poverty among most black families.[12]

—HENRY LOUIS GATES, JR.
Author and director of the W. E. B. DuBois Institute for
African American Research at Harvard University

One percent of the people owning and controlling more wealth than ninety percent of Americans, that's unsustainable. That math won't hold up long-term. There is a bubbling, there is a restlessness.

If you don't treat poor and working people with dignity now, chickens are going to come home to roost later. . . . And it won't be about love and justice. It will be about revenge, hatred, and then we all go under.[13]

—CORNEL WEST,
Author, academic archivist, and professor of
African American studies at Princeton University

We suffered a terrible blow, but we are coming back.[14]
> —TIMOTHY F. GEITHNER,
> U.S. Treasury Secretary

The party that has repeatedly saved capitalism from its own excesses and thereby preserved capitalism is the Democratic Party.[15]
> —ROBERT REICH,
> Author, political economist, and professor of public policy
> at the University of California–Berkeley

The 2010 stimulus offset a greater percentage of the recession-induced income losses than was the case in any recent recession. However, most of the safety net aspects of the stimulus bill have already expired or will expire by the end of 2012. And, even though the President has proposed extending some of them, Congress has refused and has made reducing the deficit and keeping tax rates low for millionaires a higher priority than protecting the poor and the unemployed during a slow economic recovery. The reality is that prospects for the poor and the near poor are dismal. If Congress and the states make further cuts, we can expect the number of poor and lower income families to rise in the next several years.[16]
> —SHELDON DANZIGER,
> Author and director, National Poverty Center,
> University of Michigan

In America, the culture is imbued with so many false gods and altars of worship that we must try to find new leaders who can reach the people.

I have questions about the president [Barack Obama], but I am praying that he will show us soon the evidence of the strength I know he possesses.

All that the opposition has to offer is a tangible, visible nightmare. I believe that I am still living so that I can help turn around this world we live in. And I also believe that we will eventually fall into a social rhythm that is far more embracing, far more compassionate.

It is what I have to believe. It is what we all have to believe, if we are to survive.[17]

—HARRY BELAFONTE
Activist, writer, and entertainer

"The poor" are the human shields behind whom advocates of ever bigger spending for ever bigger government advance their goal.

If poverty meant what most people think of as poverty—people "ill-clad, ill-housed, and ill-nourished," in Franklin D. Roosevelt's phrase—there would not be nearly enough people in poverty today to justify the vastly expanded powers and runaway spending of the federal government.[18]

—THOMAS A. SOWELL,
Author, economist, and the Rose and Milton Friedman Senior Fellow on
Public Policy at the Hoover Institution, Stanford University

If we can bail out banks, if we can reconstruct Iran and Afghanistan, then we can do a war on poverty that works.[19]

—REV. JESSE JACKSON,
Civil rights activist and minister

I'm not concerned about the very poor. We have a safety net there. If it needs a repair, I'll fix it. I'm not concerned about the very rich. They're doing just fine. I'm concerned about the very heart of America, the 90–95 percent of [middle-class] Americans who right now are struggling.[20]

—MITT ROMNEY,
Former Massachusetts governor and
Republican nominee for president, 2012

We live in a culture of opinion trusteeship, and my economist-trustee on matters of poverty is still John Maynard Keynes, so I would recommend that all public officials with financial responsibilities read or reread (and on talk shows, journalists should rigorously question them about), John Maynard Keynes's "The General Theory of Employment, Interest and Money." And I trust/hope that they would put Keynes's prescriptions into practice. The hoped-for result: domestically we would see (1) vastly increased investment in the public sector (what used to be called "priming the pump") to achieve full employment, and get the economy growing at significant rates again; and (2) public incentives to induce the rich to invest not in financial instruments but the real economy; and internationally I expect that would mean the allocation of massive resources to what Jeffrey Sachs (not quite my opinion trustee on these matters, but he's getting there) calls "development aid."[21]

—VICTOR NAVASKY
George T. Delacorte, professor, Columbia University
Director, Delacorte Center of Magazine Journalism,
Chair, *Columbia Journalism Review*, Publisher Emeritus, *The Nation*

NOTES

Preface

1. Michael Harrington (1928–1989) graduated Holy Cross in 1947. He attended Yale Law School and the University of Chicago. He joined the Catholic Worker Movement and a few years later the Young People's Socialist League. He wrote for magazines such as *Dissent, New Leader,* and *Commonweal.* He first wrote about poverty for *Commentary* magazine and expanded the articles into *The Other America: Poverty in the United States* (New York: Macmillan, 1962). About seventy thousand copies were sold in the first year (and more than a million copies since), while the book earned early accolades from *Business Week, Time* magazine, the *New Yorker,* and others. After *The Other America,* Harrington wrote eleven more books, including *Socialism* (1972), *The Twilight of Capitalism* (1976), and the *Decade of Decision: The Crisis of the American System* (1980). Harrington was a professor of political science at Queens College and the leader of the Democratic Socialists of America. See Danielle Kane, "Holy Cross Conference on Poverty to Mark 50th Anniversary of 'The Other America,'" News and Events, Holy Cross, February 27, 2012, http://news.holycross. edu/blog/2012/02/27/holy-cross-conference-on-poverty-to-mark-50th-anniversary-of-the-other-america/.

2. "Census Data: Half of U.S. Poor or Low Income," CBS News, December 15,2011,http://www.cbsnews.com/8301-201_162-57343397/census-data -half-of-u.s-poor-or-low-i.

3. Woody Klein, *Toward Humanity and Justice: The Writings of Kenneth B. Clark, Scholar of the 1954* Brown v. Board of Education *Decision* (Westport, CT: Praeger, 2004), 87.

4. Dwight Macdonald, "Our Invisible Poor," *New Yorker,* January 19, 1963, 82.

5. Earl Ofari Hutchinson, an author and political analyst, is a weekly cohost of the *Al Sharpton Show* on American Urban Radio Network and an associate

editor of New America Media. See his blog post, "Poverty Is America's Taboo Word," The Hutchinson Report News, September 14, 2011, http:// thehutchinsonreportnews.com/profiles/blogs/6296329:BlogPost:10901.

6. Asked to define the terms "near poor," "poor," and "deep poor," Brian Lavin, a spokesman for the U.S. Census Bureau in Suitland, Maryland, told the author in a May 15, 2012, interview: "The Census Bureau [officially] does not have standard definitions of the terms 'near poor,' 'poor,' and 'deep poor.'"

7. David Bornstein, "In the Fight against Poverty, It's Time for a Revolution," Opinionator, New York Times, January 12, 2012, http://opinionator.blogs. nytimes.com/2012/01/12/in-the-fight-against-poverty-its-time-for-a-revolution/.

8. Daniel P. Moynihan, ed., with Corinne Saposs Schelling, On Understanding Poverty: Perspectives from the Social Sciences (New York: Basic Books, 1969), 36.

9. Webster's New World Dictionary of English, 3rd college ed., s.v. "poverty."

10. The phrase "the new poor" was first published in reporter Catherine Rampell's story "The New Poor; Dwindling Prospects," the New York Times, December 3, 2010. It was one of a series of articles titled "The New Poor, examining the struggle to recover from the widespread strains of the Great Recession in 2010."

11. David Brooks, "Midlife Crisis Economics," New York Times, December 27, 2011, http://www.nytimes.com/2011/12/27/opinion/brooks-midlife-crisis-economics.html.

12. Harrington, The Other America, 118.

13. Ibid., 17.

14. "I Lived in a Slum," New York World-Telegram & Sun, published between June 23 and July 2, 1959.

15. Nathan Glazer, "Letter from East Harlem," City Journal, Autumn 1991, available at http://www.city-journal.org/printable.php?id=1584.

16. Michael Harrington, Book Week, New York Herald Tribune, November 1, 1964, 5. The review read in part: "Woody Klein's study is journalistic rather than scholarly. Klein is most compelling when he describes in insightful detail the agonizing failure of New York City to deliver on its promise—now about three decades old—to abolish the 311 East 100th Street [slum]. . . . It is good to have a report like Let in the Sun, which documents the [social and economic] trends in terms of the history of a single building [and which] is a valuable and very specific case study of the enormous national problem. The result is an excellent reportorial supplement to [other] scholarly studies. . . . As it now stands, the social tragedy described by Klein will probably become worse before it becomes better." [Italics in original.]

17. Televised on David Brinkley's Journal, NBC, November 22, 1961, and July 25, 1962. See Tom Mascaro, "They Beat the Clock—NBC's Innovative News magazine, David Brinkley's Journal (1961–63), Television Quarterly,

Television Quarterly, Summer 1964, 29. He wrote, in part: "Viewers saw a building at 311 E. 100th St. built in 1904, the kind of place that was supposed to put an end to slums. Twenty-five landlords later, the address housed 139 tenants. Brinkley explained in his clipped cadence: 'fifty-five adults and eighty-four children, most Puerto Ricans. They generally are not educated, speak not much English, and so are not able to earn much and are drawn here by the low rents,' $44.83 per month."

18. Jacob A. Riis, *How the Other Half Lives: Studies among the Tenements of New York* (New York: Charles Scribner's Sons, 1890), 296.

19. Woody Klein, "The City's Slums Are Her War, Too," *New York World-Telegram & Sun*, May 5, 1964.

20. Ibid.

21. U.S. Riot Commission, *Report of the National Advisory Commission on Civil Disorders* (New York: Bantam Books, 1968), 1.

22. Peter Singer, *The Life You Can Save: Acting Now to End World Poverty* (New York: Random House, 2009), xi–xii.

23. Ibid., 172.

24. A. G. Sulzberger, "Obama Strikes Populist Chord with Speech on G.O.P. Turf," *New York Times*, December 7, 2011.

25. Ibid.

26. Barack Obama, *The Audacity of Hope: Thoughts on Reclaiming the American Dream* (New York: Crown Publishers, 2006), 69.

27. Harrington, *The Other America*, 191.

Introduction

1. A quotation by William Shakespeare from his play *The Tempest* in The Complete Works of Shakespeare, ed. George Lyman Kittredge (Boston: Ginn and Company, 1936).

2. Author telephone interview with Kathleen S. Short, economist, U.S. Census Bureau, May 15, 2012.

3. Author telephone interview with Sheldon Danziger, Henry J. Meyer Distinguished University Professor of Public Policy, director of the National Poverty Center, and director of the Ford Foundation Program on Public Policy at the Gerald R. Ford School of Public Policy, University of Michigan, May 15, 2012.

4. Sabrina Tavernise, "Survey Finds Rising Strain Between Rich and the Poor," *New York Times*, January 11, 2012. Survey by Pew Social & Demographic Trends, conducted between December 6 and 19, 2012, of 2,048 adults. According to the *Times*, "The survey attributed the change to underlying shifts in the distribution of wealth in American society, citing a finding by the Census Bureau that the share of wealth held by the top 10 percent of the population increased 56 percent in 2009 from 49 percent in 2005."

5. Ibid.

6. Ibid.

7. "Family Homelessness in America," *American Free Press Podcast*, January 15, 2012, http://americanfreepress.net/?p=2342.

8. Robert Hartmann McNamara, ed., *Homelessness in America*, vol. 3, *Solutions to Homelessness* (Westport, CT: Praeger, 2008), xi.

9. Scott Pelley, "Hard Times Generation," *60 Minutes*, CBS, November 27, 2011, www.cbsnews.com/video/watch/?id=7389758n.

10. Department of Health and Human Services, 2012 HHS Poverty Guidelines, February 9, 2012, http://aspe.hhs.gov/poverty/12poverty.shtml/ (accessed August 31, 2012).

11. Harrington, *The Other America*, 190.

12. U.S. Bureau of the Census, Current Population Survey, *2010 Annual Social and Economic Supplement* (Washington, D.C.: U.S. Bureau of the Census, 2010). http://www.census.gov/apsd/techdoc/cps/cpsmar10.pdf.

13. Contained in a study by Mark R. Rank, PhD, the Herbert S. Hadley Professor of Social Work at the Brown School at Washington University in St. Louis. See Rank's article, "A Life Course Approach to Understanding Poverty among Older American Adults," *Families in Society: The Journal of Contemporary Social Services* (Summer 2011). He used data from the Panel Study of Income Dynamics (SID), the longest-running longitudinal data set that contains information on family demographic and economic behavior.

14. National Coalition for the Homeless, "How Many People Experience Homelessness?," Washington, D.C., July 2009, http://www.nationalhomeless.org/factsheets/How_Many.html.

15. U.S. Census Bureau data released on November 14, 2012.

16. Sabrina Tavernise, "Study Finds Big Spikes in Poorest in the U.S.," *New York Times*, November 3, 2011, http://www.nytimes.com/2011/11/04/us/extreme-poverty-is-up-brookings-report-finds.html.

17. U.S. Census Bureau, 2010 Annual Social and Economic Supplements.

18. Woody Klein, *Let in the Sun* (New York: Macmillan, 1964), 265.

19. It should be noted that in studying the early presidents, starting with George Washington, and expressly focusing on poverty, historians wrote almost entirely about slaves and Native Americans, who were seen as the people most in need of basic facilities simply to remain alive.

Chapter 1. Founding the Republic (1789–1829)

1. George Washington's first inaugural speech, April 30, 1789, Record of the United States Senate, National Archives, www.archives.gov/legislative/features/gw-inauguration/.

2. June Axinn and Mark J. Stern, *Social Welfare: A History of the American Response to Need*, 6th ed. (Boston: Pearson/Allyn and Bacon, New York, 2005), 14–17.

3. Ibid., 21.

4. Ibid., 29.
5. Ibid., 30.
6. Allan Nevins and Henry Steele Commager, *A Short History of the United States*, 6th ed. (New York: Alfred A. Knopf, 1976), 135.
7. George Washington to James Madison, letter, May 5, 1789, Teaching AmericanHistory.org,AshbrookCenteratAshlandUniversity,Ashland,Ohio, http://teachingamericanhistory.org/library/index.asp?document=390. (Hereafter TeachingAmericanHistory.org.)
8. Douglas Southall Freeman, ed., *Washington: An Abridgement by Richard Harwell of the Seven-Volume George Washington, by Douglas Southall Freeman* (New York: Charles Scribner's Sons, 1968), 139.
9. Alexis de Tocqueville, *Democracy in America*, ed. J. P. Mayer, trans. George Lawrence (New York: Doubleday, 1969), 334.
10. Henry Wiencek, *An Imperfect God: George Washington, His Slaves, and the Creation of America* (New York: Farrar, Straus and Giroux, 2003), 272; and David Humphreys, *Life of General Washington, with George Washington's Remarks*, ed. Rosemarie Zagarri (Athens: University of Georgia Press, 1991), 78.
11. Wiencek, *An Imperfect God,* 275.
12. Douglas Southall Freeman, *George Washington: A Biography*, vol. 6., *Patriot and President* (New York: Charles Scribner's Sons, 1954), 161.
13. U.S. Government, Public Acts of First Congress, statute I, August 20, 1789; and Public Acts of First Congress, statute I, August 20, 1789, in United States Congress, Government and Laws, *The Public Statutes at Large of the United States of America from the Organization of the Government in 1789, to March 3, 1945*, ed. Richard Peters (Boston: Charles C. Little and James Brown, 1945), available through the Library of Congress, *A Century of Lawmaking for a New National: U.S. Congressional Documents and Debates, 1774–1875*, http://memory.loc.gov/cgi-bin/am page?collId=llsl&fileName=001/llsl001.db&recNum=2.
14. For U.S. Statutes at Large, 2d Cong., sess. I, ch. 10 and ch. 11, March 5, 1792, see ibid.
15. William F. B. Vodrey, "George Washington: Hero of the Confederacy," *American History Magazine*, October 2004, http://www.historynet.com /george-washington-hero-of-the-confederacy.htm.
16. Michael B. Katz, *In the Shadow of the Poorhouse: A Social History of Welfare in America* (New York: Basic Books, 1986), 4–5.
17. PBS, "George Washington and the Problem of Slavery," Rediscovering George Washington, 2002, http://www.pbs.org/georgewashington/class room/slavery4.html (accessed August 31, 2012).
18. Alexis de Tocqueville first used the term with respect to the United States during his first visit to America in 1831. He noticed that the American idea of "nationality" was "different, based less on common history or ethnicity than on common beliefs." De Tocqueville stressed the advanced nature of

democracy in America, arguing that it infused every aspect of society and culture, at a time (1830s) when democracy was not in fashion anywhere else. New World Encyclopedia, s.v. "American exceptionalism," last modified November 11, 2008, http://www.newworldencyclopedia.org/entry /American_exceptionalism.

19. The History Channel, *The Presidents: The Lives and Legacies of the 43 Leaders of the United States*, produced by Craig Haffner and Donna E. Lusitana (A&E Home Video, 2005), DVD, http://shop.history.com/detail.php?p= 366781&SESSID=0cb54b7657896490cabdf81a3c6cccae&v=history (accessed August 31, 2012).

20. John Adams, "Inaugural Address," March 4, 1797, Miller Center, University of Virginia, Charlottesville, Virginia, 2012, http://millercenter.org /scripps/archive/speeches/detail/3445. (Hereafter Miller Center.)

21. John Adams, "A Dissertation on the Canon and Feudal Law," 1765, Teaching American History.org, http://www.teachingamericanhistory.org /library/index.asp?document=43.

22. John Adams, "First Annual Message," November 22, 1797, Miller Center, http://millercenter.org/president/speeches/detail/3465.

23. "John Adams: A Life in Brief," Miller Center, http://millercenter.org /president/adams/essays/biography/1.

24. Philosopher/poets Henry David Thoreau and Ralph Waldo Emerson later popularized the quote.

25. Thomas Jefferson, "First Inaugural Address," March 4, 1801, Miller Center, http://millercenter.org/president/speeches/detail/3469.

26. Tocqueville, *Democracy in America*, 176.

27. History Channel, *Jefferson*, DVD, January 11, 2011, http://shop.history .com/detail.php?p=279323&SESSID=93035f6f6ce871cf8919c351fa32fa 2d&v=history.

28. Gunnar Myrdal, with Richard Sterner and Arnold Rose, *An American Dilemma: The Negro Problem and Modern Society* (New York: Harper, 1944), 2:531; and "Note on Virginia: 1781–1782," in *The Writings of Thomas Jefferson: Being His Autobiography, Correspondence, Reports, Messages, Addresses and Other Writings, Official and Private*, ed. Henry Augustine Washington (Washington, D.C.: Taylor & Maury, 1853–1854), 8:403–4.

29. Annette Gordon-Reed, *The Hemingses of Monticello: An American Family* (New York: W. W. Norton, 2008), 112.

30. Nevins and Commager, *A Short History*, 142.

31. Ibid., 143.

32. Ibid.; Myrdal, *An American Dilemma*, 85; and Washington, *The Writings of Thomas Jefferson*, 1:85.

33. Gordon-Reed, *The Hemingses of Monticello*, 267.

34. Ibid., 17.

35. In January 2000, the Thomas Jefferson Foundation concluded in its "Report of the Research Committee on Thomas Jefferson and Sally Hemings," in

part: "The DNA study, combined with multiple strands of currently available documentary and statistical evidence, indicates a high probability that Thomas Jefferson fathered Eston Hemings, and that he most likely was the father of all six of Sally Hemings's children appearing in Jefferson's records. Those children are Harriet, who died in infancy; Beverly; an unnamed daughter who died in infancy; Harriet; Madison; and Eston." Thomas Jefferson Foundation, "Conclusions," Monticello.org., Charlottesville, Virginia, http://www.monticello.org/site/plantation-and-slavery/vi-conclusions.

36. Ralph Ketcham, *James Madison: A Biography* (New York: Macmillan, 1971), 476.

37. The History Channel, *James Madison*, DVD, http://shop.history.com/detail.php?p=366781&SESSID=0cb54b7657896490cabdf81a3c6cccae&v=history.

38. "James Monroe: Domestic Affairs," Miller Center, http://millercenter.org/president/monroe/essays/biography/4.

39. John Quincy Adams, "Inaugural Address," March 4, 1825, Miller Center, http://millercenter.org/scripps/archive/speeches/detail/3513.

40. "John Quincy Adams: A Life in Brief," Miller Center, http://millercenter.org/president/jqadams/essays/biography/1.

Chapter 2. The Era of Jackson (1829–1853)

1. James C. Curtis, *Andrew Jackson and the Search for Vindication* (Boston: Little, Brown, 1976), ix–x.

2. Arthur M. Schlesinger Jr., *The Age of Jackson* (Boston: Little, Brown, 1945), 37.

3. Jon Meacham, *American Lion: Andrew Jackson in the White House* (New York: Random House, 2008), 38–39.

4. Andrew Jackson, "First Inaugural Address," March 4, 1829, Miller Center, http://millercenter.org/scripps/archive/speeches/detail/3485.

5. Ibid.

6. History Channel, *The Presidents*.

7. Marquis James, *Andrew Jackson: Portrait of a President* (Indianapolis: Bobbs-Merrill, 1937), 219.

8. Ibid., 220; and Curtis, *Andrew Jackson*, 71.

9. Curtis, *Andrew Jackson*, ix–x.

10. Nevins and Commager, *A Short History*, 194.

11. Andrew Jackson, "Bank Veto," July 10, 1832, Miller Center, http://millercenter.org/scripps/archive/speeches/detail/3636.

12. Andrew Jackson, "Farewell Address," March 4, 1837, Miller Center, http://millercenter.org/scripps/archive/speeches/detail/3644.

13. Schlesinger, *The Age of Jackson*, 43.

14. Martin Van Buren, "Domestic Politics," Miller Center, http://millercenter.org/president/vanburen/essays/biography/4.

15. Martin Van Buren, "Inaugural Address," March 4, 1837, Miller Center, http://millercenter.org/president/speeches/detail/3486.

16. The Twenty-fifth Amendment of the U.S. Constitution reads: "In case of the removal of the President from office or of his death or resignation, the Vice President shall become President."

17. Robert Seager, *And Tyler Too* (New York: McGraw-Hill, 1963), 53.

18. Edward P. Crapol, *John Tyler: The Accidental President* (Chapel Hill: University of North Carolina Press, 2006), 5–6.

19. Ibid., 59.

20. Nevins and Commager, *A Short History*, 199.

21. James Knox Polk, "Inaugural Address," March 4, 1845, Miller Center, http://millercenter.org/president/speeches/detail/3550.

22. According to historical reports, the United States acquired more than a million square miles of land during the Polk administration. See "James K. Polk," Answers, www.answers.com/topic/james-polk.

23. John Seigenthaler, *James K. Polk: The American Presidency*, The American Presidents Series (New York: Times Books, 2004), 85.

24. John Durant and Alice Durant, *Pictorial History of American Presidents* (New York: A. S. Barnes, 1955), 88.

25. John S. D. Eisenhower, *Zachary Taylor*, The American Presidents Series (New York: *Times Books*, 1985), 1.

26. Zachary Taylor, "Inaugural Address," March 5, 1849, Miller Center, http://millercenter.org/president/speeches/detail/3551.

27. Millard Fillmore, "Domestic Policy," Miller Center, http://millercenter.org/president/fillmore/essays/biography/4.

28. Robert J. Scarry, *Millard Fillmore* (Jefferson, NC: McFarland, 2001), 59, 175.

29. Durant and Durant, *A Pictorial History*, 99.

30. Scarry, *Millard Fillmore*, 59.

31. Ibid., 177.

Chapter 3. A Nation Divided (1853–1881)

1. Michael Fitzgibbon Holt, *Franklin Pierce*, The American Presidents Series (New York: Times Books/Henry Holt, 2010), 25.

2. Holt, *Franklin Pierce*, 53.

3. Larry Gara, *The Presidency of Franklin Pierce* (Lawrence: University Press of Kansas, 1991), 181.

4. Ibid., 65.

5. Ibid., 86.

6. Holt, *Franklin Pierce*, 52.

7. Ibid., 71.

8. James Buchanan, "Inaugural Address," March 4, 1857, Miller Center, http://millercenter.org/president/speeches/detail/3554.

9. Elbert B. Smith, *The Presidency of James Buchanan* (Lawrence: University Press of Kansas, 1975), 14.

10. John Woolley and Gerhard Peters, "James Buchanan, President of the United States: 1857–1861: Fourth Annual Message to Congress on the State of the Union, December 3, 1860," The American Presidency Project, www.presidency.ucsb.edu/ws/index.php?pid=29501.

11. Doris Kearns Goodwin, *Team of Rivals: The Political Genius of Abraham Lincoln* (New York: Simon & Schuster, 2005), 90.

12. Abraham Lincoln, "A House Divided" speech, June 16, 1858, Miller Center, http://millercenter.org/president/speeches/detail/3504.

13. Abraham Lincoln, "First Inaugural Address," March 4, 1861, Miller Center, http://millercenter.org/president/speeches/detail/3507.

14. Abraham Lincoln, "Emancipation Proclamation," January 1, 1863, Miller Center, http://millercenter.org/president/speeches/detail/3509.

15. George McGovern, *Abraham Lincoln*, The American Presidents Series (New York: Times Books/Henry Holt, 2009), 89.

16. Abraham Lincoln, "Gettysburg Address," November 19, 1863, Miller Center, http://millercenter.org/president/speeches/detail/3511.

17. Abraham Lincoln, "Second Inaugural Address," March 4, 1865, Miller Center, http://millercenter.org/president/speeches/detail/3512.

18. McGovern, *Abraham Lincoln*, 89, 123.

19. Nevins and Commager, *A Short History*, 225–26.

20. Carl M. Sandburg, *Abraham Lincoln: The Prairie Years and the War Years* (New York: Harcourt, Brace, 1954), 734.

21. Goodwin, *Team of Rivals*, 91

22. Richard Striner, *Father Abraham: Lincoln's Relentless Struggle to End Slavery* (New York: Oxford University Press, 1998), 2.

23. Nevins and Commager, *A Short History*, 286.

24. Annette Gordon-Reed, *Andrew Johnson*, The American Presidents Series (New York: Times Books/Henry Holt, 2011), 3.

25. Ibid., 12.

26. Hans L. Trefousse, *Andrew Johnson: A Biography* (New York: W. W. Norton, 1989), 299.

27. William S. McFeeley, *Grant: A Biography* (New York: W. W. Norton, 1981), 305.

28. Ibid., 306.

29. Rutherford Birchard Hayes, "Inaugural Address," March 5, 1877, Miller Center, http://millercenter.org/president/speeches/detail/3558.

30. "American President: Rutherford B. Hayes (1822–1893)," Miller Center, www.millercenter.org/president/hayes/essays/biography/9.

31. Harry Barnard, *Rutherford B. Hayes and His America* (Indianapolis: Bobbs-Merrill, 1954), 433.

Chapter 4. The Golden Age (1881–1897)

1. "American President: A Reference Resource: James Abram Garfield," Miller Center, http://millercenter.org/president/garfield/essays/biography/1.
2. Robert S. Summers, "James Abram Garfield," POTUS, May 16, 2009, http://potus.com/jagarfield.html.
3. "James A. Garfield, Inaugural Address, Friday, March 4, 1881," Bartleby .com, http://www.bartleby.com/124/pres36.html.
4. Ibid.
5. Justus D. Doenecke, *The Presidencies of James A. Garfield and Chester A. Arthur*, The American Presidents Series (Lawrence: Regents Press of Kansas, 1981), 47–48.
6. Ibid., 47.
7. Ibid., 48.
8. History Channel, *The Presidents*.
9. Thomas C. Reeves, *Gentleman Boss: The Life of Chester Alan Arthur* (New York: Knopf, 1975), 271.
10. Doenecke, *The Presidencies*, 89.
11. Ibid., 90.
12. Chester Alan Arthur, "First Annual Message," December 6, 1881, Miller Center, http://millercenter.org/president/speeches/detail/3560.
13. Henry Franklin Graff, *Grover Cleveland*, The American Presidents Series (New York: Times Books, 2002), 76.
14. Ibid., 85.
15. Ibid.
16. Ibid., 91.
17. Ibid., 85.
18. Ibid., 96.
19. Ibid., 93.
20. Benjamin Harrison, "Inaugural Address," March 4, 1889, Miller Center, http://millercenter.org/president/speeches/detail/3561.
21. Graff, *Grover Cleveland*, 76.
22. Michael B. Sauter, Douglas A. McIntyre, and Charles B. Stockdale, "The 13 Worst Recessions, Depressions, and Panics in American History," 24/7 Wall St., September 9, 2010, http://247wallst.com/2010/09/09/the-13-worst-recessions-depressions-and-panics-in-american-history/#ixzz1boYbmujwa.

Chapter 5. The Progressive Movement (1897–1921)

1. Later in Bryan's career in 1925, at age sixty-five, he gained enormous prominence and was, perhaps, best remembered as the successful prosecutor in

the trial known as "The Monkey Trial" of Tennessee teacher John Scopes that determined whether evolution should be taught in American public schools.

2. Nevins and Commager, *A Short History*, 381.

3. Scott Myers-Lipton, *Social Solutions to Poverty: America's Struggle to Build a Just Society* (Boulder: Paradigm Publishers, 2006), 111.

4. Nevins and Commager, *A Short History*, 382–83.

5. William McKinley, "First Inaugural Address," March 4, 1897, Miller Center, http://millercenter.org/president/speeches/detail/3562.

6. Kevin Phillips, *William McKinley*, The American Presidents Series (New York: Times Books, 2003), 1.

7. Ibid., 113.

8. Ibid., 138.

9. Theodore Roosevelt, "Square Deal," Miller Center, http://millercenter .org/president/roosevelt/essays/biography/4.

10. Axinn and Stern, *Social Welfare*, 93.

11. Based on a West African proverb that was a favorite of Teddy Roosevelt's. When Roosevelt was governor of New York, he fought bitterly with the party bosses. Roosevelt held out, although the bosses threatened to ruin him. In the end the bosses gave in, according to Nathan Miller in his book, *Theodore Roosevelt: A Life* (New York: Morrow, 1992), 337.

12. Theodore Roosevelt, "First Annual Message," December 3, 1901, Miller Center, www.millercenter.org/president/speeches/detail/3773.

13. Theodore Roosevelt, "Second Annual Message," December 2, 1902, Miller Center, http://millercenter.org/president/speeches/detail/3774.

14. Ibid.; and Axinn and Stern, *Social Welfare*, 138.

15. Axinn and Stern, *Social Welfare*, 135.

16. Douglas Brinkley, *The Wilderness Warrior: Theodore Roosevelt and the Crusade for America* (New York: HarperCollins, 2009), 43.

17. Ibid., 313.

18. Theodore Roosevelt, "Domestic Affairs: On Race Relations and Civil Rights," Miller Center, http://millercenter.org/president/roosevelt/essays/ biography/4.

19. Ibid.; and Brinkley, *The Wilderness Warrior*, 404–5.

20. U.S. Census Bureau, 1880, http://www.census.gov/prod/www/abs/decen nial/1880.html.

21. Lincoln Steffens, published in book form, *The Shame of the Cities* (New York: McClure, Phillips, 1904), 136.

22. Jacob A. Riis, *Theodore Roosevelt, the Citizen* (New York: The Outlook Company, 1903), 13–14.

23. Ibid., 144.

24. Roosevelt, *Theodore Roosevelt*, 187.

25. Ibid., 219.

26. Riis, *Theodore Roosevelt, the Citizen*, 292–93.

27. Ibid., 354.
28. Ibid., 368.
29. Ibid., 409.
30. Theodore Roosevelt, *Theodore Roosevelt: An Autobiography* (New York: Macmillan, 1913), 707.
31. Theodore Roosevelt, "Domestic Affairs: Roosevelt and the Muckrakers," MillerCenter, http://millercenter.org/president/roosevelt/essays/biography/ 4. President Theodore Roosevelt himself originated the phrase "bully pulpit" when he referred to the White House as a "bully pulpit," or an ideal podium from which to advance his major programs. Roosevelt sometimes used the word "bully" as an adjective, meaning superb or wonderful, as in "bully for you."
32. Myers-Lipton, *Solutions to Poverty*, 117.
33. Woodrow Wilson, "First Inaugural Address," March 4, 1913, http:/miller center.org/scripps/archive/speeches/detail/3566.

Chapter 6. The Rise of Big Business (1921–1932)

1. "Warren G. Harding, Campaign Speech at Boston (1920)," http://wps .prenhall.com/wps/media/objects/107/110495/ch22_a5_d1.pdf.
2. Warren Gamaliel Harding, "Inaugural Address," March 4, 1921, Miller Center, http://millercenter.org/president/speeches/detail/3568.
3. John Fitzgerald Kennedy, "Inaugural Address," January 20, 1961, Miller Center, http://millercenter.org/president/speeches/detail/3365.
4. FDR had served in the Wilson administration as assistant secretary of the navy and helped the United States prepare the navy's involvement in World War I. His party leaders hailed Roosevelt's work, and as a result, in 1920, the Democrats named him its vice presidential candidate.
5. Eugene P. Trani and David L. Wilson, *The Presidency of Warren G. Harding* (Lawrence: Regents Press of Kansas, 1977), 38.
6. John W. Dean, *Warren G. Harding*, The American Presidents Series (New York: Times Books, 2004), 155: "Teapot Dome is the name of an oil field in Salt Creek, Wyoming, so named because of a teapot-shaped rock formation that stands atop a subterranean geological dome that contains oil. The catchy and unforgettable name Teapot Dome (like Watergate a half century later) became an identifying label for any scandal associated with the leasing of this Wyoming oil field, along with others in California."
7. Ibid., 159.
8. Trani and Wilson, *The Presidency of Warren G. Harding*, 102.
9. Ibid., 103.
10. Ibid.
11. Ibid.
12. Ibid., 105.
13. Ibid., 96.

14. Ibid., 192.
15. Dean, *Warren G. Harding*, 1.
16. Ibid.
17. Robert H. Ferrell, *The Presidency of Calvin Coolidge* (Lawrence: University of Kansas Press, 1998).
18. Calvin Coolidge, "Inaugural Address," March 4, 1925, Miller Center, http://millercenter.org/scripps/archive/speeches/detail/3569.
19. Cyndy Bittinger, "The Business of America Is Business," Calvin Coolidge Memorial Foundation, http://www.calvin-coolidge.org/html/the_business _of_america_is_bus.html. From Coolidge's speech called "The Press Under a Free Government" before the American Society of Newspaper Editors in Washington, D.C., on January 17, 1925. Coolidge, however, went on to put this statement in full context by adding this statement: "Of course the accumulation of wealth cannot be justified as the chief end of existence."
20. Ferrell, *The Presidency of Calvin Coolidge*, 41.
21. Ibid., 109.
22. Ibid., 186.
23. "Oh Yeah?: Herbert Hoover Predicts Prosperity," History Matters, http://historymatters.gmu.edu/d/5063/, citing Edward Angly's *Oh Yeah! Compiled from Newspapers and Public Records* (New York: Viking Press, 1931).
24. Herbert Clark Hoover, "Inaugural Address," March 4, 1929, Miller Center, http://millercenter.org/president/speeches/detail/3570.
25. Between 1925 and 1929, the New York Stock Exchange rose 250 percent, per Richard Norton Smith, *An Uncommon Man: The Triumph of Herbert Hoover* (New York: Simon & Schuster, 1984), 42.
26. Albert U. Romasco, *The Poverty of Abundance: Hoover, the Nation, the Depression* (New York: Oxford University Press, 1965), 3–5.
27. "President Hoover," Digital History, 2012, http://www.digitalhistory.uh.edu /disp_textbook.cfm?smtID=2&psid=3436 (accessed September 2012).

Chapter 7. The Great Depression and Social Reform (1932–1961)

1. Franklin D. Roosevelt, "The Forgotten Man, April 7, 1932," first radio address, Albany, New York, New Deal Network, http://newdeal.feri.org /speeches/1932c.htm.
2. Franklin D. Roosevelt, "Roosevelt's Nomination Address, Chicago, Illinois July 2, 1932," New Deal Network, http://newdeal.feri.org/speeches /1932b.htm.
3. "1932 Presidential General Election Results," Dave Leip's Atlas of U.S. Presidential Elections, http://www.uselectionatlas.org/RESULTS/national .php?f=0&year=1932.
4. Franklin Delano Roosevelt, "First Inaugural Address," March 4, 1933, Miller Center, http://millercenter.org/president/speeches/detail/3280.

5. Nevins and Commager, *A Short History*, 476–77.

6. James MacGregor Burns, *Roosevelt: The Lion and The Fox*, vol. 1 (New York: Harcourt, Brace, 1956), 156.

7. Doris Kearns Goodwin, "Character Above All: Franklin D. Roosevelt," Essays, PBS http://www.pbs.org/newshour/character/essays/roosevelt.html.

8. See appendix A in this volume, "Franklin D. Roosevelt and the New Deal," which is adapted from various online versions of the New Deal's timeline of legislation passed during the Great Depression. Historians distinguish two periods in the New Deal—the first as 1933 and the second as 1934–1936.

9. William E. Leuchtenburg, *Franklin D. Roosevelt and the New Deal, 1932–1940* (New York: Harper & Row, 1963), 61.

10. Burns, *Roosevelt*, 205.

11. Leuchtenburg, *Franklin D. Roosevelt*, 14.

12. World War II: Home Front Statistics, Schmoop.com, http://www.shmoop.com/wwii-home-front/statistics.html.

13. Father Coughlin, "Activism and Political Views," Old Time Radio, 2012, http://www.fathercoughlin.org/father-coughlin-anti-communism.html.

14. Huey P. Long, *Kingfish to America, Share Our Wealth: Selected Senatorial Papers of Huey P. Long*, ed. Henry M. Christman (New York: Schocken Books, 1985), 42.

15. Doris Kearns Goodwin, *No Ordinary Time: Franklin and Eleanor Roosevelt: The Home Front in World War II* (New York: Simon & Schuster, 1994), 46.

16. Harry S. Truman, "First Speech to Congress," April 16, 1945, Miller Center, http://millercenter.org/president/speeches/detail/3339.

17. Harry S. Truman, *Memoirs of Harry S. Truman*, vol. 2, *Years of Trial and Hope, 1946–1952* (Garden City, NY: Doubleday, 1956), 181.

18. Excerpted from Harry S. Truman, Address to the NAACP, at the closing session of the Thirty-eighth Annual Conference of the NAACP at the Lincoln Memorial, Washington, D.C., June 28, 1947, in "Truman," *American Experience*, WGBH-PBS, www.pbs.org/wgbh/amex/truman/psources/ps_naacphtml.

19. Truman, *Memoirs*, 2:179.

20. Truman, address to the NAACP; and Truman, *Memoirs*, 183.

21. Dwight David Eisenhower, "First Inaugural Address," January 20, 1953, Miller Center, http://millercenter.org/president/speeches/detail/3356.

22. Stephen E. Ambrose, *Eisenhower: Soldier and President* (New York: Simon & Schuster, 1990), 336.

23. Dwight D. Eisenhower, "Annual Message to the Congress on the State of the Union," February 2, 1953, www.eisenhower.archives.gov/all_about_ike/speeches/1953_state_of_the_union.pdf.

24. In *Plessy v. Ferguson*, the U.S. Supreme Court decided in 1896 that a Louisiana law mandating separate but equal accommodations for blacks and whites on interstate railroads was constitutional. This decision provided

the legal foundation to justify many other state and local governments' actions to separate blacks and whites socially.

25. Klein, *Toward Humanity and Justice*, 167. From Dr. Kenneth B. Clark's white paper, "Contemporary Realities in American Race Relations" (Hastings-on-Hudson, NY: Clark Archives, 1983).

26. Ambrose, *Eisenhower*, 409–10.

27. William Bragg Ewald Jr., *Eisenhower the President: Crucial Days, 1951–1960* (Englewood Cliffs, NJ: Prentice-Hall, 1981), 39.

28. Arthur Larson, *Eisenhower: The President Nobody Knew* (New York: Scribner, 1968), 124–26.

29. Frank Stricker, *Why America Lost the War on Poverty—and How to Win It* (Chapel Hill: University of North Carolina Press, 2007), 15; and Nevins and Commager, *A Short History*, 611.

30. Nevins and Commager, *A Short History*, 611.

Chapter 8. The War on Poverty and Its Aftermath (1961–1981)

1. John F. Kennedy, "Announcement of Candidacy, 2 January, 1960, [2 January 1960]," Papers of John F. Kennedy, John F. Kennedy Presidential Library and Museum, Boston, Massachusetts, http://www.jfklibrary.org/Asset-Viewer/Archives/JFKPOF-136-018.aspx.

2. John Fitzgerald Kennedy, "Acceptance of the Democratic Party Nomination," July 15, 1960, Miller Center, http://millercenter.org/president/speeches/detail/3362.

3. John Fitzgerald Kennedy, "Inaugural Address," January 20, 1961, Miller Center, http://millercenter.org/scripps/archive/speeches/detail/3365.

4. John Fitzgerald Kennedy, "Address on Civil Rights," June 11, 1963, Miller Center, http://millercenter.org/president/speeches/detail/3375.

5. Arthur M. Schlesinger Jr., *A Thousand Days: John F. Kennedy in the White House* (Boston: Houghton Mifflin, 1965), 1011.

6. See R. Sargent Shriver's comments in "LBJ," *American Experience*, WGBH-PBS, http://www.pbs.org/wgbh/americanexperience/features/transcriptlbj-transcript/.

7. Stricker, *Why America Lost the War*, 37.

8. Chris Matthews, *Jack Kennedy: Elusive Hero* (New York: Simon & Schuster, 2011), 264.

9. Ibid., 264–65.

10. See David Leip, "1960 Presidential General Election Results: John Kennedy vs. Richard Nixon," Atlas of U.S. Presidential Elections, 2012, http://www.uselectionatlas.org/RESULTS/national.php?year=1960&f=0.

11. Stricker, *Why America Lost the War*, 38.

12. Richard Reeves, *President Kennedy: Profile of Power* (New York: Simon & Schuster, 1993), 480.

13. Stricker, *Why America Lost the War*, 48.

14. Robert Dallek, *An Unfinished Life: John F. Kennedy, 1917–1963* (Boston: Little, Brown, 2003), 707.

15. John F. Kennedy, *Profiles in Courage* (New York: Harper & Brothers, 1956), 51.

16. Doris Kearns Goodwin, *Lyndon Johnson and the American Dream* (New York: Harper & Row, 1976), 188.

17. Robert Dallek, *Flawed Giant: Lyndon Johnson and His Times, 1961–1973* (New York: Oxford University Press, 1998), 6; and Robert Dallek, *Lone Star Rising: Lyndon Johnson and His Times, 1908–1960* (New York: Oxford University Press, 1991), passim.

18. Lyndon Baines Johnson, "State of the Union," January 8, 1964, Miller Center, http://millercenter.org/president/speeches/detail/3382.

19. Jeannie Chen, "From the Archives: The Medicare Bill of 1965," The White House Blog, July 30, 2012, http://www.whitehouse.gov/blog/2012/07/30/archives-medicare-bill-1965.

20. Dallek, *Flawed Giant*, 64.

21. U.S. Bureau of the Census, Current Population Survey, Annual Social and Economic Supplements, www.census.gov/apsd/techdoc/cps/cpsmart10pdf.

22. The war on poverty costs Americans more than a trillion dollars each year. See Edgar K. Browning, "America's Trillion-Dollar War on Poverty," BrookesNews.com, September 15, 2008, www.brookesnews.com/081509welfarepoverty.html.

23. David McCullough, on "LBJ," *American Experience*, WGBH-PBS, www.pbs.org/wgbh/americanexperience/features/transcript/lbj-transcript/?fla.

24. Dallek, *Flawed Giant*, 529.

25. William J. vanden Heuvel and Milton Gwirtzman, *On His Own: Robert F. Kennedy, 1964–1968* (Garden City, NY: Doubleday, 1970), 386.

26. Richard Milhous Nixon, "First Inaugural Address," January 20, 1969, Miller Center, http://millercenter.org/president/speeches/detail/3587.

27. Nevins and Commager, *A Short History*, 668–69.

28. Ibid., 669.

29. Ibid, 670.

30. Elizabeth Drew, *Richard M. Nixon*, The American Presidents Series (New York: Times Books, 2007), 19.

31. Excerpts from "Gerald R. Ford's inaugural address, August 9, 1974," History.com http://www.history.com/videos/inaugural-address-gerold-ford.

32. Gerald Rudolph Ford, "Domestic Affairs," Miller Center, http://millercenter.org/president/ford/essays/biography/4.

33. Ibid. The Miller Center describes itself as "a nonpartisan institute at the University of Virginia that seeks to expand understanding of the presidency, policy, and political history, providing critical insights for the nation's governance challenges." See Miller Center, http://millercenter.about/.

34. Ibid.

35. Ibid.

36. *New York Daily News* headline of October 29, 1975. See Reuven Blau, "Ford to City: Drop Dead: President's Snub Inspired, Not Discouraged, Ex-Gov. Hugh Carey," *New York Daily News*, August, 8, 2011, http://articles.nydailynews.com/2011-08-08/news/29882248_1_felix-rohatyn-president-ford-unions.

37. John Robert Greene, *The Presidency of Gerald R. Ford* (Lawrence: University Press of Kansas, 1995), 189–90.

38. John Woolley and Gerhard Peters, "Jimmy Carter: Inaugural Address, January 20, 1977," The American Presidency Project, www.presidency.ucsb.edu/ws/index.php?pid=6575.

39. Jimmy Carter, "'Crisis of Confidence' Speech," July 15, 1979, Miller Center, http://millercenter.org/scripps/archive/speeches/detail/3402.

40. American President: Jimmy Carter (1924–): Life in Brief," Miller Center, http://millercenter.org/president/carter/essays/biography/1.

41. "About Us," The Carter Center, http://www.cartercenter.org/about/index.html.

Chapter 9. The Emergence of Globalization (1981–2012)

1. Ronald Wilson Reagan, "First Inaugural Address," January 20, 1981, Miller Center, http://millercenter.org/scripps/archive/speeches/detail/3407.

2. Dr. Paul Craig Roberts is called "the father of Reaganomics." He was the former head of policy at the Department of Treasury. A columnist and the previous the editor of the *Wall Street Journal*, Roberts was assistant secretary of the treasury during Reagan's first term. Paul Craig Roberts, "Reaganomics," Inteltrends, December 20,1010, http://inteltrends.wordpress.com/2010/12/20/paul-craig-roberts-reaganomics/. It should also be noted that George H. W. Bush, in a losing challenge to Reagan for the presidential nomination in 1980, referred to Reagan's economic philosophy as "voodoo economics" or "trickle down" economics—a phrase Bush would come to regret.

3. Edmund Morris, *Dutch: A Memoir of Ronald Reagan* (New York: Random House, 1999), 422.

4. Ibid., 423.

5. Ibid., 438.

6. Ronald Wilson Reagan, "Address on the Program for Economic Recovery," April 28, 1981, Miller Center, http://millercenter.org/president/speeches/detail/544.

7. Morris, *Dutch*, 439.

8. Ronald Reagan, *An American Life* (New York: Simon & Schuster, 1990), 312.

9. Lou Cannon, *President Reagan: The Role of a Lifetime* (New York: Simon & Schuster, 1991), 232.

10. Ibid., 233.

11. Ibid., 235.
12. Ibid.
13. Ibid., 234.
14. Ibid., 83.
15. Ibid., 815.
16. U.S. Bureau of the Census, *2010 Annual Social and Economic Supplement.*
17. Ibid.; and Cannon, *President Reagan,* 74–75.
18. Reagan, *An American Life,* 401.
19. Ronald Wilson Reagan, "Impact and Legacy," Miller Center, http:/miller center.org/president/reagan/essays/biography/8.
20. Ibid.
21. Jason DeParle, "The Nation: Debris of Past Failures Impedes Poverty Policy," *New York Times,* November 7, 1993, http://www.nytimes.com /1993/11/07/weekinreview/the-nation-debris-of-past-failures-impedes -poverty-policy.html.
22. Ron Reagan, *My Father at 100* (New York: Viking, 2011), 5.
23. Herbert S. Parmet, *George Bush: The Life of a Lone Star Yankee* (New York: Scribner, 1997), 348.
24. George H. W. Bush, "Domestic Affairs," Miller Center, http://miller center.org/president/bush/essays/biography/4.
25. George H. W. Bush, "Inaugural Address," January 20, 1989, Miller Center, http://millercenter.org/president/speeches/detail/3419.
26. Doro Bush Koch, *My Father, My President: A Personal Account of the Life of George H. W. Bush* (New York: Warner Books, 2006), 218.
27. Bush, "Inaugural Address."
28. "It's the economy, stupid," is a phrase political adviser James Carville made famous during President Clinton's successful 1992 presidential race.
29. Timothy Naftali, *George H. W. Bush,* The American Presidents Series (New York: Times Books/Henry Holt, 2007), 3.
30. Nigel Hamilton, *Bill Clinton: An American Journey* (New York: Random House, 2003), 665.
31. Bill Clinton, *My Life* (New York: Alfred A. Knopf, 2004), 449.
32. Ibid., 476.
33. Ibid., 477.
34. David E. Procter and Kurt Ritter, "Inaugurating the Clinton Presidency: Regenerative Rhetoric and the American Community," in *The Clinton Presidency: Images Issues, and Communication Strategies,* ed. Robert E. Denton, Jr., and Rachel L. Holloway (Westport, CT: Praeger, 1996), 11.
35. Bill Clinton, address before a joint session of Congress, February 17, 1993, Miller Center, http://millercenter.org/presient/speeches/detail/3435.
36. Katz, *In the Shadow of the Poorhouse,* 327.
37. Clinton, *My Life,* 623.

38. Clinton, *My Life*, 624.

39. A CNN transcript of President Clinton's radio address, "The Era of Big Government Is Over," January 27, 1996, http://www.cnn.com/US/9601 /budget/01-27/clinton_radio/.

40. Bill Clinton, *My Life*, vol. 2, *The Presidential Years* (New York: Vintage Books, 2005), 720.

41. Sidney Blumenthal, *The Clinton Wars* (New York: Farrar, Straus and Giroux, 2003), 146.

42. John Iceland, *Poverty in America: A Handbook* (Berkeley: University of California Press, 2006), 126.

43. Clinton, *My Life*, 721.

44. Ibid.

45. Ibid., 862.

46. Of all the candidates who have run for president in recent years, only one—Senator John Edwards of North Carolina—made poverty his campaign theme in 2004, when he ran as vice presidential candidate with Senator John Kerry of Massachusetts. Edwards also ran a second time for president in 2008 before he was forced to leave the race because of an extramarital scandal.

47. Kevin P. Phillips, *American Dynasty: Aristocracy, Fortune, and the Politics of Deceit in the House of Bush* (New York: Viking Press, 2004), 114.

48. George W. Bush, "First Inaugural Address," January 20, 2001, Miller Center, http://millercenter.org/president/speeches/detail/3645 G.W. Bush speeches.

49. "President Bush's Acceptance Speech to the Republican National Convention," *Washington Post*, September 2, 2004, http://www.washingtonpost .com/wp-dyn/articles/A57466-2004Sep2.html.

50. George W. Bush, *Decision Points* (New York: Crown Publishers, 2010), 277.

51. Lisa Leung, "Woodward Shares War Secrets," from transcript of Correspondent Mike Wallace interviewing author Bob Woodward, *60 Minutes*, December 5, 2007, www.cbsnews.com/stories/2004/04/15/60minutes /main612067.shtml.

52. Bush, *Decision Points*, 325.

53. Ibid., 326.

54. U.S. Bureau of the Census, Annual Social and Economic Supplements.

55. Don Goyea, "Undecided We Stand: Debating Bush's Legacy," National Public Radio, January 7, 2009, http://www.npr.org/templates/story/story .php?storyId=99059614.

56. Joseph E. Stiglitz, "Reckoning: The Economic Consequences of Mr. Bush," *Vanity Fair*, December 2007, http://www.vanityfair.com/politics /features/2007/12/bush200712.

57. Barack Obama, *The Audacity of Hope: Thoughts on Reclaiming the American Dream* (New York: Crown Publishers, 2006), 231.

58. David Remnick, *The Bridge: The Life and Rise of Barack Obama* (New York: Alfred A. Knopf, 2010), 23.

59. Barack Obama, "Acceptance Speech at the Democratic National Convention," August 28, 2008, Miller Center, http://millercenter.org/president /speeches/detail/4427.

60. Barack Obama, "Inaugural Address," January 20, 2009, Miller Center, http://millercenter.org/president/speeches/detail/4453 Obama speeches.

61. Remnick, *The Bridge*, 581–83.

62. Hari Sreenivasan, "Michael Beshcloss on Obama's First Year," *Rundown*, Public Broadcasting System Channel 13, December 30, 2009, http://www .pbs.org/newshour/rundown/2009/12/michael-beschloss-on-obamas -first-year.html.

63. Doris Kearns Goodwin, "Following in JFK's Footsteps," The Daily Beast, January 19, 2010, http://www.thedailybeast.com/articles/2010/01/19/ following-in-jfks-footsteps.html.

64. Tim Mak, "Doris Kearns Goodwin: Obama Best Prez List Short," *Politico*, December 21, 2011, www.politico.com/news/stories/1211/70749.html, quoting Doris Kearns Goodwin on MSNBC's *Morning' Joe*, December 21, 2011.

65. Katrina vanden Heuvel, *The Change I Believe In: Fighting for Progress in the Age of Obama* (New York: The Nation Books, 2011), 26–27.

66. "State of the Union 2012: Full Transcript of President Obama's Speech," *The Guardian*, January 24, 2012, http://www.guardian.co.uk/world/2012 /jan/25/state-of-the-union-address-full-text.

67. Andrew Sullivan, "How Obama's Long Game Will Outsmart His Critics," *Newsweek*, January 16, 2012, http://www.thedailybeast.com/newsweek /2012/01/15/andrew-sullivan-how-obama-s-long-game-will-outsmart -his-critics.html.

68. Nicholas D. Kristof, "The White Underclass," *New York Times*, February 9, 2012, http://www.nytimes.com/2012/02/09/opinion/kristof-the -decline-of-white-workers.html.

69. Ibid.

70. Ibid.

71. Sabrina Tavernise, "Education Gap Grows Between Rich and Poor, Studies, Say," *New York Times*, February 10, 2012.

72. Michael Grabell, *Money Well Spent? The Truth Behind The Trillion-Dollar Stimulus, The Biggest Economic Recovery Plan in History* (New York: Public-Affairs, 2012,) ix.

73. Ibid., xi.

74. Ibid., x.

75. Ibid.

76. Ibid., 313.

77. Ibid., 360.

Appendix C. American Poverty

1. Peter Edelman, "The War on Poverty and Subsequent Federal Programs: What Worked, What Didn't Work, and Why? Lessons for Future Programs," *The Clearinghouse Review, Georgetown Journal on Poverty Law and Policy* 40 (2006): 7–18.

2. Statement from Katrina vanden Heuvel to the author, January 10, 2012.

3. Barbara Ehrenreich, "How America Turned Poverty into a Crime," Salon.com, August 9, 2011, http://www.salon.com/2011/08/09/america_crime_poverty/.

4. Paul Krugman, "The Slump before the Slump," *New York Times*, September 14, 2011, http://krugman.blogs.nytimes.com/2011/09/14/the-slump-before-the-slump/.

5. Statement exclusively to author from Robert Dallek, professor of History, University of California, Los Angeles, via iPhone, January 2, 2012.

6. Mark Greenberg, "From Poverty to Prosperity: A National Strategy to Cut Poverty," Center for American Progress Poverty Task Force, April 25, 2007, www.americanprogress.org/issues/2007/04/poverty_report.html.

7. Joseph Stiglitz, "Of the 1%, by the 1%, for the 1%," *Vanity Fair*, May 2011, http://www.vanityfair.com/society/features/2011/05/top-one-percent-201105.

8. Audie Cornish interview with Michael Beschloss, "Obama's Re-Election: What Are the Odds?," NPR.org., September 18, 2011, http://www.npr.org/2011/09/18/140573224/obamas-re-election-what-are-the-odds.

9. Hutchinson, "Poverty Is America's Taboo Word."

10. Tom Brokaw on the Travis Smiley program, WNET-PBS, December 2011. Transcript at http://www.pbs.org/wnet/tavissmiley/interviews/journalist-tom-brokaw-2/.

11. Congressman John Lewis (D-Ga.), April 2, 2011, quoted in Indogo Blue, "Rep. John Lewis: 'Make Some Noise, Get in the Way.' 'The Poor Have No Lobbyists To Do Their Work,'" DemocraticUnderground.com, September 11, 2008, http://journals.democraticunderground.com/indigo%20Blue/30.

12. Henry Louis Gates, "Forty Acres and a Gap in Wealth," *New York Times*, November 18, 2007, http://www.nytimes.com/2007/11/18/opinion/18gates.html?pagewanted=all.

13. Kevin Dolak, "Smiley and West: Poverty, Income Inequalities in US Could Lead to UK-like Riots," ABCNnews, August 11, 2011, http://abcnews.go.com/blogs/politics/2011/08/smiley-and-west-poverty-income-inequalities-in-us-could-lead-to-uk-like-riots/.

14. Secretary of the Treasury Timothy Geithner, "Welcome to the Recovery," *New York Times* Op-Ed, August 2, 2011, http://www.nytimes.com/2010/08/03/opinion/03geithner.html?pagewanted=all.

15. Robert Reich, "Romney's Hypocritical Attackers," Salon.com, January 10, 2012, www.salon.com/2012/01/10/romneys_hypocritical_attackers/.

16. Sheldon Danziger, director of the National Poverty Center, University of Michigan, in e-mail to author.

17. Richard Ouzounian, "Harry Belafonte Book Details Poverty, Racism and Fame," TheStar.com, January 11, 2012, http://www.thestar.com /entertainment/article/1114080--harry-belafonte-book-details-poverty -racism-and-fame.

18. Thomas Sowell, "Political Poverty: Advocates of Bigger Government Use 'the Poor' and 'Elderly' as Human Shields," *The National Review*, August 3, 2011. http://www.freerepublic.com/focus/f-news/2758006/posts.

19. "Back From The Dead? Jackson Says Revive The 'War On Poverty'" *News-One*, September 27, 2011, http://newsone.com/1551855/jesse-jackson -revive-the-war-on-poverty/.

20. Mitt Romney, quoted in Charles M. Blow, "Romney, the Rich, and the Rest," *New York Times*, February 3, 2012, http://www.nytimes.com /2012/02/04/opinion/blow-romney-the-rich-and-the-rest.html.

21. Written statement to author from Victor Navasky, February 3, 2012.

SELECTED BIBLIOGRAPHY

Books

Addams, Jane. *The Second Twenty Years at Hull-House, September 1909 to September 1929, with a Record of a Growing World Consciousness.* New York: Macmillan, 1930.

———. *Twenty Years at Hull-House, with Autobiographical Notes.* New York: Penguin Books USA, 1981.

Aikman, David. *A Man of Faith: The Spiritual Journey of George W. Bush.* Nashville, TN: W Pub. Group, 2004.

Ambrose, Stephen E. *Eisenhower: Soldier and President.* New York: Simon & Schuster, 1990.

Anderson, Judith. *William Howard Taft: An Intimate History.* New York: Norton, 1981.

Anderson, Margaret L., and Patricia Hill Collins, eds. *Race, Class and Gender: An Anthology.* 7th ed. Belmont, CA: Wadsworth, 2010.

Angelou, Maya. *Amazing Peace: A Christmas Poem.* New York: Schwartz & Wade Books, 2008.

Arrighi, Barbara A., and David J. Maume. *Child Poverty in America Today.* Praeger Perspectives. 4 vols. Westport, CT: Praeger, 2007.

Ashmore, Susan Youngblood. *Carry It On: The War on Poverty and the Civil Rights Movement in Alabama, 1964–1972.* Athens: University of Georgia Press, 2008.

Axelrod-Contrada, Joan. *Poverty in America: Cause or Effect?* New York: Marshall Cavendish Benchmark, 2010.

Axinn, June, and Mark J. Stern. *Social Welfare: A History of the American Response to Need.* 6th ed. Boston: Pearson/Allyn and Bacon, 2005.

Barnard, Harry. *Rutherford B. Hayes and His America.* Indianapolis: Bobbs-Merrill, 1954.

Baumohl, Jim, ed. *Homelessness in America.* Phoenix, AZ: Oryx Press, 1996.

Beer, Samuel H., and Richard E. Barringer, eds. *The State and the Poor.* Faculty Study Group, John F. Kennedy School of Government, Institute of Politics. Cambridge, MA: Winthrop Press, 1970.

Bennett, Robert, and Thomas Newman. *Poverty and Welfare.* Justice in America Series. Boston: Houghton Mifflin, 1969.

Blumenthal, Sidney. *The Clinton Wars.* New York: Farrar, Straus and Giroux, 2003.

Brinkley, Douglas. *Gerald R. Ford.* The American Presidents Series. New York: Times Books, 2007.

———. *The Wilderness Warrior: Theodore Roosevelt and the Crusade for America.* New York: HarperCollins, 2009.

Burch, John R. *Owsley County, Kentucky and the Perpetuation of Poverty.* Contribution to Southern Appalachian Studies. Jefferson, NC: McFarland, 2007.

Burns, James MacGregor. *Roosevelt: The Lion and the Fox.* Vol. 1, *1882–1940, the First Political Biography of FDR.* New York: Harcourt, Brace, 1956.

Burns, James MacGregor, and Susan Dunn. *George Washington.* The American Presidents Series. New York: Times Book, 2004.

Burton, C. Emory. *The Poverty Debate: Politics and the Poor in America.* New York: Greenwood Press, 1992.

Bush, George. *All the Best, George Bush: My Life in Letters and Other Writings.* New York: Scribner, 1999.

———. *Looking Forward.* With Victor Gold. Garden City, NY: Doubleday, 1987.

Bush, George W. *Decision Points.* New York: Crown, 2010.

Calhoun, Charles W. *Benjamin Harrison.* New York: Times Books, 2005.

Califano, Jr., Joseph A. *Inside: A Public and Private Life.* New York: PublicAffairs, 2004.

Cancian, Maria, and Sheldon Danziger, eds. *Changing Poverty, Changing Policies.* New York: Russell Sage Foundation, 2009.

Cannon, Lou. *Governor Reagan: His Rise to Power.* New York: PublicAffairs, 2003.

———. *President Reagan: The Role of a Lifetime.* New York: Simon & Schuster, 1991.

Capa, Cornell. *Margin of Life: Population and Poverty in the Americas.* New York: Grossman, 1974.

Caro, Robert A. *The Years of Lyndon Johnson.* Vol. 1, *The Path to Power.* New York: Knopf, 1982.

Carter, Dan T. *The Politics of Rage: George Wallace, the Origins of the New Conservatism, and the Transformation of American Politics.* New York: Simon & Schuster, 1995.

Carwardine, Richard. *Lincoln: A Life of Purpose and Power.* New York: Alfred A. Knopf, 2006.

Chafel, Judith A., ed. *Child Poverty and Public Policy.* Washington, D.C.: Urban Institute Press, 1993.

Chappell, Marisa. *The War on Welfare: Family, Poverty, and Politics in Modern America*. Politics in Culture in Modern America. Philadelphia: University of Pennsylvania Press, 2010.

Chernow, Ron. *Washington: A Life*. New York: Penguin Press, 2010.

Christman, Henry M, ed. *Kingfish to America, Share Our Wealth: Selected Senatorial Papers of Henry P. Long*. New York: Schocken Books, 1985.

Clark, Kenneth B. "Contemporary Realities in American Race Relations." White Paper. Hastings-on-Hudson, New York: Clark Archives, 1983.

Cleaves, Freeman. *Old Tippecanoe: William Henry Harrison and His Time*. New York: C. Scribner's Sons, 1939.

Clinton, Bill. *Back to Work: Why We Need Smart Government for a Strong Economy*. New York: Alfred A. Knopf, 2011.

———. *My Life*. New York: Alfred A. Knopf, 2004.

Cohen, Adam Seth. *Nothing to Fear: FDR's Inner Circle and the Hundred Days that Created Modern America*. New York: Penguin Press, 2009.

Conley, Dalton, ed. *Wealth and Poverty in America: A Reader*. Maiden, MA: Blackwell, 2003.

Cooper, John Milton. *Woodrow Wilson: A Biography*. New York: Alfred A. Knopf, 2009.

Crapol, Edward P. *John Tyler: The Accidental President*. Chapel Hill: University of North Carolina Press, 2006.

Cresson, William Penn. *James Monroe*. Chapel Hill: University of North Carolina Press, 1946.

Curtis, James C. *Andrew Jackson and the Search for Vindication*. Boston: Little, Brown, 1976.

Dallek, Robert. *Flawed Giant: Lyndon Johnson and His Times, 1961–1973*. New York: Oxford University Press, 1998.

———. *Harry S. Truman*. New York: Times Books, 2008.

———. *Lone Star Rising: Lyndon Johnson and His Times, 1908–1960*. New York: Oxford University Press, 1991.

———. *An Unfinished Life: John F Kennedy, 1917–1963*. Boston: Little, Brown, 2003.

Danziger, Sheldon H., and Robert H. Haveman, eds. *Understanding Poverty*. Cambridge, MA: Harvard University Press, 2001.

Darby, Michael R. *Reducing Poverty in America: Views and Approaches*. Thousand Oaks, CA: Sage Publications, 1995.

Davis, Bertha H. *Poverty in America: What We Do about It*. New York: Franklin Watts, 1991.

Davis, Burke. *Old Hickory: A Life of Andrew Jackson*. New York: Dial Press, 1977.

Davis, Kenneth S., ed. *The Paradox of Poverty in America*. New York: H. W. Wilson, 1969.

Dean, John W. *Warren G. Harding*. The American Presidents Series. New York: Times Books, 2004.

DeFrank, Thomas M. *Write It When I'm Gone: Remarkable Off-the-Record Conversations with Gerald R. Ford.* New York: G. P. Putnam's Sons, 2007.

DiNitto, Diane M. *Social Welfare: Politics and Public Policy.* 3rd ed. Englewood Cliffs, NJ: Prentice Hall, 1991.

Doenecke, Justus D. *The Presidencies of James A. Garfield & Chester A. Arthur.* Lawrence: Regents Press of Kansas, 1981.

Donald, David Herbert, and Harold Holzer, ed. *Lincoln in* The Times: *The Life of Abraham Lincoln, as Originally Reported in the* New York Times. New York: St. Martin's, 2005.

Drew, Elizabeth. *Richard M. Nixon.* The American Presidents Series. New York: Times Books, 2007.

Eberstadt, Nick. *The Poverty of "the Poverty Rate": Measure and Mismeasure of Want in Modern America.* Washington, D.C.: AEI Press, 2008.

Edwards, John, Marion Crain, and Arne L. Kalleberg. *Ending Poverty in America: How to Restore the American Dream.* New York: New Press, 2007.

Ehrenreich, Barbara. *Nickel and Dimed: On (Not) Getting By in America.* New York: Holt, 2008.

Eisenhower, John S. D. *Zachary Taylor.* The American Presidents Series. New York: Times Books, 2008.

Evans, Karl C., and Donella R. Evans. *And Crown Thy Good: Relieving Poverty and Struggle in Rural America.* Seattle, WA: CreateSpace Independent Publishing Platforms, 2010.

Ewald, Jr., William Bragg. *Eisenhower the President: Crucial Days, 1951–1960.* Englewood Cliffs, NJ: Prentice-Hall, 1981.

Fanelli, Vincent. *The Human Face of Poverty: A Chronicle of Urban America.* New York: Bookstrap Press, 1990.

Ferrell, Robert H. *The Presidency of Calvin Coolidge.* Lawrence: University of Kansas Press, 1998.

Fitzpatrick, Kevin, and Mark LaGory. *Unhealthy Cities: Poverty, Race and Place in America.* New York: Routledge, 2011.

Freedman, Jonathan L. *From Cradle to Grave: The Human Face of Poverty in America.* New York: Atheneum, 1993.

Freeman, Douglas Southall. *Washington: An Abridgement by Richard Harwell of the Seven-Volume* George Washington *by Douglas Southall Freeman.* New York: Charles Scribner's Sons, 1968.

Funiciello, Theresa. *Tyranny of Kindness: Dismantling the Welfare System to End Poverty in America.* New York: Atlantic Monthly Press, 1993.

Gara, Larry. *The Presidency of Franklin Pierce.* Lawrence: University Press of Kansas, 1991.

Gates, Henry Louis, Jr., and Donald Yacovone, eds. *Lincoln on Race and Slavery.* Princeton, NJ: Princeton University Press, 2009.

Gilbert, Neil, and Paul Terrell. *Dimensions of Social Welfare Policy.* Boston, MA: Allyn and Bacon, 2002.

Gillette, Michael L. *Launching the War on Poverty: An Oral History*. Oxford Oral History Series/Twayne's Oral History Series. New York: Twayne Publishers, 1996.

Glasmeier, Amy. *An Atlas of Poverty in America: One Nation, Pulling Apart, 1960–2003*. New York: Routledge, 2006.

Goodwin, Doris Kearns. *Lyndon Johnson and the American Dream*. New York: Harper & Row, 1976.

———. *No Ordinary Time: Franklin and Eleanor Roosevelt: The Home Front in World War II*. New York: Simon & Schuster, 1994.

———. *Team of Rivals: The Political Genius of Abraham Lincoln*. New York: Simon & Schuster, 2005.

Gordon-Reed. Annette. *Andrew Johnson*. The American Presidents Series. New York: Times Books/Henry Holt, 2011.

Grabell, Michael. *Money Well Spent? The Truth Behind the Trillion-Dollar Stimulus, the Biggest Economic Recovery Plan in History*. New York: PublicAffairs, 2012.

Graff, Henry Franklin. *Grover Cleveland*. New York: Times Books, 2002.

Greene, John Robert. *The Presidency of Gerald R. Ford*. Lawrence: University Press of Kansas, 1995.

Gushee, David P. *Toward a Just and Caring Society: Christian Responses to Poverty in America*. Grand Rapids, MI: Baker Books, 1999.

Hamilton, Nigel. *Bill Clinton: An American Journey*. New York: Random House, 2003.

Harrington, Michael. *The Other America: Poverty in the United States*. New York: Macmillan, 1962.

Hartman, Chester W. *Challenges to Equality: Poverty and Race in America*. Armonk, NY: M. E. Sharpe, 2001.

———. *Double Exposure: Poverty & Race in America*. Armonk, NY: M. E. Sharpe, 1997.

Hayes, Kevin J. *The Road to Monticello: The Life and Mind of Thomas Jefferson*. New York: Oxford University Press, 2008.

Herndon, Ruth Wallis. *Unwelcome Americans: Living on the Margin in Early New England*. Early American Studies. Philadelphia: University of Pennsylvania Press, 2001.

Hickok, Lorena A. *One-Third of a Nation: Lorena Hickok Reports on the Great Depression*. Edited by Richard Lowitt and Maurine Beasley. Urbana: University of Illinois Press, 1981.

Holt, Michael Fitzgibbon. *Franklin Pierce*. New York: Times Books/Henry Holt, 2010.

Iceland, John. *Poverty in America: A Handbook*. Berkeley: University of California Press, 2006.

James, Marquis. *Andrew Jackson: A Portrait of a President*. Indianapolis: Bobbs-Merrill, 1977.

Katz, Michael B. *In the Shadow of the Poorhouse: A Social History of Welfare in America*. New York: Basic Books, 1986.

Kearney, Janis F. *Conversations: William Jefferson Clinton: From Hope to Harlem*. Chicago: Writing Our World Press, 2006.

Kelso, William Alton. *Poverty and the Underclass: Changing Perceptions of the Poor in America*. New York: New York University Press, 1994.

Kendall, Diana Elizabeth. *Framing Class: Media Representations of Wealth and Poverty in America*. Lanham, MD: Rowman & Littlefield Publishers, 2005.

Kennedy, John F. *Profiles in Courage*. New York: Harper & Brothers, 1956.

Ketcham, Ralph. *James Madison: A Biography*. New York: Macmillan, 1971.

Kilty, Keith, and Elizabeth Segal, eds. *Rediscovering the Other America: The Continuing Crisis of Poverty and Inequality in the United States*. New York: Haworth Press, 2007.

Klein, Woody. *Let in the Sun*. New York: Macmillan, 1964.

———. *Toward Humanity and Justice: The Writings of Kenneth B. Clark, Scholar of the 1954* Brown v Board of Education *Decision*. Westport, CT: Praeger, 2004.

Koch, Doro Bush. *My Father, My President: A Personal Account of the Life of George H. W. Bush*. New York: Warner Books, 2006.

Kornbluh, Felicia Ann. *The Battle for Welfare Rights: Politics and Poverty in Modern America*. Philadelphia: University of Pennsylvania Press, 2007.

Korstad, Robert Rodgers, and James Leloudis. *To Right These Wrongs: The North Carolina Fund and the Battle to End Poverty and Inequality in 1960s America*. Chapel Hill: University of North Carolina Press, 2010.

Kostyal, Karen M. *Abraham Lincoln's Extraordinary Era: The Man and His Times*. Washington, D.C.: National Geographic, 2009.

Landon, Michael L. *Sweating It Out: What the "Experts" Say Causes Poverty*. Lanham, MA: University Press of America, 2006.

Larson, Arthur. *Eisenhower: The President Nobody Knew*. New York: Scribner, 1968.

Lavelle, Robert, ed. *America's New War on Poverty: A Reader for Action*. San Francisco: KQED Books, 1995.

Lawson, Russell M., and Benjamin A Lawson. *Poverty in America: An Encyclopedia*. Westport, CT: Greenwood Press, 2008.

Lens, Sidney. *Poverty: America's Enduring Paradox: A History of the Richest Nation's Unwon War*. New York: Crowell, 1969.

Leuchtenburg, William Edward. *The FDR Years: On Roosevelt and His Legacy*. New York: Columbia University Press, 1995.

———. *Franklin D. Roosevelt and the New Deal, 1932–1940*. New York: Harper & Row, 1963.

———. *Herbert Hoover*. New York: Times Books, 2009.

———. *The Perils of Prosperity, 1914–32*. Chicago: University of Chicago Press, 1958.

Levine, Daniel. *Poverty and Society: The Growth of the American Welfare State in International Comparison.* New Brunswick, NJ: Rutgers University Press, 1988.

Lincoln, Abraham. *The Portable Abraham Lincoln.* Edited by Andrew Delbanco. New York: Penguin Books, 2009.

Lindsey, Duncan. *Child Poverty and Inequality: Securing a Better Future for America's Children.* New York: Oxford University Press, 2009.

Loeb, Paul Rogat. *Soul of a Citizen: Living with Conviction in a Cynical Time.* New York: St. Martin's Press, 1999.

Loesche-Scheller, Brigitta. *Reparations to Poverty: Domestic Policy in America Ten Years after the Great Society.* European University Studies. New York: Peter Lang, 1995.

Long, Huey Pierce. *Kingfish to America, Share Our Wealth: Selected Senatorial Papers of Huey P. Long.* Edited by Henry M Christman. New York: Schocken Books, 1985.

Lustig, Nora, ed. *Coping with Austerity: Poverty and Inequality in Latin America.* Washington, D.C.: Brookings Institution, 1995.

Maeker, Nancy, and Peter Rogness. *Ending Poverty: A 20/20 Vision Guide for Individuals and Congregations.* Minneapolis: Augsburg Fortess, 2006.

Mandell, David. *Obama: From Promise to Power.* New York: Amistaad, 2007.

McCullough, David. *John Adams.* New York: Simon & Schuster, 2001.

———. *Truman.* New York: Simon & Schuster, 1999.

McElvaine, Robert. *The Great Depression: America, 1929–1941.* New York: Times Books, 1984.

McFate, Katherine, Roger Lawson, and William Julius Wilson, eds. *Poverty, Inequality, and the Future of Social Policy: Western States in the New World Order.* New York: Russel Sage Publications, 1995.

McFeely, William S. *Grant: A Biography.* New York: W. W. Norton, 1981.

McGovern, George Stanley. *Abraham Lincoln.* The American Presidents Series. New York: Times Books/Henry Holt, 2009.

McNamara, Robert Hartmann, ed. *Homelessness in America.* 3 vols. Westport, CT: Praeger, 2008.

Meacham, Jon. *American Gospel: God, the Founding Fathers, and the Making of a Nation.* New York: Random House, 2006.

———. *American Lion: Andrew Jackson in the White House.* New York: Random House, 2008.

Mead, Lawrence M. *The New Politics of Poverty: The Nonworking Poor in America.* New York: Basic Books, 1993.

Means, Howard B. *The Avenger Takes His Place: Andrew Johnson and the 45 Days that Changed the Nation.* Orlando, FL: Harcourt, 2006.

Meltzer, Milton. *Poverty in America.* New York: William Morrow, 1986.

Miller, Joshua L., and Ann Marie Garran. *Racism in the United States: Implications for the Helping Profession.* Belmont, CA: Thomson Brooks/Cole, 2008.

Miller, William. *A New History of the United States*. New York: G. Braziller, 1958.

Milton, Cynthia E. *The Many Meanings of Poverty: Colonialism, Social Compacts, and Assistance in Eighteenth-Century Ecuador*. Stanford, CA: Stanford University Press, 2007.

Minutaglio, Bill. A. *First Son: George W. Bush and the Bush Family Dynasty*. New York: Three Rivers Press, 1999.

Mohl, Raymond A. *Poverty in New York, 1783–1825*. New York: Oxford University Press, 1971.

Morris, Edmund. *Dutch: A Memoir of Ronald Reagan*. New York: Random House, 1999.

Murray, Charles. *Losing Ground: American Social Policy, 1950–1980*. New York: Basic Books, 1984.

Myers-Lipton, Scott J. *Social Solutions to Poverty: America's Struggle to Build a Just Society*. Boulder: Paradigm Publishers, 2006.

Myrdal, Gunnar. *An American Dilemma: The Negro Problem and Modern Democracy*. With Richard Sterner and Arnold Rose. New York, London: Harper, 1944.

Naftali, Timothy J. *George H. W. Bush*. The American Presidents Series. New York: Times Books/Henry Holt, 2007.

Nagel, Paul C. *John Quincy Adams: A Public Life, A Private Life*. New York: Knopf, 1997.

Nevins, Allan, and Henry Steele Commager. *A Short History of the United States*. 6th ed. New York: Alfred A. Knopf, 1976.

New York Times correspondents. *Class Matters*. Introduction by Bill Keller. New York: Times Books, 2005.

Newman, Barbara M., and Philip R. Newman. *Development Through Life: A Psychosocial Approach*. Belmont, CA: Wadsworth/Cengage Learning, 2009.

O'Brien, Conor Cruise. *First in Peace: How George Washington Set the Course for America*. Cambridge, MA: Da Capo Press, 2009.

Otfinoski, Steven. *William Henry Harrison: America's 9th President*. New York: Children's Press, 2003.

Parmet, Herbert S. *George Bush: The Life of a Lone Star Yankee*. New York: Scribner, 1997.

Patterson, James T. *America's Struggle Against Poverty in the Twentieth Century*. Cambridge, MA: Harvard University Press, 2000.

———. *America's Struggle Against Poverty in the Twentieth Century, 1900–1985*. Cambridge, MA: Harvard University Press, 1986.

———. *America's Struggle Against Poverty, 1900–1994*. Rev. ed. Cambridge, MA: Cambridge University Press, 1994.

Phillips, Kevin P. *American Dynasty: Aristocracy, Fortune, and the Politics of Deceit in the House of Bush*. New York: Viking, 2004.

———. *William McKinley*. The American Presidents Series. New York: Times Books, 2003.

Pimpare, Stephen, and Howard Zinn. *A People's History of Poverty in America.* New York: New Press, 2008.

Procopio, Mariellen, and Frederick J. Perella, Jr. *Poverty Profile, USA: Poverty in America, the Statistics, and the People Who Make Up the Poor in the World's Most Affluent Nation.* New York: Paulist Press, 1976.

Procter, David E., and Kurt Ritter. "Inaugurating the Clinton Presidency: Regenerative Rhetoric and the American Community." In *The Clinton Presidency: Images, Issues, and Communication Strategies,* edited by Robert E. Denton Jr., and Rachel L. Holloway. Westport, CT: Praeger, 1996.

Randall, Willard Sterne. *Thomas Jefferson: A Life.* New York: H. Holt, 1993.

Reagan, Ron. *My Father at 100.* New York: Viking, 2011.

Reagan, Ronald. *An American Life.* New York: Simon & Schuster, 2011.

Rector, Robert, and William F Lauber. *America's Failed $5.4 Trillion War on Poverty.* Washington, D.C.: Heritage Foundation, 1995.

Reef, Catherine. *Poverty in America.* New York: Facts on File, 2007.

Reeves, Richard. *President Reagan: The Triumph of Imagination.* New York: Simon & Schuster, 2005.

Reeves, Thomas C. *Gentleman Boss: The Life of Chester Alan Arthur.* New York: Knopf, 1975.

Remnick, David. *The Bridge: The Life and Rise of Barack Obama.* New York: Alfred A. Knopf, 2010.

Riis, Jacob A. *Theodore Roosevelt, the Citizen.* New York: The Outlook Company, 1903.

Robbins, Susan P., Pranab Chatterjee, and Edward R. Canda. *Contemporary Human Behavior Theory: A Critical Perspective for Social Work.* 2nd ed. Boston: Pearson/A and B, 2006.

Rodgers, Harrell R., ed. *Beyond Welfare: New Approaches to the Problem of Poverty in America.* Armonk, NY: M. E. Sharpe, 1988.

Romasco, Albert U. *The Poverty of Abundance: Hoover, the Nation, the Depression.* New York: Oxford University Press, 1965.

Roosevelt, Theodore. *Theodore Roosevelt: An Autobiography.* New York: Macmillan, 1913.

Rubin, Allen, and Earl R. Babbie. *Research Methods for Social Work.* 6th ed. Belmont, CA: Thomson Brooks/Cole, 2008.

Rutkow, Ira M. *James A. Garfield.* The American Presidents Series. New York: Times Books, 2006.

Sachs, Jeffrey. *The End of Poverty: Economic Possibilities for Our Time.* New York: Penguin Press, 2005.

Sandburg, Carl M. *Abraham Lincoln: The Prairie Years and the War Years.* New York: Harcourt, Brace, 1954.

Sandel, Michael J. *Justice: What's the Right Thing to Do?* New York: Farrar, Straus and Giroux, 2009.

Savage, Michael. *Trickle Up Poverty: Stopping Obama's Attack on Our Borders, Economy, and Security.* New York: William Morrow, 2010.

Scarry, Robert J. *Millard Fillmore*. Jefferson, NC: McFarland, 2001.

Schiller, Bradley R. *The Economics of Poverty and Discrimination*. Englewood Cliffs, NJ: Prentice Hall, 1989.

Schlesinger, Jr., Arthur M. *The Age of Jackson*. Boston, Little, Brown, 1945.

———. *A Thousand Days: John F. Kennedy in the White House*. Boston: Houghton Mifflin, 1965.

Schmitt, Edward R. *President of the Other America: Robert Kennedy and the Politics of Poverty*. Amherst: University of Massachusetts Press, 2010.

Schriver, Joe M. *Human Behavior and the Social Environment: Shifting Paradigms in Essential Knowledge for Social Work Practice*. Boston, MA: Allyn and Bacon, 2011.

Schwartz, Joel. *Fighting Poverty with Virtue: Moral Reform and America's Urban Poor, 1825–2000*. Bloomington: Indiana University Press, 2000.

Schweizer, Peter, and Rochelle Schweizer. *The Bushes: Portrait of a Dynasty*. New York: Doubleday, 2004.

Seager, Robert. *And Tyler Too*. New York: McGraw-Hill, 1963.

Segalman, Ralph, and Asoke Basu. *Poverty in America: The Welfare Dilemma*. Westport, CT: Greenwood Press, 1981.

Seigenthaler, John. *James K. Polk*. The American Presidents Series. New York: Times Books, 2004.

SenGupta, Gunja. *From Slavery to Poverty: The Racial Origins of Welfare in New York, 1840–1918*. New York: New York University Press, 2009.

Sherman, Jennifer. *Those Who Work, Those Who Don't: Poverty, Morality, and Family in Rural America*. Minneapolis: University of Minnesota Press, 2009.

Shipler, David K. *The Working Poor: Invisible in America*. New York: Vintage Books, 2005.

Sider, Ronald J. *Just Generosity: A New Vision for Overcoming Poverty in America*. Grand Rapids, MI: Baker Books, 1999; reprint, 2007.

Sinclair, Upton. *EPIC Answers: How to End Poverty in California*. Los Angeles: End Poverty League, 1934.

Singer, Peter. *The Life You Can Save: Acting Now to End World Poverty*. New York: Random House, 2009.

Smith, Elbert B. *The Presidency of James Buchanan*. Lawrence: University Press of Kansas, 1975.

Smith, Richard Norton. *An Uncommon Man: The Triumph of Herbert Hoover*. New York: Simon & Schuster, 1984.

Snyder, Larry. *Think and Act Anew: How Poverty in America Affects Us All and What We Can Do about It*. Maryknoll, NY: Orbis Books, 2010.

Sreenivasan, Jyotsna. *Poverty and the Government in America: A Historical Encyclopedia*. 2 vols. Santa Barbara, CA: ABC-CLIO, 2009.

Steffens, Lincoln. *The Shame of the Cities*. New York: McCure, Phillips, 1904.

Stricker, Frank. *Why America Lost the War on Poverty—and How to Win It*. Chapel Hill: University of North Carolina Press, 2007.

Striner, Richard. *Father Abraham: Lincoln's Relentless Struggle to End Slavery.* New York: Oxford University Press, 1998.

Sweetman, Caroline, ed. *Gender and Poverty in the North.* Oxfam Focus on Gender Series. Oxford, UK: Oxfam, 1997.

Thernstorm, Stephan. *The Other Bostonians: Poverty and Progress in the American Metropolis, 1988–1970.* Harvard Studies in Urban History. Cambridge, MA: Harvard University Press, 1973.

Toqueville, Alexis de. *Democracy in America.* Edited by J. P. Mayer. Translated by George Lawrence. New York: Doubleday, 1969.

Trager, Oliver, ed. *Poverty in America: The Forgotten Millions.* New York: Facts on File, 1989.

Trani, Eugene P., and David L. Wilson. *The Presidency of Warren G. Harding.* Lawrence: Regents Press of Kansas, 1977.

Trefousse, Hans L. *Andrew Johnson: A Biography.* New York: W. W. Norton, 1989.

Truman, Henry S. *Memoirs of Harry S. Truman.* Vol. 2, *Years of Trial and Hope, 1946–1952.* Garden City, NY: Doubleday, 1956.

Tugwell, Rexford Guy. *Grover Cleveland.* New York: Macmillan, 1968.

Turner, Jonathan H., and Charles E. Starns. *Inequality: Privilege & Poverty in America.* Goodyear Series in American Society. Pacific Palisades, CA: Goodyear, 1976.

Unger, Harlow G. *America's Second Revolution: How George Washington Defeated Patrick Henry and Saved the Nation.* Hoboken, NJ: John Wiley & Sons, 2007.

vanden Heuvel, William J., and Milton Gwirtzman. *On His Own: Robert F. Kennedy, 1964–1968.* Garden City, NY: Doubleday, 1970.

Ward, John William. *Andrew Jackson, Symbol for an Age.* New York: Oxford University Press, 1955.

Washington, Henry Augustine, ed. *The Writings of Thomas Jefferson: Being His Autobiography, Correspondence, Reports, Messages, Addresses and Other Writings, Official and Private.* 9 Vols. Washington, D.C.: Taylor & Maury, 1853–1854.

White, Craig C. *Toward the Resolution of Poverty in America.* Dubuque, IA: Kendall/Hunt Pub Co., 1993.

Wicker, Tom. *Dwight D. Eisenhower.* New York: Times Books, 2002.

———. *George Herbert Walker Bush.* New York: Lipper/Viking, 2004.

Widmer, Edward L. *Martin Van Buren.* New York: Times Books, 2005.

Wiencek. Henry. *An Imperfect God: George Washington, His Slaves, and the Creation of America.* New York: Farrar, Straus and Giroux, 2003.

Will, George F. *With a Happy Eye, but—America and the World, 1997–2002.* New York: Free Press, 2003.

Wilson, William Julius. *The Truly Disadvantaged: The Inner City, the Underclass, and Public Policy.* Chicago: University of Chicago Press, 1987.

Woodward, Bob. *Plan of Attack.* New York: Simon & Schuster, 2004.

Zelizer, Julian E. *Jimmy Carter*. New York: Times Books/Henry Holt, 2010.

Audio Recordings

Connelly, Michael. *The Lincoln Lawyer*. Santa Ana, CA: Books on Tape, 2005.
Fishman, Ethan, William D. Peterson, and Mark J. Rozell, eds. *George Washington: Foundation of Presidential Leadership and Character*. Westport, CT, Praeger, 2001.
Montreal Guitar Trio. *Once Upon a Time in America: Poverty*. Arranged by G. Levesque. ATMA Classique, 1999. MP3 Download.

Articles

O'Hare, William P. "Poverty in America: Trends and New Patterns." *Population Bulletin* 40, no. 3 (1985).
Vodrey, William F. B. "George Washington: Hero of the Confederacy?" *American History Illustrated* 39, no. 4 (2006): 58+. http://www.historynet.com /george-washington-hero-of-the-confederacy.htm.

Websites

Adams, John. "A Dissertation on the Canon and Feudal Law." TeachingAmericanHistory.org. Ashbrook Center at Ashland University, Ashland, Ohio. www.teachingamericanhistory.org/library/index.asp?document=43.
Adams, John Quincy. "Inaugural Address," March 4, 1825. Miller Center, University of Virginia, Charlottesville, 2012. http://millercenter.org/scripps /archive/speeches/detail/3513.
Arthur, Chester Alan. "Annual Message," December 6, 1881. Miller Center, University of Virginia, Charlottesville, 2012. http://millercenter.org /president/speeches/detail/3560.
Bittinger, Cyndy. "The Business of America Is Business?" Calvin Coolidge Memorial Foundation. http://calvin-coolidge.org/html/the_business_of _america_is_bus.html.
Buchanan, James. "Inaugural Address," March 4, 1857. Miller Center, University of Virginia, Charlottesville, 2012. http://millercsnter.org/president /speeches/detail/3554.
"The Clinton Presidency: A Historic Era of Progress and Prosperity." The Clinton-Gore Administration, Record of Progress. White House. http:// clinton5.nara.gov/WH/Accomplishments/eightyears-01.html.
Coolidge, Calvin. "The Press Under a Free Government." Speech given before the American Society of Newspaper Editors, Washington, D.C., January 17, 1925. TeachingAmericanHistory.org, Ashbrook Center at Ashland University, Ashland, Ohio. http://teachingamericanhistory.org/library/index .asp?documentprint=1604.

Coughlin, Father. "Activism and Political Views." Old Time Radio, 2012. http:www.fathercoughlin.org/father-coughlin-ant-communism.html.

Ford, Gerald R. "Domestic Affairs." Miller Center, University of Virginia, Charlottesville, 2012. http://millercenter.org/president/ford/essays/biography/4.

———. "State of the Union Address," January 20, 1975. Miller Center, University of Virginia, Charlottesville, 2012. http://millercenter.org/president/speeches/detail/5499.

Goodwin, Doris Kearns. "Character Above All: Franklin D. Roosevelt." Essays. PBS. http://www.pbs.org/newshour/character/essays/roosevelt.html.

Harrison, Benjamin. "Inaugural Address to Congress," March 4, 1889. Miller Center, University of Virginia, Charlottesville, 2012. http://millercenter.org/president/speeches/detail/.

Johnson, Lyndon B. "First State of the Union Address," January 8, 1964. Miller Center, University of Virginia, Charlottesville, 2012. http://millercenter.org/president/speeches/detail/3382.

Kennedy, John F. "Acceptance of the Democratic Party Nomination," July 15, 1960. Miller Center, University of Virginia, Charlottesville, 2012. http://millercenter.org/president/speeches/detail/3362.

———. "Address on Civil Rights," June 11, 1963. Miller Center, University of Virginia, Charlottesville, 2012. http://millercenter.org/president/speeches/detail/3375.

———. "Announcement of Candidacy for President." Washington, D.C., January 2, 1960. John F. Kennedy Presidential Library and Museum. www.jfklibrary.org/Research/Ready-Reference/JFK-Miscellaneous-Information/Announcement-of-Candidacy.aspx.

Monroe, James. "Domestic Affairs." Miller Center, University of Virginia, Charlottesville, 2012. http://millercenter.org/president/monroe/essays/biography /4.

Nixon, Richard M. "Inaugural Speech," January 20, 1969. Miller Center, University of Virginia, Charlottesville, 2012. http://millercenter.org.

Roosevelt, Theodore. "Domestic Affairs: On Race and Civil Rights." Miller Center, University of Virginia, Charlottesville, 2012. http://millercenter.org/president/roosevelt/essays/biography/4.

Thomas Jefferson Foundation. "Report of the Research Committee on Thomas Jefferson and Sally Hemings, January 2000." Monticello.org (Charlottesville, Virginia). http://www.monticello.org/site/plantation-and-slavery/report-research-committee-thomas-jefferson-and-sally-hemings.

United States Congress. Government and Laws. *The Public Statutes at Large of the United States of America from the Organization of the Government in 1789, to March 3, 1945.* Edited by Richard Peters. Boston: Charles C. Little and James Brown, 1945. Available through the Library of Congress, *A Century of Lawmaking for a New National: U.S. Congressional Documents and Debates, 1774–1875,* http://memory.loc.gov/cgi-bin/ampage?collId=llsl&fileName=001/llsl001.db&recNum=2.

U.S. Demographic Data. http://www.demograhicsnow.com.
Washington, George. "First Inaugural Address, April 30, 1789." Records of
    United States Senate. Center for Legislative Archives, National Archives,
    Washington. http://www.archives.gov/legislative/features/gw-inauguration/.
    ———. Letter to James Madison, May 6, 1789. TeachingAmericanHistory.org,
    Ashbrook Center at Ashland University, Ashland, Ohio. http://Teaching
    AmericanHIstory.org/library/Index.asp?documentprint=390.

Video Recordings

History Channel. *The Presidents: The Lives and Legacies of the Leaders of the
    United States.* Produced by Craig Haffner and Donna E. Lusitana. A&E
    Home Video, 2005. DVD. http://shop.history.com/detail.php?p=366781
    &SESSID=ddefe0cd2967c6d4b8ba2146fef80467&v=history.

INDEX

ABOUT THE AUTHOR

WOODY KLEIN is an award-winning investigative newspaper reporter and author. He has written about poverty, race relations, politics, and civil rights. A former reporter for the *Washington Post* and the *New York World-Telegram & Sun*, he covered poverty, the slums, the civil rights movement, and was a Pulitzer Prize nominee for his 1959 series "I Lived in a Slum" about East Harlem, New York. He graduated from Dartmouth College (BA) and the Graduate School of Journalism at Columbia University (MS). He is the author or editor of eight books, including *The Inside Stories of Modern American Scandals: How Investigative Reporters Have Changed the Course of American History* (2010); *All the Presidents' Spokesmen: Spinning the News, White House Press Secretaries from Franklin D. Roosevelt to George W. Bush* (2008); *Toward Humanity and Justice: The Writings of Dr. Kenneth B. Clark, Scholar of the* Brown v. Board of Education *Decision in 1954* (2004); *Liberties Lost: The Endangered Legacy of the ACLU* (2006); *Lindsay's Promise: The Dream That Failed* (1970); *Westport, Connecticut: The Story of a New England Town's Rise to Prominence* (2000); and *Let in the Sun* (1964), the anatomy of an East Harlem slum building. He served as New York mayor John V. Lindsay's press secretary in 1965–1966 and worked as editor of *Think*, IBM's international magazine. Klein has taught journalism as an adjunct professor at several colleges and universities. He lives with his wife, Audrey, in Westport, Connecticut.